Getting to Know Ourselves and Others Through the ABCs

A Journey Toward Intercultural Understanding

A volume in
Literacy, Language, and Learning
Claudia Finkbeiner, Althier M. Lazar, and Wen Ma, *Series Editors*

Getting to Know Ourselves and Others Through the ABCs

A Journey Toward Intercultural Understanding

edited by

Claudia Finkbeiner

University of Kassel

Althier M. Lazar

Saint Joseph's University

INFORMATION AGE PUBLISHING, INC.
Charlotte, NC • www.infoagepub.com

Library of Congress Cataloging-in-Publication Data

A CIP record for this book is available from the Library of Congress
http://www.loc.gov

ISBN: 978-1-62396-768-0 (Paperback)
   978-1-62396-769-7 (Hardcover)
   978-1-62396-770-3 (ebook)

To my mother Ria, who taught me everything in life and whose love and wisdom I will always miss.
—Claudia

To Mitch, Aaron, and Zachary, the principal players in my life story.
—Althier

To all of the TRANSABCs participants whose work advances knowledge about human understanding and communication.
—Claudia and Althier

CONTENTS

FOREWORD

The number of books about linguistic and cultural diversity seems to be expanding exponentially, and it has become almost ritualistic to introduce such books by reference to globalization and internationalization. The mantra that young people today are in constant contact with others in distant places through the new social media is often repeated but seldom analyzed.

In an informal and opportunistic survey of university teachers working with students in languages and cultures, one response ran as follows:

> Regarding your question about whether 15–20 year olds are connected to people all over the world, in our experience this is not so—most teenagers we are familiar with use social networks to talk to their local friends. In Ana's doctoral research, the informants had practically no foreign friends before they did their Erasmus programme. It is true that, during study abroad, they all had to start writing and speaking in other languages with their new contacts (mostly other Erasmus). But we also need to remember that only about 2% of students in Europe study abroad, and this reflects the percentage of Europeans who move to another European country to work—leaving the other 98% at home . . . food for thought! (Claudia Borghetti and Ana Beavan, University of Bologna, Italy)

One of the significant features of this book is to recognize, as the authors of one article say, that many students have never entered "the world of diversity," whether in Europe or the United States. When those students are going to be teachers—or are indeed already teachers and simultaneously students of in-service courses—working in classrooms where diversity is the norm, this lack of personal experience and reflection is a poor

Getting to Know Ourselves and Others Through the ABCs, pages ix–xi
Copyright © 2015 by Information Age Publishing
All rights of reproduction in any form reserved.

starting point for them and their learners. The ABCs instrument is revealed throughout the book to be a powerful means of helping future and present teachers to understand diversity: by analyzing their own and other people's experience, by comparing and contrasting—always an effective means of challenging what has hitherto been taken for granted—and by inciting them to plan and implement their own methods and techniques for teaching groups of diverse learners.

This is a book about teachers and diversity, but diversity of all kinds. Diversity exists within societies as well as among societies. Diversity is a matter of recognizing the ways in which individuals belong to many social groups within society. It is also a matter of recognizing that in the contemporary world many individuals belong to social groups of more than one society, as a consequence of mobility and migration as well as diversity across societies.

Diversity is also a matter of power relations and social statuses. It becomes evident to the learners described in the various chapters of this book that they themselves usually belong to high-status social groups in their society and that this gives them advantages of which they have perhaps not been conscious. There is however evidence in the book that people who are teachers or wish to be teachers have a propensity to help those who are disadvantaged. There is a strong sense of social justice running through this book, something which we should not take for granted, even though those of us who have been teacher educators for many years have seen it again and again in the teaching profession. The commitment to social justice of the vast majority of teachers is something to treasure.

This is a book about writing stories. The ABCs instrument stimulates people to write stories about themselves and about other people. As one of the authors says, story writing is also a matter of creating identities, the identities of the writer—how they present themselves from the past, how the discourse of their story is itself a presentation of a writing identity—for story writers always have a readership in mind even if it is only the writers themselves. As another author says, writing stories about someone else when that someone else has been selected because they are "different," in some sense representing "diversity," leads at least initially to the relationship of "otherizing," but the significance of the ABC instrument is to bring this relationship into the open and, by comparison and contrast, to dissolve it. This third stage of the ABC instrument, the process of comparison and contrast, is one that the authors of the book clearly see as significant but also in need of constant reflection and analysis. As another author says, those few students who, after completing the ABC process, still feel uncomfortable in the norms of other cultures, pose an unsolved problem that the success of working with the majority of teachers should not occlude.

Complementing the telling of stories and the comparative process with the requirement to think about but also actively plan for the impact of the

ABCs process on teaching activities in classrooms is a crucial element of the book that will make it stimulating reading not just for researchers but also for other teachers. Although limitations of space do not allow authors to describe their learners' plans for teaching in detail, there are plenty of indications of what they have in mind, of how they will ensure the recognition of the identities and statuses of their learners, of how they will bring the world into the classroom, or how they will help their learners to become active members of their own society and perhaps ultimately of that international world when it becomes more than a mantra.

Finally, but not least, this is a book about the authors themselves, as researchers in an international project discovering the ABC instrument, and as teachers introducing innovation, sometimes easily, sometimes with difficulty, always with perseverance. As members of the project, they had to find some common ground, a common framework, which nonetheless does not constrain, since they are working in not just different societies with different kinds of diversity but also different education systems and traditions where learners' expectations may not fit easily with the assumptions of the autonomous learner in the ABCs instrument. I have no doubt that the project had its ups and downs as all projects do, particularly with so many members involved, both teachers and learners, and they are to be congratulated on bringing to fruition a publication that will allow readers to dip into diversity not just as a topic but as an experience in teaching and learning.

The fact that this was a transatlantic project was doubtless significant for the participants, but ultimately it is evident, to me at least, that in the comparison across the Atlantic, and also within the societies on each side of the Atlantic, there is a common need for teachers to find practical ways of responding to their learners that are founded on their own position and purpose in the societies and education systems in which they live and work. This book points the way.

—**Michael Byram**

INTRODUCTION

FROM THE ABCs
TO THE TRANSABCs

Claudia Finkbeiner and Althier Lazar

The wing of a butterfly can change the world.
—Lorenz (1963)

The TRANSABCs project[1] is an international autobiographical and biographical project involving more than a dozen researchers and several hundred study participants. Despite its large-scale character, at the heart of the project are individual life stories and their profound impact on how humans change the way they see and understand one another. Thus, we relate the TRANSABCs project to the "butterfly effect" (Lorenz, 1963), which metaphorically means that a small cultural change can have a huge effect.

The TRANSABCs project described in this book is based on the original ABCs model (Ruggiano Schmidt, 1998) as well as on its international adaptations (Ruggiano Schmidt & Finkbeiner, 2006). It follows a narrative approach, including the writing of an autobiography, interviewing someone different with respect to one's own self and writing that person's biography, comparing the autobiography and biography for similarities and differences, conducting a cross-cultural in-depth analysis, and finally following up with the development of culturally responsive ideas (Ruggiano Schmidt, 1998; Ruggiano Schmidt & Finkbeiner, 2006). The ABCs have been implemented in various adaptations (Finkbeiner & Knierim, 2006; Finkbeiner &

Getting to Know Ourselves and Others Through the ABCs, pages xiii–xvii
Copyright © 2015 by Information Age Publishing

Koplin, 2002; Leftwich & Madden, 2006; Wilden, 2007, 2008; Xu, 2006). These studies and others have demonstrated the ability of the ABCs to bridge the divide between people of different cultural orientations. So far, however, a large-scale project involving multiple international partners implementing the ABCs at the same time and according to the same standards has been missing.

Patricia Ruggiano Schmidt, U.S. director, and her colleague Claudia Finkbeiner, EU director, pursued this ambitious goal by cooperating with a linguistically and culturally diverse group of university professors who would help implement, test, and disseminate the model in different sociocultural settings on a large scale. They applied for the FIPSE/Atlantis (Fund for the Improvement of Post-Secondary Education) grant to implement the TRANSABCs. The acronym TRANSABCs consists of two parts: The first, "TRANS," implies that it is a transatlantic project. The second, "ABCs," indicates that it is a project that employs the ABCs model (Ruggiano Schmidt, 1998; Ruggiano Schmidt & Finkbeiner, 2006).

When Finkbeiner and Ruggiano Schmidt received word that the grant would be funded, they were thrilled. At the FIPSE and ATLANTIS Project Directors' Meeting in Boston in September 2009, they learned that being a recipient of the FIPSE/Atlantis grant was considered highly prestigious. Of 75 proposals, only 25 were selected, and only 2 of those were from small colleges. All projects involved professors and university staff at the highest levels, and many "flagship" research universities were chosen. The FIPSE-ATLANTIS grant is a bilateral matching fund scheme of the U.S. Department of Education and the European Commission's Directorate General for Education and Culture (DGEAC) as well as the European Education Audiovisual and Culture Executive Agency (EACEA) in Brussels.

The TRANSABCs group has been actively involved within the ABCs framework since the study formally ended. Grant team members have continued to contribute to the project with presentations, workshops, follow-up training and dissemination courses, and finally with their own chapters in this book, which give insight into the individual work over the two grant years.

The contents of this book are based on the adaptations of the ABCs model on college and university campuses in Bulgaria, Germany, Poland, Sweden, and Spain in Europe and New York, California, Michigan, Oklahoma, and Pennsylvania in the United States, as well as in one of the participant's partner universities in Quebec, Canada. Committed scholars across the world participated in the project, including the U.S. partners Althier Lazar, Patricia Ruggiano Schmidt,[2] Jane Neer and William Neer, Patricia Edwards, Jeining Ruan, and Shelley Hong Xu. The EU partners included Claudia Finkbeiner,[3] Sylvia Fehling, Josep Maria Cots, Ewa Bandura, Ulla Lundgren, and Lilia Ratcheva-Stratieva. Each of the authors of these studies looked at the model through a particular theoretical or practical lens.

As a result, readers are able to see various ways in which the participating professors have used the model to enhance candidates' cultural awareness and the different meanings professors have assigned to this growth.

The Foreword is by Michael Byram, who contributed feedback to the project after the first year.

In the first chapter, Patricia Ruggiano Schmidt describes the origins of the ABCs model and highlights how it has shaped her students' attitudes from 1992 to the present at Le Moyne College.

With Chapter 2 "Responding to Cultural and Linguistic Diversity: The TRANSABCs Project," Claudia Finkbeiner introduces the TRANSABCs project and a survey of its implementation as well as its most important results. Particular emphasis is put on the empirical evidence gained from the analyses of the survey data.

The third chapter is introduced by Claudia Finkbeiner. It is a tribute by Troy Davidson, who was an ABCs participant in Claudia Finkbeiner's intense M.A. summer course in Montreal, Canada, in 2011. It is a powerful example of a practical application of the ABCs and was chosen because it is highly authentic and a true testimony to the role of identity in a multilingual world. Furthermore, the author testifies that the ABCs have made a big impact on him.

In "The ABCs Model: A Foundation for Culturally Responsive Teaching," Jane Neer and William Neer describe how they implemented the ABCs as an integral part of their literacy courses.

In Chapter 5, Althier Lazar writes about putting a face on power and inequality through the ABCs project and how she implemented the project in her graduate-level classes on cultural aspects of literacy.

In his chapter, Josep M. Cots discusses writing about ANOTHER woman: difference, gender, and face-work. With four colleagues, he incorporated the ABCs in four different courses at the University of Lleida, Catalonia: two English studies programs, one in business administration, and one in applied linguistics with a focus on intercultural communication.

In Chapter 7, Sylvia Fehling describes the construction of identity through the ABCs of cultural understanding and communication in an English as a foreign language class at the University of Kassel, Germany.

In Shelley Hong Xu's chapter, she elaborates on an implementation of the ABCs model in a reading methods course with the goal of learning to read and reading to learn through literacy memories.

In Chapter 9, Ulla Lundgren explains how to integrate the ABCs model into the curriculum of an international undergraduate teacher course in Sweden focusing on intercultural action readiness.

In her chapter, Jiening Ruan describes the use of the ABCs in two different contexts to support cultural awareness and sensitivity development.

She implemented the ABCs in one graduate class about understanding different cultures and issues and one undergraduate literacy methods class.

In Chapter 11, Ewa Bandura describes how the ABCs are a tool for intercultural critical development. She elaborates on the implementation of the ABCs in her Teaching English as a Foreign Language seminar as well as in a writing class in Krakow, Poland.

In Chapter 12, Patricia Edwards and Susan Piazza describe literacy coaches who use the ABCs model to work effectively in diverse school settings.

In Chapter 13, "To Open Doors," Lilia Ratcheva-Stratieva writes about how she incorporated the ABCs in three separate seminars in Bulgaria and two seminars in Austria.

In Chapter 14, we summarize the contributions from the chapter authors and provide ideas for possible adaptations of the ABCs model.

The TRANSABCs project was an exciting collaborative journey. Together we learned so much more than we could have if we had conducted this research by ourselves. Only through lively, frank, and often intense discussions could we succeed. In this way we found out about underlying contrasting and differing preconceptions with respect to phenomena we discussed about the world and about intercultural education, literacy development, and multilingualism. And we learned about differences of learned codes and scripts with respect to these important issues when comparing the United States and the European Union as a whole, as well as individual EU countries on each side of what was once labeled as the Iron Curtain, or simply single campuses. The differences included our beliefs about what constitutes a good lesson, a good teacher, successful cultural learning, multiculturalism, cultural and linguistic differences, and many other issues.

The biggest effect of the project can be seen in the narratives that our students produced during their TRANSABCs journeys. Most important, the TRANSABCs project helped elicit and trigger both language and cultural awareness with respect to different underlying concepts that most likely would have remained untouched and even unnoticed. The biggest lesson we learned was that together we have started a journey that will never end, for cultures just as personalities, are dynamic systems, constantly changing and adapting, becoming hybrid and thus remaining unpredictable.

NOTES

1. The full title of the P116J090029 Policy Project is "Dissemination and Adaptation of the ABC's of Cultural Understanding and Communication," EU-US

Cooperation Program ATLANTIS under Action 3 Policy-oriented Measures Reference: 156403-DE-2009USAPOM.
2. Patricia Ruggiano Schmidt was the TRANSABCs U.S. director.
3. Claudia Finkbeiner was the TRANABCs EU director.

REFERENCES

Finkbeiner, C., & Knierim, M. (2006). The ABC's as a starting point and goal: The online intercultural exchange project. In P. Ruggiano Schmidt & C. Finkbeiner (Eds.), *The ABC's of cultural understanding and communication: National and international adaptations* (pp. 213–244). Greenwich, CT: Information Age.

Finkbeiner, C., & Koplin, C. (2002). A cooperative approach for facilitating intercultural education. *Reading Online, 6*(3). Retrieved from http://www.readingonline.org/newliteracies/lit_index.asp?HREF=/newliteracies/finkbeiner

Leftwich, S., & Madden, M. (2006). Doing the ABC's. In P. Ruggiano Schmidt & C. Finkbeiner (Eds.), *The ABC's of cultural understanding and communication: National and international adaptations* (pp. 73–92). Greenwich, CT: Information Age.

Lorenz, E. N. (1963, March). Deterministic nonperiodic flow. *Journal of the Atmospheric Sciences, 20*(2), 130–141.

Ruggiano Schmidt, P. (1998). The ABC's of cultural understanding and communication. *Equity and Excellence in Education, 31*(2), 28–38.

Ruggiano Schmidt, P., & Finkbeiner, C. (Eds.). (2006). *The ABC's of cultural understanding and communication: National and international adaptations.* Greenwich, CT: Information Age.

Ruggiano Schmidt, P., & Lazar, A. (2011). *Practicing what we teach: How culturally responsive literacy classrooms make a difference.* New York, NY: Teachers College Press.

Wilden, E. (2007). Voice chats in the intercultural classroom: The ABC's on-line project. In R. O'Dowd (Ed.), *Online intercultural exchange: An introduction for foreign language teachers* (pp. 271–277). Clevedon, UK: Multilingual Matters.

Wilden, E. (2008). *Selbst- und Fremdwahrnehmung in der interkulturellen Onlinekommunikation. Das Modell der ABC's of cultural understanding and communication online. Eine qualitative Studie.* Frankfurt/Main, Germany: Peter Lang.

Xu, S. H. (2006). The complexity and multiplicity of pre-service teachers' exploring diversity issues. In P. Ruggiano Schmidt & C. Finkbeiner (Eds.), *The ABC's of cultural understanding and communication: National and international adaptations* (pp. 143–160). Greenwich, CT: Information Age.

ACKNOWLEDGMENT

We express our deep gratitude to the U.S. Department of Education and the European Commission's Directorate General for Education and Culture (DGEAC) as well as the Education, Audiovisual and Culture Executive Agency (EACEA) in Brussels for selecting and funding the TRANSABCs project. Acknowledgments also go to Steven Kulick, Le Moyne College, Director of Institutional Advancement for his administrative support as well as to PD Dr. Gerhard Schnaitmann, private lecturer emeritus, University of Heidelberg, for his help with the text analyses. We thank Dr. Christoph Schneider and Andrea Stuck from the University of Koblenz-Landau for their help with the final analyses that turned out to be so important. We also thank Bjoern Bierschenk who was most supportive in creating the cover, as well as his students who volunteered to be part of the cover. A thousand thanks go to all the TRANSABCs professors, lecturers, and teacher participants on the different campuses and in different schools across the world. Their contributions are highly valued. Without their engagement this project would not have been possible; without their dedication the underlying idea of a peaceful culturally and linguistically diverse world would not continue living; without their understanding of a respectful and meaningful tone in cooperation the hope for a better world would not be sustainable.

CHAPTER 1

THE ORIGINS OF THE ABCs

A Crusade to Develop
Compassionate Educators

Patricia Ruggiano Schmidt

In the fall of 1992, I was completing my dissertation, entitled "Cultural Conflict and Struggle: Literacy Learning in a Kindergarten Program." It was a year-long ethnography that described blatant and subtle discriminatory practices occurring in a kindergarten classroom. Children from Southeast Asia, who attended a suburban school, were harassed and bullied by their classmates without the awareness of the teacher or her assistants.

At the time, I was a research fellow and teaching assistant in the Syracuse University Reading and Language Arts Center with responsibility for two literacy courses. Thanks to the chair of the department, Dr. Peter Mosenthal, I was given an office among the stellar literacy professors, Drs. Hal Herber, Don Leu, Susan Hynds, and Kathy Hinchman. Dr. Mosenthal claimed that I belonged with this group because of my 20-year teaching experience in public schools. He believed that the length of my tenure as an educator was an important credential to be recognized in research circles. I was thrilled and humbled.

Getting to Know Ourselves and Others Through the ABCs, pages 1–9
Copyright © 2015 by Information Age Publishing
All rights of reproduction in any form reserved.

So it was, on an autumn afternoon in 1992, that a textbook salesman sauntered into the department looking for the person who taught the multicultural literacy courses. I quickly summoned Dr. Mosenthal and requested an answer. Dr. Mosenthal noticed how nervous I was, and said, "You, Patty, are the one to do it. Your dissertation explains multicultural literacy; you can write the course." Stunned, I returned to the salesman and responded, "I have been elected to teach the course; please show me your texts." He handed me several books and I happily discovered authors cited in my dissertation literature review. I felt optimistic about this new venture. The year before, I had taught graduate and undergraduate literacy courses and even modified syllabi, with the help of professors at the Reading and Language Arts Center. However, I had never actually created a course, so was happily challenged and again began reading my dissertation research sources and others.

My ethnographic research demonstrated the stereotypical behaviors of well-meaning, highly educated teachers and the difficulties associated with changing dispositions regarding stereotypes (Ruggiano Schmidt, 1998a). Other previous studies in education suggested similar results (Heath, 1983; Ladson-Billings, 1995; Paley, 1989; Reyhner & Garcia, 1989; Tatum, 1992). Therefore, I believed that this new course should provide a process that would modify attitudes; I did not realize that this new course would become my research agenda for the next 20 years.

The understandings gained from my dissertation research and applied to this multicultural literacy course motivated me and propelled me toward a crusade to develop compassionate educators: teachers who could learn from their students and their families; teachers who could walk in the shoes of others; teachers who would not merely tolerate differences; but actually appreciate and celebrate differences in their classrooms and schools; and finally, teachers who could connect student differences to the required curriculum and be capable of bringing relevancy to learning. These teachers would be considered culturally responsive educators (Au, 1993, Ladson-Billings, 1995; Ruggiano Schmidt & Lazar, 2011; Ruggiano Schmidt & Ma, 2006).

ABCS OF CULTURAL UNDERSTANDING AND COMMUNICATION

As I studied information for the new course, I discovered research that led to the first implementation of the model known as the ABCs of Cultural Understanding and Communication (Ruggiano Schmidt, 1998b). In this chapter I have also included current research that has influenced changes in the ABCs process. In brief, the ABCs model includes the writing of an autobiography, interviewing people from other language, economic, ethnic, and cultural backgrounds, analyzing life stories with an emphasis on understanding differences, and creating culturally responsive literacy ideas across the curriculum. The model may be summarized in the statement, "Know thyself and understand others."

Teacher education programs that use reading, writing, listening, viewing, and speaking to create consciousness-raising experiences help teachers gain a knowledge of self and others through autobiographies, biographies, reflection on diversity issues, and cross-cultural analysis (Cochran-Smith, 1995; Lazar, 2004; Noordhoff & Kleinfield, 1993; Osborne, 1996; Spindler & Spindler, 1987; Tatum, 1992). However, those programs have not linked self-knowledge to teachers' implementation of home, school, and community connections for literacy instruction. Therefore, the ABCs of Cultural Understanding and Communication is a model designed to fill this gap in teacher education. Current and prospective K–12 teachers who experience the model's process often begin to successfully connect home, school, and community for literacy learning (Finkbeiner & Koplin, 2001, 2002; Izzo & Ruggiano Schmidt, 2006; Leftwich, 2002; Ruggiano Schmidt, 1999, 2000b, 2001, 2005; Ruggiano Schmidt & Finkbeiner, 2006; Ruggiano Schmidt & Ma, 2006; Xu, 2000a, 2000b). The following paragraphs explain the model's five-step process.

Autobiography

First, each present or prospective teacher writes an autobiography in his or her lingua franca (Gunderson, 2007), starting from earliest memories, which include key life events related to education, family, religious tradition, recreation, victories, defeats, and so on. This helps to build awareness of personal beliefs and attitudes that form the traditions and values of cultural autobiographies (Banks, 1994). Since it is well documented that writing is linked to knowledge of self within a social context (Emig, 1971; Finkbeiner, 2006; Yinger, 1985), writing one's life story seems to construct connections with universal human tenets and serves to lessen negative notions about different groups of people (Progoff, 1975). Also, the autobiographies are confidential: only the teacher educator (professor) sees them. The autobiography is seen as a mirror of one's own identity and so remains protected. Quality is determined by the details written, but no evaluation is given, only encouragement to write more, if possible. (This promotes more candid responses.) The autobiography experience sets the stage for the second step: learning about the lives of culturally different people (Banks, 1994; Sjoberg & Kuhn, 1989).

Biography

Present and prospective teachers practice an interviewing process in class, with partners, to gain the confidence necessary to interview someone from a different culture. After several in-depth, audiotaped, unstructured or semistructured interviews (Spradley, 1979) of a person who is culturally different, each present or prospective teacher constructs a biography from key events in that selected person's life. (Practicing teachers choose a student's parent or guardian.) They may begin the interview by asking the parent to tell what he or she would want their child to learn this year. This is a way of allowing parents to voice their ideas and begin developing a comfort level with the teacher. During the interview, the teacher also shares some relevant personal life events. This allows for a give and take that creates a more democratic interview setting. Also, it is recommended that the interviews occur in a place that the parent requests—neutral ground, such as a park, coffee shop, or recreation center. (School may be considered hostile or intimidating. The power structure of schools may intimidate those with little formal education and from lower socioeconomic levels.) Another recommendation is for teachers to interview someone who has a significantly different skin tone, since this physical feature has implications for underrepresented groups in society. As a result, when present and prospective teachers meet those who are from different ethnic, cultural, economic, and linguistic groups, they learn about their lives and begin to develop the cultural sensitivity necessary to analyze similarities and differences between life stories (Ruggiano Schmidt, 1998b, 2000b; Ruggiano Schmidt & Finkbeiner, 2006; Spindler & Spindler, 1987).

CROSS-CULTURAL ANALYSIS

For the third step in the process, each present or prospective teacher studies the autobiography and biography and charts a list of similarities and differences. This may be accomplished in a table or Venn diagram and leads to the fourth step, or self-analysis of differences, a key component of the process (Finkbeiner, 2005, 2006; Osetek, 2006; Ruggiano Schmidt, 1999; Spindler & Spindler, 1987; Trueba, Jacobs, & Kirton, 1990).

Appreciation of Differences

Then the present or prospective teacher carefully examines the diagram that lists similarities and differences and writes an in-depth self-analysis of cultural differences. He or she explains how the differences make him or her feel; that is, "Why am I feeling uncomfortable about this difference? Why do I admire this difference?" Present and prospective teachers write about these feelings in specific detail. Through this process, they begin to acquire insights about others and sense their own ethnocentricity (Osetek, 2006; Ruggiano Schmidt, 2000a, 2001; Ruggiano Schmidt & Finkbeiner, 2006; Spindler & Spindler, 1987).

Home/School/Community Connection Plans for Literacy Development

After experiencing the previous steps, Kindergarten through Grade 12, present and prospective teachers design year-long plans for connecting home, school, and community for students' reading, writing, listening, speaking, and viewing based on numerous modifications of the ABCs model. Working with a partner while exploring the Internet is helpful in the search for ideas that relate to curriculums. Together, partners see ways to design culturally relevant or culturally responsive lessons and unit plans. For example, a math teacher studies ethnomathematics and uses indigenous people's designs to teach geometry; a biology teacher explains DNA through human cell characteristics and their adaptations to environments; and a 1st-grade teacher celebrates an appreciation of differences through multicultural self-portraits in crayon. The myriad examples are inspiring when teachers learn to take notice and see that true unity comes with an appreciation of differences (Izzo & Ruggiano Schmidt, 2006; Ruggiano Schmidt & Ma, 2006).

Those present and prospective teachers who follow the structure of these assignments produce excellent work that makes an impact on them personally and in their present and future classrooms (Ruggiano Schmidt & Lazar, 2011). Of course, as with any personal reflective activities, there are challenges for the professor and present and prospective teachers. First, professors must gently deal with those who resist the ABCs assignments. Some may think the ABCs assignments are useless, so they plod through and do the minimum; it seems typical in many courses that one or two students are unable to appreciate certain assignments. Others may not want to deal with their life stories, so they can be asked to write about their present lives. However, over the 20 years of ABCs implementation, only two teachers could not write their autobiographies. Most students write 20 to 30 pages, typed and with pictures, and many have even shared horrific past events that they have overcome. Second, professors may have to find interviewees for students, but this is a rare occurrence. Third, many are also challenged by the large amount of work involved in these assignments. Students study basic theories of literacy learning and critical race theory and then must see how the ABCs model connects with their particular teaching content areas. Once they have created at least 40 lesson ideas, they see the patterns in culturally responsive lessons and understand the significance of connecting the known to the new for relevant teaching and learning. Ultimately, course evaluations show that this is an extremely worthwhile requirement in their education programs as evidenced by the following typical statements:

"Everyone in this college should take this course. It helps you understand people."

"This course is perfect. It is truly a Jesuit experience."

"The work was demanding, but the learning was unforgettable."

"I will never be the same after this course. It was life changing."

Meeting Dr. Claudia Finkbeiner

In 1998, after teaching, writing, and presenting at conferences concerning the ABCs of Cultural Understanding and Communication, I met Dr. Claudia Finkbeiner at the World Conference in Jamaica. She approached me to discuss our research. And so began a terrific partnership! We traveled around the world spreading the original ABCs model and its adaptations throughout the United States, Europe, Australia, and Asia. Dr. Finkbeiner modified the ABCs and implemented it in numerous interesting ways, and many of the authors included in this book appreciated learning about the model's adaptability. Moreover, the graduate students that Dr. Finkbeiner and I followed, as part of doctoral and master's programs in education, demonstrated their expertise in noteworthy ways while creating unique adaptations of the ABCs of Cultural Understanding and Communication.

Two of the major results of Dr. Finkbeiner and my collaboration were the edited book, ABCs of Cultural Understanding and Communication: National and International Adaptations and our authored 2009–2011 FIPSE-Trans-Atlantic Policy Grant, which included professors from Europe and the United States. These accomplishments were joyous and rewarding endeavors.

This new ABCs book, edited by Dr. Claudia Finkbeiner and Dr. Althier Lazar, is the first "child" of the FIPSE Grant. It showcases the work of professors from Europe and the United States who implemented the ABCs model in a variety of contexts and time periods. For two years the professors studied the ABCs of Cultural Understanding and Communication as participants in the FIPSE-Atlantis Policy Grant. Their interesting depictions of the motivational powers of the ABCs of Cultural Understanding and Communication seem to validate much of the research related to the fields of educational anthropology, multicultural education, and literacy learning.

The ABCs model has evolved over time and belongs to those who want to make a difference in this world—compassionate people who care about others and wish for a more just existence for all. It appears that the ABCs of Cultural Understanding and Communication is needed now more than ever, but it takes courage and determination to implement it successfully. It also involves more work for the student and the professor, more than most would care to do for and in a university course, but those who implement the model in its purest form, with the greatest rigor, have the satisfaction of making significant differences in the lives of present and prospective teachers as they connect with their students, families, and communities for a more just academic and social classroom environment.

So this is my ABCs story. It has been a rich experience for me and my colleagues who examine and implement this model. Presently, I have left the world of research and am working for refugee families and children, and traditionally underrepresented groups in an urban community on the verge of revitalization. With the help of the Roman Catholic Church, Le Moyne College newly graduated teachers, master teachers, families, and community members, we are attempting to create a model international school, where spiritual and academic growth are seen as major factors in realizing the full meaning of being human. We are guided by the fundamental principle that true unity comes with an appreciation and celebration of linguistic, economic, ethnic, and cultural diversity.

REFERENCES

Au, K. (1993). *Literacy instruction in multicultural settings.* New York, NY: Harcourt Brace Jovanovich College Publishers.

Banks, J. (1994). *An introduction to multicultural education.* Boston, MA: Allyn & Bacon.

Cochran-Smith, M. (1995). Uncertain allies: Understanding the boundaries of race and teaching. *Harvard Educational Review, 65*(4), 541–570.

Emig, J. (1971). Writing is a mode of learning. *College Composition and Communication, 28,* 122–128.

Finkbeiner, C. (2005). *Interessen und Strategien beim fremdsprachlichen Lesen. Wie Schülerin und Schüler englische Texte lesen und verstehen.* [Interest and Strategies in Foreign Language Reading: How Students Read and Comprehend English Texts]. Tuebingen, Germany: Narr.

Finkbeiner, C. (2006). Constructing third space. The principles of reciprocity and cooperation. In P. Ruggiano Schmidt & C. Finkbeiner (Eds.), *The ABCs of cultural understanding and communication: National and international adaptations* (pp. 19–42). Greenwich, CT: Information Age.

Finkbeiner, C., & Koplin, C. (2001). Fremdverstehensprozesse und interkulturelle Prozesse als Forschungsgegenstand. In A. Mueller-Hartmann & M. Schocker-v.-Ditfurth, (Eds.), *Qualitative Forschungsansatze im Bereich Fremdsprachen lehren und lernen* (pp. 114–136). Tuebingen, Germany: Narr.

Finkbeiner, C., & Koplin, C. (2002). *A cooperative approach for facilitating intercultural education.* Reading Online. Retrieved from http://www.readingonline.org/newliteracies/lit_index.asp?HREF=/newliteracies/finkbeiner

Gunderson, L. (2007). *English-only instruction and immigrant students in secondary schools: A critical examination.* Mahwah, NJ: Lawrence Erlbaum.

Heath, S. B. (1983). *Ways with words: Language life and work in communities and classrooms.* Cambridge, UK: Cambridge University Press.

Izzo, A., & Ruggiano Schmidt, P. (2006). Successful ABCs in-service project: Supporting culturally responsive teaching. In P. Lazar, A. (Ed.), *Learning to be literacy teachers: Stories of growth and change.* Newark, DE: International Reading Association.

Ladson-Billings, G. (1995). Toward a theory of culturally relevant pedagogy. *American Educational Research Journal, 32,* 465–491.

Lazar, A. (2004). *Learning to be literacy teachers: Stories of growth and change.* Newark, DE: International Reading Association.

Leftwich, S. (2002). Learning to use diverse students' literature in the classroom: A model for preservice teacher education. *Reading Online, 6*(2). Retrieved from www.readingonline.org

Noordhoff, K., & Kleinfield, J. (1993). Preparing teachers for multiculturalclassrooms. *Teaching and Teacher Education, 9*(1), 27–39.

Osborne, A. B. (1996). Practice into theory into practice: Culturally relevant pedagogy for students we have marginalized and normalized. *Anthropology and Education Quarterly, 27*(3), 285–314.

Osetek, J. (2006). ABCs: A journey toward making a positive difference. In P. Ruggiano Schmidt & C. Finkbeiner (Eds.), *ABCs of cultural understanding and communication: National and international adaptations* (pp. 43–72). Greenwich, CT: Information Age.

Paley, V. G. (1989). *White teacher.* Cambridge, MA: Harvard University Press.

Progoff, I. (1975). *At a journal workshop: The basic text and guide for using the intensive journal.* New York, NY: Dialogue House Library.

Reyhner, J., & Garcia, R. L. (1989). Helping minorities read better: Problems and promises. *Reading Research and Instruction, 28*(3), 84–91.

Ruggiano Schmidt, P. (1998a). *Cultural conflict and struggle: Literacy learning in a kindergarten program.* New York, NY: Peter Lang.

Ruggiano Schmidt, P. (1998b). The ABCs of cultural understanding and communication. *Equity and Excellence in Education, 31*(2), 28–38.

Ruggiano Schmidt, P. (1999). Focus on research: Know thyself and understand others. *Language Arts, 76*(4), 332–340.

Ruggiano Schmidt, P. (2000a). Emphasizing differences to build cultural understandings. In V. Risko & K. Bromley (Eds.), *Collaboration for diverse learners: Viewpoints and practices.* Newark, DE: IRA.

Ruggiano Schmidt, P. (2000b). Teachers connecting and communicating with families for literacy development. In T. Shanahan & F. Rodriguez-Brown (Eds.), *National Reading Conference yearbook, 49th* (pp. 194–208). Chicago, IL: National Reading Conference.

Ruggiano Schmidt, P. (2001). The power to empower. In P. R. Schmidt and P.B. Mosenthal (Eds.), *Reconceptualizing literacy in the new age of multiculturalism and pluralism.* Greenwich, CT: Information Age.

Ruggiano Schmidt, P. (2005). Culturally responsive instruction: Promoting literacy in secondary content areas. Adolescent literacy. American Institutes for Research. Retrieved from http://www.learningpt.org

Ruggiano Schmidt, P., & Finkbeiner, C. (2006). ABCs of cultural understanding and communication: National and international adaptations. Greenwich, CT: Information Age.

Ruggiano Schmidt, P., & Lazar, A. (2011). Practicing what we teach: How culturally responsive literacy classrooms make a difference. New York, NY: Teachers College Press.

Ruggiano Schmidt, P., & Ma, W. (2006). 50 literacy strategies for culturally responsive teaching. Thousand Oaks, CA: Corwin.

Sjoberg, G., & Kuhn, K. (1989). Autobiography and organizations: Theoretical and methodological issues. *The Journal of Applied Behavioral Science, 25*(4), 309–326.

Spindler, G., & Spindler, L. (1987). The interpretive ethnography of education: At home and abroad. Hillsdale, NJ: Lawrence Erlbaum.

Spradley, J. (1979). The ethnographic interview. New York, NY: Holt, Rinehart & Winston.

Tatum, B. (1992). Talking about race, learning about racism: The application of racial identity theory in the classroom. *Harvard Educational Review, 62,* 1–24.

Trueba, H. T., Jacobs, L., & Kirton, E. (1990). Cultural conflict and adaptation: The case of the Hmong students in American society. New York, NY: Falmer.

Xu, H. (2000a). Preservice teachers integrate understandings of diversity into literacy instruction: An adaptation of the ABCs model. *Journal of Teacher Education, 51*(2), 135–142.

Xu, H. (2000b). Preservice teachers in a literacy methods course consider issues of diversity. *Journal of Literacy Research, 32*(4), 505–531.

Yinger, R. (1985). Journal writing as a learning tool. *Volga-Review, 87*(5), 21–33.

CHAPTER 2

RESPONDING TO CULTURAL AND LINGUISTIC DIVERSITY THROUGH THE TRANSABCs PROJECT

Report and Results

Claudia Finkbeiner

INTRODUCTION

The TRANSABCs project is situated in the framework of the EU-US cooperation program Atlantis.[1] It is a large-scale research study that is rooted in experiences with various applications of the ABCs model (Ruggiano Schmidt, 1998; Ruggiano Schmidt & Finkbeiner, 2006). Its power and challenge lie in the commitment of a strongly interwoven network of people from different parts of the world who have joined with each other on a journey to some of the most valuable and exciting world heritages: language, culture, and literacy (Finkbeiner & Svalberg, 2012).

What the travelers at the start of the journey might unquestionably label as *their* language, *their* culture, and *their* literacy, in contrast to those of

Getting to Know Ourselves and Others Through the ABCs, pages 11–46
Copyright © 2015 by Information Age Publishing
11

others, often turns out to be a lot more complex. The individual paths chosen prove to be less travelled, and concepts or ideas about the world have to be refined, and as a result something new emerges as a third domain (Bhabha, 1994). It seems as if life stories are individual puzzle pieces flying through space and time, meeting other pieces, discovering similarities and differences, and producing a common thread between people who might coincidentally or intentionally meet on this rocky journey.

TRANSABCs draws on the *ABC's Model of Cultural Understanding and Communication* (Ruggiano Schmidt, 1998; Ruggiano Schmidt & Finkbeiner, 2006) as well as on the Human GPS model (Finkbeiner, 2009). The ABCs model consists of several steps: A = autobiography, B = biography based on interviews, and C1 = cross-cultural comparison, C2 = cultural self-analysis of differences, and C3 = culturally responsive ideas (see below). This model allows people of all walks of life to take a path usually not chosen. The ABCs journey encourages self-discovery and discovery of others with respect to cultural differences and similarities.

The ABCs cannot only be used on a local but also on a global level, thus offering opportunities to meet individual needs as well as public demands in a diversifying world. In this way it is also suitable for global education programs. This is the key to its value.

TRANSABCS PARTICIPANTS, SOCIOCULTURAL CONTEXT, AND TIME FRAME

Our call for active participation in this project was responded to by far more people interested in language, culture, and literacy (Finkbeiner & Svalberg, 2012) than those we were finally allowed to select: Seven scholars from the United States and six from Europe were chosen from different EU regions in Northern, Eastern, Central and Southern Europe and from different U.S. states. Furthermore, the model was implemented in an M.A. summer course in one of the participant's partner universities in Montreal, Canada (see Chapter 3). All partners are academically comparable. They work at public and private colleges and universities across the United States and Europe and are experts in culture, language, and literacy (Finkbeiner & Svalberg, 2012).

The ABCs model was implemented by professors in their university classes several times over a two-year period (see Appendix). Beyond the TRANSABCs grant group an external group of additional five professors voluntarily implemented the model. The project was officially launched September 1, 2009 and ended August 31, 2011. More than 700 students participated. We were able to gather the complete data set (see below) from all professors and from 557 students. All professors and lecturers worked with college and university students who find positions in another professional settings. Most of the participants shared the belief that in today's world—no matter whether one works at school, in the community, or in the workplace—one needs to be well prepared to work with heterogeneous groups consisting of members from diverse cultural, socioeconomic, and linguistic backgrounds (Finkbeiner, 2006a, 2006b).

The Diversity Factor

Diversity preparation is a key qualification for learning to cherish the inherent wealth of variety in differing worlds and create meaningful and authentic environments to motivate and empower individuals and groups in schools, the community, and the workplace. Diversity and migration are by no means new phenomena. History shows that complete tribes migrated across Europe. This is evident in the words *Völkerwanderung* in German, *migration des barbares* in French, and *invasion of the barbarians* in English (Finkbeiner & Fehling, 2006). This example underlines the importance of language awareness and perspective when creating cultural awareness in a multilingual and multicultural world (Finkbeiner, 2008). Whereas the German expression for the phenomenon described above is neutral, the French and English languages use the Roman sense of the barbarian as someone uncivilized. Accordingly, underlying concepts may differ, and therefore words do not always carry the same meanings from one language to another. It all depends on one's perspective (Finkbeiner, 2008, 2009).

We need to carefully look beyond the one seventh of the iceberg that lies on the surface (Weaver, 1993) and dive deep to find out about the six sevenths below the surface that contain the exciting concepts and ideas underlying what was said or expressed (Finkbeiner, 2009).

Human GPS Approach: Multi-Perspectives

A multi-perspective approach as modeled in the "Human GPS" can be helpful (Finkbeiner, 2009). Just as in a GPS, it takes at least three different perspectives to locate one's own self. This approach can be facilitated in learning environments that encourage the inclusion of different and even opposing perspectives. Differences in socialization and acculturation contribute to the development of different values, beliefs, attitudes, and traditions (Finkbeiner, 2006a, 2006b). These hidden traits mostly remain uncovered because they belong to personal life stories that are usually not taken into account in professional or educational settings.

This is the starting point of the ABCs model (Finkbeiner & Koplin, 2001, 2002; Ruggiano Schmidt & Finkbeiner, 2006), which takes life stories seriously and uses them as a springboard into meta-cognitive reflection of perceived differences of cultural processes. Such reflection is key to one's cultural awareness, especially language awareness (Fehling, 2008; Finkbeiner & Svalberg, 2012; James & Garrett, 1992). The ABCs model is an important trigger for such meta-cognitive processes, bearing in mind that the linguistic, economic, and cultural differences of populations have challenged educators all across the world (Finkbeiner, 2006a; Nieto, 1996, 1999).

There are educators in the United States and the EU who do not feel adequately prepared to teach in culturally and linguistically diverse classroom settings. Cultural conflicts and struggles—observable or hidden—can disconnect children, families, and communities and therefore have to be taken seriously (Ogbu, 2003; Ruggiano Schmidt, 1998a; T. Trueba, 2002; Trueba, Jacobs, & Kirton, 1990).

Literacy

Literacy was another factor that played a role in the design of the TRANS-ABCs project. The poor results for several student populations in the *Progress in International Reading Literacy Study* (PIRLS) and the *Program for International Student Assessment* (PISA) stimulated concerns in the United States and Europe regarding children's literacy learning (http://www.bmbf.de/en; www.oecd.org/pisa).

Beginning in 2000 and 2003, countries whose children did not perform well on PISA and PIRLS initiated a strong emphasis on reading, writing, and math skills. But in spite of the stress on reading and math, test results continued to indicate that a certain group of children, particularly those in underserved communities, had made little progress, especially in the area of literacy development.

In order to fully understand this lag in achievement, researchers have gone beyond the study of test scores. Other qualitative factors from the PIRLS and PISA reports indicate that the influence of home, school, and community must be considered when attempting to improve literacy learning (Brozo, Shiel, & Topping, 2007). Further analyses of this influence show that linguistic, cultural, and economic differences—even though they bear potential for a cognitively demanding learning process—may at the same time hinder the academic progress of many of the students. The PISA study illustrated that immigrant children in the participating countries also have a performance disadvantage (Lindholm-Leary, 2000). These are important concerns, because children with a migration background are by no means a minority. In 2010 more than 210 million people lived in a country other than the one in which they were born, with one fourth living in the United States and Europe (Bundeszentrale für politische Bildung, 2013).

The Role of Language in the ABCs Process

Finkbeiner and Koplin (2002) explained that the language issue is an important factor in the ABCs process. The role of language cannot be underestimated in intercultural communication because it is linked to power relationships (Finkbeiner, 2008; James & Garrett, 1992). English was the language used across all campuses in the TRANSABCs project. It was important to agree on a language everybody could share so that talk about the stories was possible. For some TRANSABCs participants, English was the native language, for others it was a second or foreign language or the *lingua franca*.

With diverse classes that share the heritage of about 10 to 15 different languages, we find a lot of speakers that are not on a proficiency level of a native speaker in English. We, therefore, have to be aware of the fact that the solution to write the stories in English as the *lingua franca* is quite some compromise due to proficiency level and the issue of feeling comfortable enough to express one's most personal and private ideas in a language other than one's own (Finkbeiner & Koplin, 2002).

According to Finkbeiner and Koplin (2002), we have to consider the fact that even highly proficient speakers of English might find it alienating to tell and write down their stories in a language different from the one in which their life stories were situated. We face differences in schemata and scripts or even gaps across languages. Direct verbatim translation is not really possible.

The language issue is even more important in ABCs applications in the school setting. In the kindergarten, primary, and secondary level I, as well as in other learning environments, most new migrants do not yet speak the official language. This target group often faces speech difficulties or does not even speak the "new" language at all. In such cases, media used in conjunction with the ABCs are very helpful as they compensate for the lack of language with pictures, graphs, music, and such.

Telling or writing down the stories in a language other than one's own can also be easier than telling or writing them in one's own language. When one writes the story down or tells it, the language can be used as a tool to place oneself in what seems to be another person's shoes. We have learned this lesson in interviews with participants who have told horrific war stories or traumatic life stories.

Quite a few participants explain that they adopt another identity when talking about their lives in another language. Someone talking to a person from a different cultural or linguistic background might also change roles or adopt another identity even though the discourse happens in that person's native language.

Validation

Validation of what was said by the interviewee and understood by the interviewer is very important to avoid misinterpretation. The validation follows after the biography has been written about the other person based on an initial interview and a follow-up interview. In this phase, the biography will be presented to the interviewees: it will either be read to them, translated for them or read by the interviewees themselves, depending on the language situation. The validation phase has to take place in a context of mutual respect and acceptance. It has to allow the interviewees to pass if issues turn out to be too private or difficult. Validation ought to never be about justification, but rather clarification.

Relevant Research Studies

Research and practice demonstrate that strong home, school, and community connections promote students' literacy development (Au, 1993; P. A. Edwards, 1996; Faltis, 1993; Finkbeiner, 2005; McCaleb, 1994; Moll, 1992; Reyhner & Garcia, 1989; Ruggiano Schmidt, 2000; Ruggiano Schmidt & Finkbeiner, 2006). School populations on either side of the Atlantic have become increasingly diverse both culturally and ethnically; however, teaching populations often have remained fairly homogeneous.

School curricula, methods, and materials sometimes reflect mainstream European or European American culture and do not always take into account the backgrounds and experiences of students from low income families (Howard, 2001; Ladson-Billings, 1994, 1995; Nieto, 1996). Many teacher-education as well as business programs do not adequately prepare students for "culturally relevant pedagogy" (Ladson-Billings, 1995) nor for a culturally relevant workplace. This has become an international problem as the influence of this factor has been linked to poor literacy development and high dropout rates among students from urban poverty areas (Au, 1993; Banks, 1994; Cummins, 1986; Edwards, Pleasants, & Franklin, 1999; Nieto, 1999; Ruggiano Schmidt, 1998c; H. T. Trueba et al., 1990). In Germany, for example, the results of the second wave of the PISA study revealed the educational disadvantage children from low-income families and families with a migration background might face. Obviously, this information concerning educational programs makes urgent the promotion of cultural understanding and communication. The ABCs model and its adaptations provide opportunities for participants to learn how to make connections and create culturally responsive ideas.

Culturally relevant teaching (Ladson-Billings, 1995) connects the curriculum to the knowledge and experiences of the diverse cultures in the classrooms by taking account of students' family backgrounds and experiences and by using the literacies found in the students' cultures.

Teachers who reach out to families and connect students' experiences and backgrounds to the curriculum implement *culturally relevant pedagogy* or *culturally responsive teaching* (Ruggiano Schmidt & Lazar, 2011). This can result in a narrowing of the student academic achievement gap and an increase in positive attitudes toward learning (P. A. Edwards et al., 1999; Faltis, 1993; Moll, 1992; Ruggiano Schmidt & Finkbeiner, 2006). However, many educators do not have an understanding of the literacies related to particular cultures. Cultural funds of knowledge often remain tacit and ignored (Moll, Amanti, Neff, & Gonzalez, 1992).

There is evidence that self-knowledge may be the first and foremost consideration when attempting to help teachers understand diverse groups of students (Banks, 1994; Finkbeiner, 2003; Osborne, 1996). This self-knowledge is promoted in the ABCs of Cultural Understanding and Communication. According to Byram (2009), this self-knowledge ought to be critical. Drawing on Barnett (1997), he suggests that "students should critique the knowledge they are acquiring, become involved in a process of reflection on self, in a process of reconstruction of self, and become engaged through critique in action 'in a collective reconstruction of the world'" (Byram, 2009, p. 212).

Exploratory studies of the ABCs model on both sides of the Atlantic indicate that this journey to the self is a valuable process (Finkbeiner & Knierim, 2008; Leftwich, 2002; Ruggiano Schmidt, 1998c, 1999; Ruggiano Schmidt & Finkbeiner, 2006; Ruggiano Schmidt & Ma, 2006; Wilden, 2007, 2008; Xu, 2000a, 2000b). However, there is a need for larger cohorts of present and future teachers and for systematic evaluations using qualitative and quantitative data.

The ABCs Model

Critical literacy (Fairclough, 1992; Powell, Cantrell, & Adams, 2001) and the sociocultural perspective (Purcell-Gates, L'Allier, & Smith, 1995; Rogoff, 1990; H. T. Trueba et al., 1990; Vygotsky, 1978) serve as the foundation for the *ABCs of Cultural Understanding and Communication* (Finkbeiner, 2006a; Ruggiano Schmidt & Finkbeiner, 2006). According to Clark et al. (1991), critical literacy sees language as discourse. The ABCs process triggers discourse between two or more participants who may be different from each other with respect to age, gender, skin color, ethnicity, language, religion, physical appearance, and more.

Critical literacy puts an emphasis on three perspectives that are important in the ABCs process:

a. Social context with respect to each specific situation, institution, and society in general: taking account of the social context can help ABCs participants understand differences better;
b. Sociocognitive processes that play a role in discourse production and interpretation: this is an important hint as to the role of culture in reciprocal knowledge construction via the ABCs;
c. Spoken and written text, which form the basic corpus for the ABCs.

The theoretical framework of culture, equity, and democracy in the classroom and school environments (Feng, Byram, & Fleming, 2009; Finkbeiner, 2009) match the ABCs model.

ABCs Target Groups

The ABCs model can be used and adapted for all age and target groups. So far the model has been applied in classes with primary school children; secondary, college, and university students; university professors; business people; and parents. It can be done online (Finkbeiner & Knierim, 2006; Wilden, 2007) and face-to-face, in written, oral, or hybrid forms including pictures, drawings, and online features. It can be mono-directional, with clear roles of researcher and research subject, or it can be reciprocal, with all partners adopting interchangeable roles (Finkbeiner, 2004).

The ABCs can be done in pairs or groups of three (Finkbeiner & Koplin, 2002). Participants who become involved in the ABCs process begin to critically discuss and evaluate their own life experiences. They look inward and outward simultaneously and often describe a discomfort, disequilibrium, or anxiety associated with learning new information that may conflict with old ideas and norms.

Focused and Non-Focused Life Stories

The process can be initiated via non-focused life stories that one remembers and are therefore relevant to that person. However, in specific settings, one might decide to put a special focus on the life stories. For example, in applied linguistics classes, the center of attention can be on language-learning theories. Relevant episodes of one's own language learning and literacy development would be triggered and written down. In content and language integrated or bilingual classes, such as in biology, the focal point can be on ecology and nature and the role it has played in the participants' lives as well as the way it has changed one's attitudes over the years. In history classes, the focus can be on personal, local, national, and international historical events and signs, monuments, and places as well as special personal, local, national, or international days of these events and their impact on daily life. In geography, the attention can be on locations, places, and climate and the images and preferences we have about them as well as the influence they have had on people's lives as their often tacit geoculture. In physical education, the focus can be on memories of physical activities at home, at school, or in nature as well as on role models one adored as a child. In the ABCs process, episodes in one's own life can be compared with somebody else's biography or the biographies of famous sportsmen and -women.

ABCs Requirements

It is mandatory that ABCs teachers or instructors have gone on an ABCs journey themselves. Since not all TRANSABCs partners had been acquainted with the ABC's model right from the start, a week-long workshop was held at the beginning at the University of Kassel in the fall of 2009. This workshop was a necessary precondition for the implementation of the grant goals. It is a basic but highly important principle of the ABCs that ABCs instructors can only convincingly and authentically teach the ABCs model if they have experienced it themselves.

Prospective ABCs instructors can take part in a preparatory instructors' ABCs online course before the actual class exchange. This is the way we practiced it with the instructors involved in an ABCs online exchange between classes in the Netherlands and in India[2] as well as in Germany and Pakistan.

The TRANSABCs Courses

A key goal for the study investigators was to standardize the implementation of the TRANSABCs model across the courses. While all university courses were based on *The ABCs of Cultural Understanding and Communication* (Ruggiano Schmidt & Finkbeiner, 2006) some variation existed in the educational level of the course participants (undergraduate vs. graduate/professional), the number of participants in each course, and the length of time these projects were conducted (see Appendix, "TRANSABCs Project 2009–2011"). In addition, these courses were required in most university programs, but in a few cases they were elective courses. Given these variations which come naturally with ecological validity, we sought to maximize consistency by educating all instructors to conduct the project the same way, and to ask instructors to follow the steps of the ABCs in a particular sequence. The aim was to explore cultural similarities and differences in the life stories of individuals from different cultural backgrounds through intercultural exchange and discourse. On the basis of this experience, students were encouraged to develop their own concepts and strategies of multicultural education as an important part of the school curriculum and/or the workplace. Students preparing for industry and commerce became aware of cultural differences and potential conflicts when negotiating and communicating with business partners.

Each TRANSABCs class followed a 5-step process to produce the following documents (Ruggiano Schmidt & Finkbeiner, 2006):

A = Autobiography: writing or narrating relevant events from one's own life.

B = Biography: interviewing someone different from oneself, e.g., with respect to culture, language, ethnicity, religion, age, political viewpoint, and/or sexual orientation and writing down that person's story. This step included the validation of the interviews and the presentation of the biography draft to the interviewee to clarify misinterpretations (Finkbeiner & Koplin, 2002).

It usually required three meetings at a place that was both neutral and safe for both the interviewer and interviewee (such as a park, coffee shop, or recreation center; schools may be considered hostile or intimidating for some participants who fear educational settings).

The "C" parts of the project include:

C1 = Cross-cultural comparison, writing a chart, Venn diagram (A. W. F. Edwards, 2004) or Cultural Venn Diagram (Finkbeiner, 2009, p. 165; see Table 1) of similarities and differences.

C2 = Cultural self-analysis of differences that ought to lead to an appreciation of differences. C1 and C2 entail analyzing the interview partner's life story with an emphasis on understanding differences.

C3 = Development of at least five culturally responsive ideas for the school or the workplace.

Follow-up interviews were conducted a year later with a selected focus group from each ABCs group.

A = Autobiography

First, each TRANSABCs participant wrote an autobiography that included key life events related to education, family, religious tradition, recreation, victories, and defeats. The goal was awareness raising with respect to values and beliefs, likes and dislikes, attitudes and preferences, cognition and affection, life philosophies, and wills (Finkbeiner, 2006a). These traits form the traditions and values of cultural autobiographies (Banks, 1994). Literacy activities can help trigger knowledge of the self (Finkbeiner, 2006a, 2009; Yinger, 1985). Most ABCs participants reported that for the first time in their lives they halted, sat down, and started reflecting on themselves and their life stories.

The autobiographies are considered highly confidential documents; only the teacher-educator/instructor (professor) sees them if not agreed upon differently at the outset. The autobiography is seen as a mirror of one's identity and thus remains protected. Quality is determined by the details written, but no evaluation is given, only encouragement to write more, if possible.

The autobiography experience sets the stage for step "B": learning about the lives of culturally different people (Banks, 1994; Sjoberg & Kuhn, 1989). Sometimes these stories reveal traumatizing events participants might have gone through. ABCs instructors need to be reminded that they are neither psychologists nor psychiatrists; their role is to guide and perhaps advise the participant to seek professional help if the event seems an unresolved burden in life.

Often participants will spend a lot of effort on their stories, and they might want to share these with their families and or friends. It is their decision whether to do so.

B = Biography

After several in-depth, audio- or video-taped, unstructured or semi-structured interviews (Bogdan & Biklen, 1994; Spradley, 1979) with a person who is culturally different, each present or future teacher constructs a biography from key events in that person's life. Teachers can choose a student's parent or guardian. University students can choose a person who is different from themselves along at least a few significant cultural dimensions. These dimensions may include dominant language, class, skin color, gender, and religion. High school or primary students can chose a student from another part of the world in the classroom, outside the classroom in the same city, or even beyond; in the latter case the meeting will be online.

Interviewing a parent is a way of allowing parents to voice their ideas and begin developing a comfort level with the teacher. During the interview, the interviewer can also share some personal, relevant life events. When teachers meet with family members and learn about their lives, they might begin to develop the cultural sensitivity necessary to analyze similarities and differences between life stories (Borschel, 2012; Ruggiano Schmidt, 1998b; Spindler & Spindler, 1987).

In iPad and tablet-based ABCs pilot studies with a senior lady of 87, a graduate student of 30, and a secondary level I student of 15, we found out about the positive effects of the use of the iPad and/or any other tablet PC on different age groups. These new media suit the ABCs process well, as one cannot only tape others (B) but also oneself (A) by reversing the picture. Furthermore, this medium is less threatening, particularly for seniors and children, as it is small in size. It can be put on an integrated keyboard stand, allows ad hoc use and the storage of many single mini-episodes, and has an instant gratification and motivation effect as the interviewee can watch the episodes right away in a stimulated recall phase (Gass & Mackey, 2000). As the tool allows direct haptic manipulation of the screen, it is attractive both for young and old learners.

C1 = Cross-Cultural Comparison

For the third step in the process, each participant studies the autobiography and biography and charts a list of similarities and differences. Formerly, this was accomplished in a list or Venn diagram (Edwards, 2004). The Venn diagram consists of two intersecting circles clearly showing differences and similarities. In order to not only elicit surface but also deep level comparisons the Venn diagram has been integrated into Weaver's iceberg (Weaver, 1993) by Finkbeiner (2009, p. 165; see Table 1) and developed into the "Cultural Venn Diagram." Furthermore, a hybrid zone has been added to this new Cultural Venn Iceberg, as it might be sometimes difficult to allocate phenomena simply to the above or the below domain. These different layers allow us to more carefully look at the specific language used to express certain experiences and to find out about similarities and differences above, below, and within the hybrid zone.

Davidson (Finkbeiner & Davidson, this volume) expresses it like this:

> As I stated at the end of my mother's biography, the motivation to have her participate as an interviewee was to open a dialog about her personal history that had often been shrouded in silence. This silence and subsequent search for self are common themes in literature written by second-generation immigrants in North America. Two who come immediately to mind are Canada's Nino Ricci in his trilogy *The Lives of the Saints* and the Chinese American author Amy Tan; both write about characters who grapple with what is unspoken, confronting their parents' past and its secrets. I liken this process to a storm that stirs the waters at sea; each wave that comes to shore carries elements that were previously hidden on the sea floor beneath murky waters. What was once invisible or unknown is now available for closer inspection, which can lead to new realizations, associations, memories, and questions, some of which are discussed in this paper, the cross-cultural analysis phase of this ABCs process.

There are a lot of intertextual clues in the paragraph. In ABCs texts there might also be a preference for adjectives, verbs, or nouns that might be neutral or emotionally loaded in a positive or negative way. Or there might be a preference for certain pronouns (e.g., we, our, and us versus I, mine, and me), which indicate the belonging to what Hofstede (1980) labels as collective culture versus individual culture.

The form that has been developed (Figure 2.1) integrates text indicators on the surface, hybrid, and deep structures in all three mandatory texts: autobiography, biography, and cross-cultural comparison. This new form has proven to be a useful tool as it not only makes participants consider the surface structure of the text but also helps to illuminate its deep structure as well as the intertextual clues among A, B, and C. This helps participants move away from a vague interpretation towards an in-depth text and evidence-based analysis.

C2 = Cross-Cultural In-Depth Analysis and Appreciation of Differences

This leads us to the fourth step, which is a self-analysis of differences. It is the heart and core of the ABCs model (Ruggiano Schmidt, 1998; Finkbeiner & Koplin, 2002; Ruggiano Schmidt & Finkbeiner, 2006). Participants carefully examine the Cultural Venn Iceberg (Finkbeiner, 2009), which lists similarities and differences as well as quotes the sources in the autobiographies and/or biographies. They write their individual in-depth self-analyses of cultural differences in the chart (Figure 2.1).

Participants explain how the differences make them feel, for example, "Why am I feeling uncomfortable about this difference? Why do I admire this difference?" Beliefs and feelings are described in specific detail. Through this process, ABCs participants begin to acquire insights about others and sense their own ethnocentricity (Spindler & Spindler, 1987).

C3 = Culturally Responsive Ideas for Home-School or Workplace-Community Connections

After experiencing the previous steps, ABCs participants develop culturally responsive ideas either for home–school or workplace–community connections (Ruggiano Schmidt & Lazar, 2011). For example, K–12[3] present and future teachers design plans for connecting home, school, and community for students' reading, writing, listening, speaking, and viewing. They envision ways to design culturally relevant or culturally responsive lessons and unit plans. For example, a math teacher would help students study ethnomathematics and use indigenous peoples' designs to grasp geometry. A language teacher would teach the Brothers Grimms' fairy tales in a Human GPS approach (Finkbeiner, 2009), which would include the reception and adaptation of specific fairy tales in different cultures and languages across the world. A geography teacher would teach geolocalization and what impact the specific geolocation might have on one's daily life. Business or vocational participants would develop ideas for the workplace. For example, in order to develop nurses, doctors, and patients' cultural health literacy awareness in a diverse dermatology practice, participants would develop a program where ethnic hair and skin as well as the values connected to them would be studied.

The participants wrote one paragraph for each idea in which they described the idea as precisely as possible. They described the target group and the intended goal and had to make sure that the idea complied with curricular validity. Furthermore, they used the following self-assessment checklist to make sure they included the most important key data:

- Lesson or Workplace Implementation: Have you provided enough information so that another person will be able to implement your idea with the aid of your description?
- Home/School/Community Connection: Is there an obvious connection between the content area of your idea and the ethnic, linguistic, and/or cultural diversity of the classroom/staff?

Name: .... Course: .... Date: .... Term: .... Place: ....

Cross Cultural Analysis C1

| Autobiography (A) | | Cross Cultural Comparison (A and B) | | Biography (B) | |
Themes/ Categories	Notes Reference (Page A)	Differences Above A	Similarities Above A and B	Differences Above B	Notes Reference (Page B)	Themes/ Categories
			ABOVE → SURFACE Zone			
		In Between → HYBRID ZONE				

Themes/ Categories	Notes Reference (Page A)	Differences Below A	Similarities Below A and B	Differences Below B	Notes Reference (Page B)	Themes/ Categories
			BELOW → DEEP ZONE			
	Autobiography (A)		Cross Cultural Comparison (A and B)		Biography (B)	

Figure 2.1 Simplified Cultural Venn Iceberg. *Source:* Finkbeiner (2009, 2012)

- Components of Literacy Learning: Does your idea include literary components, such as reading, writing, listening, speaking and viewing? How many components does your idea include? Just one? Three or even more components?
- Source of the Idea: Is it your own idea or did you use a reliable source, such as a journal or a textbook, etc.?
- Organization/Appearance/Editing: Is the organization of your idea clear and easy to follow?
- Level of Variety and Engagement: Does the content area for the lesson or your idea for the workplace demonstrate great variety and require students'/employees' active involvement? Or does your idea incorporate repetitious activities with little student/employee involvement?
- Evaluation: Did you mention how a teacher or employer would evaluate the outcome of the students'/employees' work?

Participants were encouraged to be as creative as possible and write about a "real" project, which could be implemented in the school or at the workplace. They were reminded to dive deeply under the water level (Finkbeiner, 2009) when developing their idea and to try to think about projects other than just food, folklore, or festivities. They had to write at least 300 words and attach an appendix if they had further material that could help illustrate their idea. A lot of wonderful culturally responsive ideas were developed over the two years.

European Adaptation of the ABCs Model

Ruggiano Schmidt's ABCs model has been adapted by Finkbeiner and colleagues (Finkbeiner, 2006a, 2006b, 2009; Finkbeiner & Fehling, 2006; Finkbeiner & Knierim, 2006, 2008; Finkbeiner & Koplin, 2002; Wilden, 2007, 2008) within the European context in order to take into account the special sociocultural characteristics in a continuously changing Europe. These are (a) geographic closeness of the European countries, (b) multilingual and multicultural perspectives (Finkbeiner & Fehling, 2006), (c) European dimension (Finkbeiner, 1995) as expressed in the Maastricht treaty, (d) permanent political and socioeconomic changes that have taken place in Europe since 1989, and (e) challenges that can be seen in the continuous expansion and growth of the European Union.

After preparing their autobiographies, conducting interviews, and writing biographies of their partners, the ABCs participants discover that their perspectives are bound to their cultural knowledge. A cross-cultural analysis follows, in which participants reflect on differences and similarities between autobiographies and biographies as well as biographies and biographies. While transcribing their conversations, participants reflect in detail on their learning processes. In addition, they are asked to look for communication strategies as well as linguistic preferences that the transcriptions reveal: What do you do when you have to talk about misunderstandings, differences, or similarities with someone from a different cultural background? And, finally, an intercultural diary is written to reflect on the learning process and/or certain language awareness and cultural awareness-raising activities are added. Furthermore, a phase is added for communicative validation of the biography. In such a phase the interviewee will have the chance to point out and clarify misunderstanding and/or misinterpretation of his or her story.

Implementation of the Framework of TRANSABCs

The dissemination and adaptation of the *ABC's of Cultural Understanding and Communication* (TRANSABCs) was designed to prepare college and university professors from Europe and the United States to teach present and future educators as well as present business students and future businessmen and -women to successfully communicate with students, families, and communities in the workplace.

One goal was to enable participants to make connections to the school curriculum or to the demands of the workplace. L1, L2, or L3 language teachers were to develop into culturally responsive instructors.

Future business students and international students were included to become better prepared for a diverse workplace and for making decisions in the labor market that were culturally responsive. The project was embedded in teacher education programs as well as business and vocational programs at universities in the United States and Europe. Every partner was involved in every step of the project's implementation.

Some professors brought students together from different parts of the world. The online participants were matched in a cooperative effort by the professors.

Very interesting results were obtained through follow-up online ABCs between, for example, between primary schools in Calcutta, India, and in Zwolle, the Netherlands (Goebel, 2012).

Diversity of Educational Systems and Core Curriculum

The TRANSABCs were implemented in teaching English as a foreign language, literacy methods and literacy classes, as well as in classes on applied linguistics, business administration, and intercultural competence. While the core curriculum varied across 12 different campuses, the common core curriculum was literacy. The educational systems of the participating countries are described in the different chapters of this volume (also see Appendix).

Time Frame of the TRANSABCs Project

The project started with a TRANSABCs Workshop in Kassel, Germany, from the end of September to October 4, 2009. In this workshop the participants experienced and learned about the underlying theories of the ABCs, decided on ABCs participants, studied evaluation forms and procedures, planned data recording and collection as well as group communication procedures, and discussed the TRANSABCs webpage (www.transabcs.org). The goals of the workshop were to find out about how to implement the ABCs and evaluate its effectiveness in teacher education programs as well as how to develop a curriculum across the different European and American institutions within the *Common European Framework of Reference for Languages*. Directly after the Kassel workshop, the EU and U.S. Project Directors[4] participated in the ATLANTIS annual conference and the Project Directors meeting in Boston, from October 11 to 13, 2009. Formal issues on how to implement the project as well as budget issues were clarified. The conference also allowed for an exchange between different partners and the sharing of information about FIPSE-Atlantis projects.

In the first and second runs, the *ABCs of Cultural Understanding and Communication* were implemented into the general coursework of each instructor. This phase lasted from winter 2009/2010 until summer 2010. During the seminars, the data were collected from cultural competency survey pre- and post-tests (Ruggiano Schmidt & Finkbeiner, 2009) and polarity profiles (pre- and post; Finkbeiner, 2005), the ABCs data from each student in each EU and U.S. partner's classroom, as well as from the lesson evaluations. In July 2010, the Atlantis Symposium took place during the international Conference of the *Association for Language Awareness* (www.languageawareness.org), which entailed meetings and discussions, a colloquium, and reports by the lead directors and a select number of U.S. and EU participants, as well as the external evaluator.

During the third and fourth run of seminars, the *ABCs of Cultural Understanding and Communication* were implemented and disseminated in the coursework that took place in winter 2010/2011 and summer 2011. In the seminars, data were collected again from cultural competency survey pre- and post tests (Ruggiano Schmidt & Finkbeiner, 2009) and polarity profiles (pre- and post; Finkbeiner, 2005), as well as the ABCs data collection from each student in each EU and U.S. partner's classroom and the data collection from lesson evaluations.

From October 13 to 15, 2010, the Directors Conference took place in Berlin, Germany. The U.S. and EU TRANSABCs directors participated. The goal was to share information on further project management in the second year, plan the book publication and the workshop that was to be held in Syracuse, New York, as well as discuss how to analyze the data corpus. Subsequently, the project participants sent data for initial statistical and qualitative analyses. Moreover, each project partner interviewed five students who participated in the first or second run to measure a follow-up effect.

Initial quantitative and qualitative analyses of data were conducted, and the web-based and e-learning-based technologies were updated. Furthermore, a website for International Cultural Competency concerning the *ABC's of Cultural Understanding and Communication* was developed (www.transabcs.org).

After a detailed evaluation of the EU project in July 2011, a workshop concerning data analyses from the ABCs dissemination took place in Syracuse. All participants contributed to the interpretation and discussion of preliminary statistical and qualitative analyses, as well as ABCs process and products over two years. A further run of seminars with partner students followed to collect data from cultural competency surveys (pre- and post) (Ruggiano Schmidt & Finkbeiner, 2009), polarity profiles (pre- and post) (Finkbeiner, 2005), lesson evaluations, and random sample interviews and to compare and contrast online ABCs with face-to-face ABCs. This run was also meant to discover how effective the online procedure was in comparison to the face-to-face procedure.

In July 2012, a select group of TRANSABCs participants from Spain, Poland, Germany, and the United States presented their results to the scientific community of the *Association for Language Awareness* at the 11th international conference in Montreal, Canada. Furthermore, qualification papers and MA and teacher exam theses were written on the TRANSABCs project. More presentations at international conferences will follow, and an international follow-up research project is planned. In 2013 and 2014, all data collected had to be re-entered for SPSS analyses and were subject to various analyses. Re-analyses were conducted and discussed with colleagues from the University of Koblenz-Landau. The results will be presented in the next section.

Instruments, Procedure, Research Questions, and Sample

The project aimed at answering the following research questions: After experiencing the *ABCs of Cultural Understanding and Communication* in their one-semester coursework, would present and future teachers as well as students targeted for the workplace

- claim to be more knowledgeable about communicating and connecting with their students and clients as well as colleagues' diverse home and community cultures? (Question 1)

- know how to create and adapt culturally responsive literacy ideas that relate to the required school curriculum as well as the workplace? (Question 2)
- know how to implement culturally responsive teaching in their classrooms, schools, and in the workplace? (Question 3)

The mixed-method research design approach (Creswell & Plano Clark, 2007) seemed appropriate for this project. Quantitative and qualitative data were collected and analyzed from different test instruments:

- The TRANSABCs data contained autobiographies, biographies, cross-cultural comparisons of similarities and differences, and cultural in-depth analyses as well as culturally responsive ideas;
- Cultural competency surveys (pre- and post) (Ruggiano Schmidt & Finkbeiner, 2009);
- Polarity profiles (pre- and post) (Finkbeiner, 2005);
- Rubric designed for evaluating culturally responsive literacy teaching and learning ideas;
- List of questions for the semi-structured follow-up interviews.

The MAXQDA and NVivo software was very helpful for the qualitative data analysis of the impact of the ABCs model. SPSS version 22 served as software for the quantitative analyses. Furthermore, the evaluation sheet mentioned before (see Figure 2.1) was developed to facilitate the look below the surface of language and culture and to support the detection of the hidden or hybrid in order to be able to combine probable similarities on the surface with possible hidden similarities down below in Step C.

Professors taught student cohorts of varied sizes (see Appendix, "TRANSABCs Projects 2009–2011") over a two year period. At the end of the project, 763 present and future teachers as well as business students had experienced the *ABC's of Cultural Understanding and Communication* (Ruggiano Schmidt & Finkbeiner, 2006). The population was university or college students enrolled in the programs of the professors. All of these programs were literacy, EFL/ESL, or business and intercultural learning programs.

In the end, we obtained a complete set of all data, including autobiographies, biographies, cross-cultural analyses, culturally responsive ideas, cultural competency survey pre- and post-tests (Ruggiano Schmidt & Finkbeiner, 2009) and polarity profiles (pre- and post; Finkbeiner, 2005) from 557 students, and qualitative follow-up interviews after a year with 40 participants.

Results as to Research Question 1—The Transcultural Competence Scale (TCS)

After experiencing the ABC's of Cultural Understanding and Communication in their one-semester coursework, would present and future teachers as well as students targeted for the workplace claim to be more knowledgeable about communicating and connecting with their students' and clients' as well as colleagues' diverse home and community cultures?

Triangulated data sources assisted in data analyses and interpretations to bring greater credibility to the findings. Two of these sources were the cultural survey and the polarity profile (Finkbeiner, 2005).[5] Here I will summarize the outcomes of the survey (Ruggiano Schmidt & Finkbeiner, 2009).

The focus of the survey is on declarative cultural knowledge as well as perceptions connected to it (Finkbeiner, 2006, p. 27). It is about what participants declare they actually think, do, perceive, and believe in. As the cultural survey used in the TRANSABCs project[7] mirrors the subjective beliefs, worldviews, and perception structures of the participants, one might argue that it may not be such a suitable instrument after all. For example, perception of the world might not be stable over time and be vague as a construct. However, subjective worldviews and perception structures have to be taken very seriously: they strongly determine how we interpret the world and can develop into self-fulfilling prophecies and, thus, influence future actions (Finkbeiner, 2005; Ludwig, 1991).

The cultural competency survey pre- and post-test (Ruggiano Schmidt & Finkbeiner, 2009), tested by Ruggiano Schmidt at Le Moyne College during four consecutive semesters, provided highly valuable information on probable changes in the TRANSABCs participants' perceptions and their declarative cultural knowledge over time. It was administered before and after the ABCs treatment and allowed direct testing of the hypothesis, that is, whether the ABCs of Cultural Understanding and Communication as a treatment would actually show an effect, for example, in the way participants perceived the world. Participants had to spontaneously decide what they thought about the survey statements, circle their responses accordingly, and comment on their answers. Four response options were possible: strongly agree, agree, disagree, and strongly disagree.

Together with our colleagues from the University of Koblenz-Landau, we conducted several statistical analyses[7] with the SPSS version 22 software with all survey data, considering the whole sample as well as the subsamples by gender and national subgroups. The factor analyses resulted in five meaningful categories of cultural competency which not only grouped similar items but also were stable across time, that is, both in the pre- and post-test. These categories are (a) "high value of cultural diversity," (b) "cultural/religious monoperspective," (c) "cultural homogeneity of the social environment,"

(d) "strong expectation of immigrants' assimilation," and (e) "immigrants' cultural adaptivity." As (d) and (e) are rather similar in nature, they could be merged into one category.

The four remaining stable categories are very helpful as they allow a closer look at certain subgroups and their change over time with respect to these dimensions. Of the four categories, the first one turned out to have the most acceptable internal consistency (Cronbach's $\alpha > .8$). The following items loaded in the first factor, which we label the *Transcultural Competence Scale (TCS)*: 12, 14, 16, 17, 19, 20, 21, 22, 23, 24, 25, 28, 29 (see Table 2.1). As this scale has turned out to be statistically reliable and with 13 quantitative items easy to administer, it can be recommended for future intercultural projects (and be combined with other scales if necessary) that need to test cultural competence.

The Transcultural Competence Scale (TCS) facilitates examining students' perceptions and the change they might experience due to an intercultural program, such as for example the TRANSABCs program. Probable changes can, for example, be determined with the paired *Student's t-test*, which

TABLE 2.1 *Scale One:* **The Transcultural Competence Scale (TCS)**

Survey Item	Item Description
12. Teachers/Colleagues must reach out to people struggling with our nation's culture.	Openness toward cultural diversity Cultural awareness
14. We should respect physical differences.	Openness toward (physical) difference
16. We should celebrate physical differences.	Appreciation/value of (physical) difference
17. We should celebrate cultural differences.	Appreciation/value of (physical) difference
19. We should use students' languages in our classrooms.	Language awareness: power domain
20. We should help students connect their backgrounds with the school curriculum.	Cultural awareness
21. We should communicate, face to face, with our children's families even if we don't know their languages.	Language awareness Awareness of appreciation of individual and his/her family
22. My nation has many cultures.	Cultural self-awareness
23. When we include our students' backgrounds, languages, and experiences in the classroom, they will be more motivated to learn their school subjects.	Openness toward cultural diversity Cultural awareness
24. I am committed to social justice.	Cultural, social self-awareness
25. My family has a culture.	Cultural, social self-awareness
28. I learn more when I study different perspectives of different groups of people	Openness toward cultural diversity Cultural, social self-awareness
29. When I study and learn, I change my attitudes.	Cultural, social self-awareness

measures mean differences in a test before and after a treatment as well as the level of their significance.

In order to find out about certain profiles, we need to look at individual groups. This is why we subdivided the total sample into sub-samples by gender and national group. Then we took a closer look at the perception of the quartiles within these groups before and after the ABCs treatment and whether they changed over time. The highest quartile (highest 25%) scored highest in mean value of the pre- and/or post-test of the *Transcultural Competence Scale (TCS)*, the second quartile (second highest 25%) scored second highest, the second lowest quartile (second lowest 25%) scored second lowest, and the lowest quartile (lowest 25%) scored lowest.

With respect to the *Transcultural Competence Scale,* the lowest quartile can be described as the least open group with respect to cultural diversity. It is particularly interesting to look at the development of "extreme" profiles (either highly open toward cultural heterogeneity or highly attracted by cultural homogeneity, very narrow-minded cultural worldview) before the ABCs process started in order to answer the question of whether the ABCs process really causes a "change." Pedagogically speaking, the subgroup with very low openness toward cultural homogeneity (cultural phobia) is particularly crucial as they might be the ones facing enormous difficulties as they do not feel prepared, have not accommodated their perceptions, and might face difficulties adjusting to a more diversifying world.

Table 2.2 shows the results of the Student's t-Test with respect to selected national samples as well as the subsamples and extreme groups (highest and lowest quartiles). The change of perception with respect to an increase in their openness toward more cultural heterogeneity between pretest and posttest is highly significant. This result is complementary with the national subgroup results for the United States and Germany.

The interesting question is how the extreme groups develop. Out of the total sample ($n = 557$), 158 participants are in the top quartile (highly open toward cultural heterogeneity) and 129 are in the lowest quartile (highly attracted by cultural homogeneity). The change of the perception of the lowest quartile with an increase in their openness toward more cultural heterogeneity between pretest and posttest is highly significant ($p < .01$) for the total sample as well as the sample of the participating groups from Germany, the United States, and Poland, and it is significant ($p < .05$) for the group from Spain.

In looking at gender differences in response to the ABCs project (see Table 2.3), we found significant changes among women in their acceptance of cultural heterogeneity. Despite the smaller sample size of the men we still have significant changes in the total sample. What is more important, however, is the effect within the lowest quartiles of both men and women. Both the male and the female groups that had an explicit preference for

TABLE 2.2 Transcultural Competence Scale (TCS): Mean Value and Standard Deviation for Total Sample, Selected National Samples, and Extreme Groups

	Mean value (Standard deviation)		N	T	p
	Pre	Post			
Total sample					
Lowest 25%	2.87	3.02	158	−7.05	< .01
(AM$_{t1}$ ≤ 3.00)	(.12)	(.27)			
Highest 25%	3.75	3.73	129	1.071	> .05
(AM$_{t1}$ ≥ 3.54)	(.12)	(.24)			
Total (all quartiles)	**3.27**	**3.34**	**557**	**−5.735**	**< .01**
	(.34)	**(.38)**			
Germany					
Lowest 25%	2.87	3.04	28	−4.133	< .01
(AM$_{t1}$ ≤ 3.0)	(.18)	(.23)			
Highest 25%	3.58	3.47	29	.794	> .05
(AM$_{t1}$ ≥ 3.38)	(.12)	(.29)			
Total (all quartiles)	**3.19**	**3.27**	**105**	**−2.975**	**< .01**
	(.27)	**(.30)**			
USA					
Lowest 25%	2.93	3.15	55	−4.536	< .01
(AM$_{t1}$ ≤ 3.08)	(.12)	(.38)			
Highest 25%	3.81	3.76	75	1.509	> .05
(AM$_{t1}$ ≥ 3.69)	(.10)	(.25)			
Total	**3.41**	**3.52**	**237**	**−5.303**	**< .01**
	(.35)	**(.37)**			
Spain					
Lowest 25%	2.75	2.88	15	−2.348	< .05
(AM$_{t1}$ ≤ 2.82)	(.04)	(.23)			
Highest 25%	3.42	3.27	19	2.572	< .05
(AM$_{t1}$ ≥ 3.20)	(.19)	(.31)			
Total	**3.08**	**3.04**	**64**	**1.327**	**> .05**
	(.28)	**(.29)**			
Poland					
Lowest 25%	2.70	2.89	13	−3.371	< .01
(AM$_{t1}$ ≤ 2.83)	(.09)	(.18)			
Highest 5%	3.26	3.17	20	1.578	> .05
(AM$_{t1}$ ≥ 3.20)	(.10)	(.25)			
Total	**3.0**	**3.04**	**65**	**−1.252**	**> .05**
	(.22)	**(.23)**			

Note: AM = Arithmetic Mean

TABLE 2.3   Transcultural Competence Scale (TCS): Mean Value and Standard Deviation for Gender and Gender Extreme Groups

	Mean value (Standard Deviation)				
	Pre	Post	N	T	p
Total sample					
Women	3.28 (.34)	3.35 (.38)	453	−5.359	< .01
Men	3.22 (.34)	3.28 (.38)	102	−2.034	< .05
Total (all quartiles)	**3.27**	**3.34**	**557**	**−5.735**	**< .01**
Subsamples					
Women					
Lowest 25% ($AM_{tl} \leq 3.0$)	2.88 (.12)	3.03 (.26)	124	−6.674	< .01
Highest 25% ($AM_{tl} \geq 3.54$)	3.75 (.12)	3.73 (.25)	106	.814	> .05
Men					
Lowest 25% ($AM_{tl} \leq 2.92$)	2.76 (.10)	2.95 (.21)	17	−3.965	< .01
Highest 25% ($AM_{tl} \geq 3.46$)	3.69 (.12)	3.65 (.26)	27	.883	> .05

Note: AM = Arithmetic Mean

cultural homogeneity before the ABCs process started had a highly significant increase in their awakened or elicited "openness" toward cultural heterogeneity.

What is striking is the slight decrease of the openness toward cultural heterogeneity among the top 25%. Even though the decrease is insignificant (except for one subsample), this mirrors the results of other studies where sometimes one of the two top quartiles stagnates over time or even experiences a slight decline (Finkbeiner, 1995; Finkbeiner, Knierim, Smasal & Ludwig 2012). A possible explanation is, that the ABCs treatment might not have had the same significant effect on participants that were already open towards cultural heterogeneity at the beginning of the treatment. It is plausible that participants that were already culturally open at the beginning of the ABCs treatment might not have been challenged in the same way as participants that favored cultural homogeneity. However, the slight decrease of the highest 25% from the pre- to the post-test makes the effect of the lowest 25% seem even stronger. Still, it is worth mentioning that overall the differences between the highest and the lowest quartiles are still most highly significant before and after the ABCs process.

In order to get a better picture of the overall effect of the ABCs process, random sample semistructured interviews were conducted at the end of 2 years. The goal was to test the hypothesis that the ABCs had really helped present and future teachers and other professionals become more knowledgeable about communicating and connecting with culturally diverse students or co-workers. The results show that a high proportion of the TRANS-ABCs participants not only claimed to be more knowledgeable but also gave proof of this, for example, by implementing the ABCs in their internships or practical studies as well as in the workplace or by even following up with their own study (Borschel, 2012; Goebel, 2012).

Results of Research Question 2

After experiencing the ABC's of Cultural Understanding and Communication in their one semester coursework, would present and future teachers as well as students who would be situated in the workplace know how to create and adapt culturally responsive literacy ideas that related to the required school curriculum as well as the workplace?

The evaluation of the data of the two student follow-up projects mentioned above, as well as follow-up face-to-face projects by former TRANS-ABCs participants as ABCs instructors, proves how strong the impact of the project was (Borschel, 2012; Goebel, 2012).

An interesting study is by ABCs alumna Goebel (2012) who conducted an exploratory study on an online ABCs between Dutch and Indian primary school children. Sulagna Mukhopadhyay volunteered with her class in Calcutta, India. Goebel's (2012) focus was on the construction of the self and other in the online discourse triggered though the ABCs. Goebel (2012) developed and implemented online literacy activities that supported the children in conducting the ABCs. The children were guided in how to start thinking and reflecting about their own selves and the others. They prepared group presentations to present their class to the children of the ABCs partner school in India and in the Netherlands. Additionally, the children met via Skype, showed their presentations and started a discourse on the self and other. Finally, the children started reflecting on the differences and similarities they discovered. Goebel applied qualitative content analysis on eight case studies. Her results are most revealing.

Borschel (2012), an ABCs alumnus, for example, investigated the family-teacher discourse in a mulitethnic 10th grade in a comprehensive school in Germany. He argues that due to the multicultural, multinational and multilingual situation in German schools intercultural learning is of great importance. His study aimed at including students and siblings as equal discourse members according to the cooperative and reciprocal elements of the European Adaption of the ABCs model (Finkbeiner & Koplin, 2002) which draws on the original model by Ruggiano Schmidt (1998). Borschel used the explorative single case study method and collected quite a large data corpus of individual discourse sessions between an English teacher and ten individual families. His study shows that the ABCs method cannot only help initiate and foster family-teacher discourse but also contribute to a higher degree of contentedness among all participants.

Examples like the ones from Borschel (2012) and Goebel (2012) show, that ABCs alumni did not only change their views, but they initiated their own projects in highly complex and demanding settings.

Furthermore, the data from the rubric created to evaluate lesson and unit plan ideas, as well as random sample semistructured interviews at the end of two years, provided information in answer to the second research question.

All professors and lecturers in Europe and the United States evaluated the culturally responsive literacy ideas using the designated rubric, performed random sample interviews, and coded the collected random sample interview data (see, for example, Chapter 4). On average, all students scored high, and professors agreed that they had developed their ability to produce multiperspective approaches (Finkbeiner, 2009) for culturally responsive teaching or workplace management environments.

Result of Research Question 3

After experiencing the ABC's of Cultural Understanding and Communication in their one-semester coursework, would present and future teachers as well as students targeted for the workplace know how to implement culturally responsive teaching in their classrooms, schools, and the workplace?

The third research question is the most difficult as it still takes time to follow the participants' careers. Those who are on the job talk about a multitude of examples of how they implement the project or ideas from the project across the world. For example, in Montreal, one of my former ABCs students approached me and said, "You know, there is one thing I really want to tell you: The ABCs stayed with me," and he is now sharing his ABCs with the readers of this book (Finkbeiner & Davidson, this volume).

Records of emails, journals, participation in the workshops, and participation in the creation of follow-up projects are used to answer the final question: How would a group of education professors and lecturers successfully achieve the goals and objectives stated in the proposal and continue to collaborate after the project is completed? The two directors facilitated the workshops at Le Moyne College and Kassel University as well as follow-up workshops at international conferences such as at the international conferences of the *Association for Language Awareness.* Beyond the project, friendship and colleagueship developed: There is still strong ongoing exchange and cooperation between most of the participants, and new projects are being launched.

SUMMARY

This study has had an impact on implementing global culturally responsive teaching and learning on a large scale. Its effect has been demonstrated by the significant changes the participating students went through. This holds especially true for those students who, at the beginning of the project, comprised what I would call the *cultural risk group*. The model's dissemination affected numerous teacher education, business education, and international student exchange programs in the United States and Europe (see Appendix). It helped present and future teachers and future business people become more culturally and linguistically aware and gain confidence in communicating and connecting with people from diverse backgrounds and experiences (Finkbeiner, 2008, 2012). This scale-up study demonstrated how the model works in different nations of Europe, different regions in the United States, New Zealand, and Canada, as well as on the school level in Germany, the Netherlands, Pakistan, and India.

The participants now know the ABCs of Cultural Understanding and Communication. They use and will go on using these experiences and the knowledge they have gained in their teaching and in their daily work. The intercultural education programs that aim at facilitating cultural awareness and language awareness that use this approach have become an integral part of language classes as well as business communication settings in the United States, Europe, and beyond, and they will positively influence students as well as business people's intercultural competence and literacy development.

We have aimed at and succeeded in improving literacy development in Europe and the United States by drawing upon students and people's backgrounds and making connections with the required curriculum. We do not know of any study that would have given voice to so many people and produced so many high quality learner-generated authentic texts that document the specific time and thus carry huge historical value.

In this book, we present evidence that the study has had and will have an important impact on global culturally responsive teaching and learning as well as acting and negotiating in the workplace. Evidence is given by the results gained from the *Transcultural Competence Scale*, in the follow-up interviews, and in the ABCs data themselves, as well as in the meta-cognitive reflection during classes and in the class evaluations.

The dissemination of the model helped connect people from diverse backgrounds and experiences. Previous unsystematic studies and small exploratory studies had demonstrated that the *ABCs of Cultural Understanding and Communication* (Ruggiano Schmidt & Finkbeiner, 2006) was an effective model for developing culturally responsive literacy teaching and learning. However, this large study demonstrated how the model—after socioculturally adequate adaptation—worked in different European countries and different regions in the United States as well as with different subject matters and in different time spans.

Since this project was embedded in teacher-training programs and business programs as well as international exchange programs at universities, the project also had an impact on everyday teaching in schools and in the workplace in the transatlantic dimension. TRANSABCs has contributed to the fact that cultural diversity has become a topic in language classes as well as in classes preparing students for the business world and has positively influenced their intercultural competence and literacy development.

What we discovered led us and our students to new ideas with respect to pedagogies as well as business and marketing approaches that will assist educators and business people in their teaching and negotiating and students in their literacy learning in the future (Erler & Finkbeiner, 2007; Finkbeiner, 2008, 2009). And the sooner diverse populations become educated in a "new" location's language and culture, the sooner they can become productive, respected, and happy members of society (Finkbeiner, 2006a).

The success of the model lies in its highly individual approach; it is about each single individual story and about personal "funds of knowledge" (González, Moll, & Amanti, 2005, p. 72). As mentioned in the introduction, "The wing of a butterfly can change the world" (Lorenz, 1963). The fact that a wing of a butterfly can be so powerful implies that the journey can be rocky: it takes the voyager on windy and bumpy roads and less travelled paths. Those who have the chance to join the ABCs travel never want to miss this mind-altering experience.

APPENDIX

The TRANSABCs Project 2009–2011

Participating instructors, locations, sample size, course type and time frame

Investigator	Book Chapter	FIPSE-Atlantis Partner	Country	Federal State, City, and University	Participants N =	Course type: U = undergraduate G = graduate	Time period Duration in w = weeks, h= hours
Claudia Finkbeiner	Introduction, 2, 3, 14	EU	Germany	Hesse, Kassel, University of Kassel	68	G	w = 15; h = 30
Claudia Finkbeiner	Introduction, 2, 3, 14	EU	Canada*	Quebec, Montreal, Concordia University	20	G	w = 2; h = 30
Claudia Finkbeiner	Introduction, 2, 3, 14	EU	New Zealand*	Wellington, University of Wellington	19	G	w = 2; h = 30
Jane Neer	4	USA	USA	New York, Syracuse, Le Moyne College	47	U	w = 3; h = 13
William Neer	4	USA	USA	New York, Syracuse, Le Moyne College	24	G	w = 3; h = 13
Althier Lazar	Introduction, 5, 14	USA	USA	Philadelphia, PA, Saint Joseph's University	51	G	w = 15; h = 45
Josep M. Cots and colleagues	6	EU	Spain	Catalonia, University of Lleida	10	U	w = 15; h = 45
					6	G (online)	w = 15; h = 62
					35	U	w = 15; h = 60
					25	U	w = 15; h = 60
					25	U	w = 15; h = 60
Sylvia Fehling	7	EU	Germany	Hesse, Kassel, University of Kassel	87	G	w = 15; h = 30

#	Name	Region	Country	Institution	Count	U & G	w/h
8	Shelley Xu	USA	USA	California, Long Beach, California State University	75	U & G	w = 15; h = 45
9	Ulla Lundgren	EU	Sweden	Jönköping, School of Education and Communication, Jönköping University	54	U	w = 5
10	Jiening Ruan	USA	USA	Oklahoma, University of Oklahoma	51	G	w = 15; h = 45
11	Ewa Bandura	EU	Poland	Kraków, Jagiellonian University	64	U, G	w = 20; h = 25
12	Patricia A. Edwards	USA	USA	Michigan, Michigan State University	23	G	w = 16; h=48
12	Susan V. Piazza	USA	USA	Michigan, Western Michigan University	18	G	w = 16; h=48
13	Lilia Ratcheva	EU	Bulgaria	Ruse, The Luben Karavelov Regional Library	10	G	w = 3; h = 9
			Bulgaria	Varna, The Pencho Slaveykov Regionl Library, American Corner	15	U	w = 3; h = 9
			Bulgaria	The Sofia City Library, American Corner	24	G	w = 3; h = 9
			Austria	Vienna, Bulgarian-Austrian Free Time School	6	U	w = 3; h = 9
			Austria	Professional Trainers, Austria	6	G	w = 1; h = 3
Total over two years		USA and EU*			763	U, G	w = 230
Total of participants with complete data set		USA and EU			557	U, G	

* Including additional ABCS courses in the framework of the partner university cooperation with the University of Kassel

NOTES

1. Reference: 156403-DE-2009USAPOM
2. Thanks go to Sulagna Mukhopadhyay and Ann-Kristin Goebel.
3. K–12 = Kindergarten through grade 12
4. These are Claudia Finkbeiner and Patricia Ruggiano Schmidt.
5. The polarity profile or semantic differential exists of pairs of opposing adjectives, such as good–bad, exciting–boring etc., that participants have to rate on a scale from one to seven. It is a nice tool to be used in research as it does not take much time and it is not too complex.
6. Information learned for the survey came from Gay, 2000; Lindsey, Roberts, & Campbell Jones, 2005; Schmidt & Finkbeiner, 2006; Trumbull, Rothstein-Fisch, Greenfield, & Quiroz, 2001.
7. Acknowledgments to Dr. Christoph Schneider and Andrea Stuck, University of Koblenz-Landau, Germany, for their help with the statistical analyses as well as to Prof. Dr. Peter Ludwig, University of Koblenz-Landau and Markus Knierim, M.A. for their valuable comments on the final proofs.

REFERENCES

Au, K. (1993). *Literacy instruction in multicultural settings.* New York, NY: Harcourt, Brace Javanovich College Publishers.

Banks, J. (1994). *An introduction to multicultural education.* Boston, MA: Allyn & Bacon.

Barnett, R. (1997). *Higher education: A critical business.* Buckingham: Open University Press.

Berggren, N., Richards, A., Taylor, J. & Derakshan, N. (2013). Affective attention under cognitive load: reduced emotional biases but emergent anxiety related costs to inhibitory control. *Frontiers in Human Neuroscience.* Open access journal, May 2013. http://journal.frontiersin.org/Journal/10.3389/fnhum.2013.00188/full [retrieved September 6th 2014].

Bhabha, H. (1994). *The location of culture.* London, UK: Routledge.

Bogdan, R. C., & Biklen, S. K. (1994). *Qualitative research for education: An introduction to theory and methods* (2nd ed.). Needham Heights, MA: Allyn & Bacon.

Borschel, M. (2012). *Familie-LehrerInnen-Diskurs in einer multiethnischen 10. Schulklasse: Eine explorative Studie im Rahmen des interkulturellen Modells ABC's of Cultural Understanding and Communication.* (Non-published teacher state examination thesis) Kassel, Germany: University of Kassel.

Brozo, W. G., Shiel, G., & Topping, K. (2007). Engagement in reading: Lessons learned from three PISA countries. *Journal of Adolescent & Adult Literacy, 51*(4), 304–315.

Bundeszentrale für politische Bildung. (2013). *Zahlen und Fakten. Die soziale Situation in Deutschland. Bevölkerung mit Migrationshintergrund.* Retrieved from http://www.bpb.de/nachschlagen/zahlen-und-fakten/soziale-situation-in-deutschland/61646/migrationshintergrund-i

Byram, M. (2009). Afterword—Education, training and becoming critical. In A. Feng, M. Byram, & M. Fleming (Eds.), *Becoming interculturally competent through education and training* (pp. 211–213). Bristol, UK: Multilingual Matters.

Clark, R., Fairclough, N., Ivanic, R., & Martin-Jones, M. (1991). Critical language awareness, Part II. Towards critical alternatives. *Language and Education 5*(1), 41–54.

Creswell, J. W., & Plano Clark, V. L. (2007). *Designing and conducting mixed methods research.* Thousand Oaks, CA: Sage.

Cummins, J. (1986). Empowering minority students: A framework for intervention. *Harvard Educational Review, 56*(1), 18–36.

Edwards, A. W. F. (2004). *Cogwheels of the mind: The story of Venn diagrams.* Baltimore, MD; London, UK: Johns Hopkins University Press.

Edwards, P. A. (1996). Creating sharing-time conversations: Parents and teachers work together. *Language Arts, 73,* 344-349.

Edwards, P. A., Pleasants, H., & Franklin, S. (1999). *A path to follow: Learning to listen to parents.* Portsmouth, NH: Heinemann.

Erler, L., & Finkbeiner, C. (2007). A review of reading strategies: Focus on the impact of first language. In A. D. Cohen & E. Macaro (Eds.), *Language learner strategies: 30 years of research and practice* (pp. 187–206). Oxford, UK: Oxford University Press.

Fairclough, N. (Ed.). (1992). *Critical language awareness.* London, UK: Longman.

Faltis, C. J. (1993). *Joinfostering: Adapting teaching strategies for the multilingual classroom.* New York, NY: Maxwell Macmillan International.

Fehling, S. (2008). *Language Awareness und bilingualer Unterricht: Eine komparative Studie* (2nd ed.). Frankfurt, Germany: Peter Lang.

Feng, A., Byram, M., & Fleming, M. (Eds.). (2009). *Becoming interculturally competent through education and training.* Bristol, UK: Multilingual Matters.

Finkbeiner, C. (1995). *Englischunterricht in europaeischer Dimension. Zwischen Qualifikationserwartungen der Gesellschaft und Schuelereinstellungen und Schuelerinteressen.* Bochum, Germany: Dr. Brockmeyer.

Finkbeiner, C. (2003). Cooperative learning and teaching in Germany. In *International Association for the Study of Cooperation in Education* newsletter, *22*(3), 14–16.

Finkbeiner, C. (2004). Cooperation and collaboration in a foreign language teacher training program: The LMR Plus model. In E. Cohen, C. Brody, & M. Sapon-Shevin (Eds.), *Learning to teach with cooperative learning: Challenges in teacher education* (pp. 111–127). Albany: State University of New York Press.

Finkbeiner, C. (2005). *Interessen und Strategien beim fremdsprachlichen Lesen. Wie Schülerinnen und Schüler englische Texte lesen und verstehen.* [Interests and strategies in foreign language reading: How students read and comprehend English texts]. Tuebingen, Germany: Narr.

Finkbeiner, C. (2006a). Constructing third space: The principles of reciprocity and cooperation. In P. R. Schmidt, P. Ruggiano, & C. Finkbeiner (Eds.), *The ABC's of cultural understanding and communication: National and international adaptations* (pp. 19–42). Greenwich, CT: Information Age.

Finkbeiner, C. (2006b). EFL and ESL knowledgeable reading: A critical element for viable membership in global communities. *Babylonia, 3,* 45–50.

Finkbeiner, C. (2008). Culture and good language learners. In C. Griffiths (Ed.), *Lessons from good language learners* (pp. 131–141). Cambridge, UK: Cambridge University Press.

Finkbeiner, C. (2009). Using "Human Global Positioning System" as a navigation tool to the hidden dimension of culture. In A. Feng, M. Byram, & M. Fleming (Eds.), *Becoming interculturally competent through education and training* (pp. 151–173). Bristol, UK: Multilingual Matters.

Finkbeiner, C. (2012). Research and scholarship in multilingualism: An interdisciplinary multi-perspective framework. *Die Neueren Sprachen, 2,* 82–96.

Finkbeiner, C., & Fehling, S. (2006). Investigating the role of awareness and multiple perspectives in intercultural education. In P. R. Schmidt, P. Ruggiano, & C. Finkbeiner (Eds.), The *ABC's of cultural understanding and communication: National and international adaptations* (pp. 93–110). Greenwich, CT: Information Age.

Finkbeiner, C., & Knierim, M. (2006). The ABC's as a starting point and goal: The online intercultural exchange project (ICE). In P. R. Schmidt, P. Ruggiero, & C. Finkbeiner (Eds.), *The ABC's of cultural understanding and communication: National and international adaptations* (pp. 213–244). Greenwich, CT: Information Age.

Finkbeiner, C, & Knierim, M. (2008). Developing L2 strategic competence online. In F. Zhang & B. Barber (Eds.), *Handbook of research on computer-enhanced language acquisition and learning* (pp. 377–402). Hershey, PA: IGI Global.

Finkbeiner, C., & Koplin, C. (2002). A cooperative approach for facilitating intercultural education. *Reading Online, 6*(3). Retrieved from http://www.readingonline.org/newliteracies/lit_index.asp?HREF=/newliteracies/finkbeiner

Finkbeiner, C., & Svalberg, A. (Eds.). (2012). Culture language literacy. Special issue. *Language Awareness.*

Gass, S. M., & Mackey, A. (2000). *Stimulated recall methodology in second language research.* Mahwah, NJ: Lawrence Erlbaum.

Gay, G. (2000). *Culturally responsive teaching: Theory, research, and practice.* New York, NY: Teachers College Press.

Goebel, A. (2012). *The self and the other in an intercultural online encounter: An explorative study between Dutch and Indian primary school children based on the ABC's of cultural understanding and communication.* (Unpublished teacher state examination thesis) Kassel, Germany: University of Kassel.

González, N., Moll, L. C., & Amanti, C. (Eds.). (2005). *Funds of knowledge: Theorizing practices in households, communities, and classrooms.* Mahwah, NJ: Lawrence Erlbaum.

Hofstede, G. (1980). *Culture's consequences—International differences in work related values.* Newbury Park, CA; London, UK; New Delhi, India: Sage.

Howard, T. (2001). Telling their side of the story: African American students' perceptions of culturally relevant teaching. *The Urban Review, 33*(2), 131–149.

James, C., & Garrett, P. (1992). *Language awareness in the classroom.* London, UK; New York, NY: Longman.

Ladson-Billings, G. (1994). *The dreamkeepers: Successful teachers of African American students.* San Francisco, CA: Jossey-Bass.

Ladson-Billings, G. (1995). Toward a theory of culturally relevant pedagogy. *American Educational Research Journal, 32*, 465–491.

Leftwich, S. (2002). Learning to use diverse students' literature in the classroom: A model for preservice teacher education. *Reading Online, 6*(2). Retrieved from www.readingonline.org

Lindholm-Leary, K. (2000). *Biliteracy for a global society: An idea book on dual language education.* Washington, DC: National Clearinghouse for Bilingual Education.

Lindsey, R. B., Roberts, L. M., & Campbell Jones, F. (2005). *The culturally proficient school: An implementation guide for school leaders.* Thousand Oaks, CA: Corwin.

Lorenz, E. N. (1963, March). Deterministic nonperiodic flow. *Journal of the Atmospheric Sciences, 20*(2), 130–141.

Ludwig, P. H. (1991). *Sich selbst erfüllende Prophezeiungen im Alltagsleben. Theorie und empirische Basis von Erwartungseffekten und Konsequenzen für die Pädagogik* (Geleitwort von Robert Rosenthal, Harvard). Stuttgart: Verlag für Angewandte Psychologie (Hogrefe).

McCaleb, S. P. (1994). *Building communities of learners.* New York, NY: St. Martin's.

Moll, L. C. (1992). Bilingual classroom studies and community analysis: Recent trends. *Educational Researcher, 21*(2), 20–24.

Moll, L. C., Amanti, C., Neff, D., & Gonzalez, N. (1992). Funds of knowledge for teaching: Using a qualitative approach to connect homes and classrooms. *Theory into Practice, 31*(2), 132–141.

Nieto, S. (1996). *Affirming diversity: The sociopolitical context of multicultural education.* New York, NY: Longman.

Nieto, S. (1999). *The light in their eyes.* New York, NY: Teachers College Press.

Ogbu, J. U. (2003). *Black American students in an affluent suburb: A study of academic disengagement.* Mahwah, NJ: Lawrence Erlbaum.

Osborne, A. B. (1996). Practice into theory into practice: Culturally relevant pedagogy for students we have marginalized and normalized. *Anthropology and Education Quarterly, 27*(3), 285–314.

Powell, R., Cantrell, S. C., & Adams, S. (2001). Saving Black Mountain: The promise of critical literacy in a multicultural democracy. *The Reading Teacher, 54*(8), 772–781.

Purcell-Gates, V., L'Allier, S., & Smith, D. (1995). Literacy at the Harts' and the Larsons': Diversity among poor inner-city families. *The Reading Teacher, 48*(7), 572–578.

Reyhner, J., & Garcia, R. L. (1989). Helping minorities read better: Problems and promises. *Reading Research and Instruction, 28*(3), 84–91.

Rogoff, K. (1990). *Apprenticeship in thinking: Cognitive development in social context.* New York, NY: Oxford University Press.

Ruggiano Schmidt, P. (1998a). *Cultural conflict and struggle: Literacy learning in a kindergarten program.* New York, NY: Peter Lang.

Ruggiano Schmidt, P. (1998b). The ABC's of cultural understanding and communication. *Equity and Excellence in Education, 31*(2), 28–38.

Ruggiano Schmidt, P. (1998c). The *ABC's model*: Teachers connect home and school. In T. Shanahan & F. V. Rodriguez-Brown (Eds.), *National Reading Conference yearbook 47* (pp. 194–208). Chicago, IL: National Reading Conference

Ruggiano Schmidt, P. (1999). Focus on research: Know thyself and understand others. *Language Arts, 76*(4), 332–340.

Ruggiano Schmidt, P. (2000). Teachers connecting and communicating with families for literacy development. In T. Shanahan & F. Rodriguez-Brown (Eds.), *National Reading Conference yearbook 49* (pp. 194–208). Chicago, IL: National Reading Conference.

Ruggiano Schmidt, P., & Finkbeiner, C. (2006). *ABC's of cultural understanding and communication: National and international adaptations.* Greenwich, CT: Information Age.

Ruggiano Schmidt, P., & Finkbeiner, C. (2009). *Cultural Competency Test.* In the FIPSE-USA/EU Transatlantic Policy Grant and the FIPSE EU/USA Transatlantic Policy Grant, 2009–2011.

Ruggiano Schmidt, P., & Ma, W. (2006). *50 literacy strategies for culturally responsive teaching, K–8.* Thousand Oaks, CA: Corwin.

Ruggiano Schmidt, P., & Lazar, A. (Eds.). (2011). *Practicing what we teach: How culturally responsive literacy classrooms make a difference.* New York, NY; London, UK: Teachers College Press.

Sjoberg, G., & Kuhn, K. (1989). Autobiography and organizations: Theoretical and methodological issues. *The Journal of Applied Behavioral Science, 25*(4), 309–326.

Spindler, G., & Spindler, L. (1987). *The interpretive ethnography of education: At home and abroad.* Hillsdale, NJ: Lawrence Erlbaum.

Spradley, J. (1979). *The ethnographic interview.* New York, NY: Holt, Rinehart & Winston.

Trueba, H. T., Jacobs, L., & Kirton, E. (1990). *Cultural conflict and adaptation: The case of the Hmong students in American society.* New York, NY: Falmer.

Trueba, T. (Ed.). (2002). *Ethnography and schools. Qualitative approaches to the study of education.* Lanham, MD: Rowman & Littlefield.

Trumbull, E., Rothstein-Fisch, C., Greenfield, P. M., & Quiroz, B. (2001). *Bridging cultures between home and school: A guide for teachers.* Mahwah, NJ: Lawrence Erlbaum.

Vygotski, L. S. (1978). *Mind in society.* Cambridge, MA: Harvard University Press.

Weaver, G. R. (1993). Understanding and coping with cross-cultural adjustment stress. In R. M. Paige (Ed.), *Education for the intercultural experience* (pp. 137–167). Boston, MA: Intercultural Press.

Wilden, E. (2007). Voice chats in the intercultural classroom: The ABC's on-line project. In R. O'Dowd (Ed.), *Online intercultural exchange: An introduction for foreign language teachers* (pp. 271–277). Clevedon, UK: Multilingual Matters.

Wilden, E. (2008). *Selbst- und Fremdwahrnehmung in der interkulturellen Onlinekommunikation. Das Modell der* ABC's *of Cultural Understanding and Communication Online.* Eine qualitative Studie. (Series Language Culture Literacy, Claudia Finkbeiner series editor). Frankfurt/Main, Germany: Peter Lang.

Xu, H. (2000a). Preservice teachers integrate understandings of diversity into literacy instruction: An adaptation of the ABC's model. *Journal of Teacher Education, 51*(2), 135–142.

Xu, H. (2000b). Preservice teachers in a literacy methods course consider issues of diversity. *Journal of Literacy Research, 32*(4), 505–531.

Yinger, R. (1985). Journal writing as a learning tool. *The Volta Review, 87*(5), 21–33.

CHAPTER 3

AN EXEMPLARY
ABCs PROJECT

Claudia Finkbeiner and Troy Davidson

INTRODUCTION
Claudia Finkbeiner

We would like to take you to the heart and core of this book by sharing one adapted ABCs project with you (Ruggiano Schmidt & Finkbeiner, 2006). The ABCs presented here will expose you to a world that was hidden to the author, Troy Davidson, before he started the project. This is typical for the ABCs journey. It is about discovery of the alleged known that in reality turns out to be unknown. It is also about developing an awareness with respect to things we often take for granted. And it is about issues that finally turn out to be so different than first expected once we dive under the surface.

Troy Davidson's ABCs were written in my graduate education course, "Language, Culture, Literacy" in the summer of 2011 at Concordia University in Montreal where I held a position as visiting professor. After a week in Syracuse where we conducted our final TRANSABCs workshop, I traveled up to Montreal to teach this intense class over a 2-week period. It was a hot and beautiful August. The atmosphere at the university was special, as the campus was unusually quiet because most of the university's faculty and students were away for their summer break. Left there was a class of highly

Getting to Know Ourselves and Others Through the ABCs, pages 47–70
Copyright © 2015 by Information Age Publishing
47

motivated language and literacy teachers who had decided to come back to the university to complete a course for their graduate education degree.

The focus of the class was on the role of culture in language learning and literacy development in a multilingual world. The class was exciting, exhilarating, and most rewarding. It was a true privilege to teach the class. None of the participants was ever late or would have missed a class. Breaks never were fully used. Everybody seemed to stay around in the classroom and continued lively discussions of language and culture after a short 5-minute break. The course was divided into three parts, which were related to (a) preparing, assisting and evaluating the different steps of the ABCs; (b) conducting culture and language activities; and (c) reading and discussing theoretical input and implementing theories into practice.

Montreal as a multilingual thriving cosmopolitan hub is an ideal location for this topic. It is densely populated by a heterogeneous group of people: on average there are nearly 900 persons per square kilometer in Montreal, which compares to around 4 persons per square kilometer in the national land area (Statistics Canada, 2011). Even though Canada has a law that supports official bilingualism both for French and English as equal legal languages, Quebec declares French the first official constitutional language. However, with enormous migration into Quebec, the language diversity is huge: Nearly a quarter of the population reported a language other than French and English as their mother tongue in 2011.

The students in my course taught in this rich linguistic setting. As all but one participant had a bilingual or multilingual background, they could relate to the situation to a certain degree. However, even though they could be considered experts in at least two languages and were professionally established, many did not have not a first-generation migration background. Therefore they expected a cultural and linguistic gap between themselves and their newly immigrated students.

Troy's ABCs were powerful for helping him discover his cultural and linguistic heritage in relation to another person's. Troy goes back to his own family language roots and finds these in Italian, a language, which, together with Spanish and Arabic, belongs to the three most spoken unofficial languages in Montreal (Statistics Canada, 2011). Usually the steps A and B are not shared in a verbatim manner as they are very personal; as both participants of these particular ABCs agreed on this we are really happy to give you deeper insight into what the ABCs actually mean.

Although we chose Troy's ABCs for this book, all ABCs handed in by the participants turned out to be most revealing and intriguing reads. The ABCs of those who agreed in their letters of consent that their work could be used for teaching and research will definitely be subject to further analyses. They are trustworthy and authentic documentations of the teachers' own stories on language acquisition, language learning, and literacy development.

One year later I met Troy at the Conference of the Association for Language Awareness in Montreal. He approached me with a smile saying: "You know, the ABCs really stayed with me." If you wonder why, just read his ABCs.

REFERENCES

Ruggiano Schmidt, P., & Finkbeiner, C. (2006). *The ABC's of Cultural Understanding and Communication: National and International Adaptations*. Greenwich, CT: Information Age.

Statistics Canada. (2011). *Focus on Geography Series. Census 2011*. Retriexed from http://www12.statcan.gc.ca/census-recensement/2011/as-sa/fogs-spg/Facts-cma-teng.cfm?LANG=Eng&GK=CMA&GC=462; retrieved on 9/04/2013

MY ABCs

Troy Davidson

AUTOBIOGRAPHY

To write my autobiography from the perspective of language and learning seems natural for a life that has been shaped so much by language experiences. My earliest childhood memory, in fact, involves language. Somewhere around the age of 3, I can recall observing my mother styling her mother's hair in our family's home. Mesmerized, I watched my mother's fingers dance deftly between potions and sprays, curlers and combs, transforming my nonna's tired locks into a sculpture, as she had every week since long before I was born, and would every week in her long career as a hairdresser. What was special about this week was not so much my nonna's hairstyle. For the first time, I noticed my mother and nonna conducted this magical ritual in their central Italian dialect, Maceratese, which was different from the English I heard from my father and brother and neighbors. Moreover, I realized that I was somehow excluded from this conversation, the rhythm of their speech ricocheting through my ears at lightning speed, not slowing down enough for me to catch. Once my mother had finished her work, my nonna dashed out in the rain, taking care to place a plastic bonnet on her fresh hairdo. I squealed with laughter at the site of her with a plastic bag on her head!

The episode I have just described characterizes much of my early language experience: I associated Italian with my mother's side of the family, and English for my father's side, or the community at-large. My father was not bilingual, and my brother was not interested in Italian, so my mother most frequently used English at home, the language she had learned when she immigrated to Canada as an adolescent. Since my father's family lived a considerable distance away from our community, however, the influence from the Italian side of my family was undeniable. Extended family dinners featured endless food, and a chorus of Italian-speaking relatives, all eager to give me a vigorous pinch on the cheek. I delighted in the warm chaos and spirited discussions of these dinners. Also, while my parents were at work, I was often in the care of my Italian-speaking grandparents. I was only able to contribute simple phrases to our conversations in Italian, so I would often speak to them in a simplified version of English I was sure they would understand. In turn, they spoke to me in a blend of Italian and English. I still recall how much I enjoyed spending time at my grandparents' home, being part of their nightly ritual: nonna crocheting and nonno passing the yarn to her while watching an episode of their Italian soap opera on television. Intriguingly, while I was sufficiently curious about picking up some Italian, my older brother seemed completely disinterested in such endeavors, limiting his Italian to stock swear words with shock value. Around this same time, I noticed that the grocery store I went to with my grandparents was different from the one where my parents went. It smelled and sounded different. My grandparents spoke to their butcher in Italian. The same was true for church: with my grandparents, the priest spoke Italian (and everyone there seemed so old to me at the time), whereas with my parents, the priest spoke English.

As I got a little older, my world began to include more people, and I made friends with other children on the street where we lived in Toronto; many of them heard or spoke a language other than English at home, such as my best friend Aimée, who spoke Haitian Creole (when she heard me call my English-speaking grandfather "grandpa," she also called him "grandpa," which seemed to make some people smile). Regardless of our home situation, there seemed to be a tacit agreement among us to speak English together. How we spoke English was actually subtly policed at times by older brothers and sisters, who would point out our "mistakes" to us. I recall quite vividly one such episode that occurred between my brother and me around the time I had turned 4, shortly after my family had moved to the suburb of Scarborough. We had just returned from our friend Thad's house down the street, when my brother mockingly pointed out my inability to produce the English "th" sound at the beginning of our friend's name. My version at the time was something more of a cockney "Fad" rather than a Toronto "Thad." By making fun of me, my brother had unwittingly added himself to a long list of language teachers in my life. Not only had he assisted me in "noticing the gap" between my pronunciation and his, but he had provided sufficient humiliation to motivate me to practice my "th" sounds obsessively until mastery. Around this same age, I can recall my mother reading a story to me about a bird and its nest: "I love my house, I love my nest, in all the world, this nest is best." The mother bird in the story had eyelashes and wore a scarf on her head. I thought she was pretty.

Moving to our new home in Scarborough brought about another significant change: beginning formal schooling. At the age of 4, half-day sessions of junior kindergarten began at an English-medium Catholic elementary school. My first best friend was Rose, whose parents were from Trinidad; I loved the intricate braids in her hair and the way she sometimes imitated her mother's sing-song way of speaking. I generally enjoyed most activities in class, especially artistic ones, such as painting, sculpting with modeling clay, or role-playing. Learning letters and numbers was a new activity for me, and sometimes I wondered how other classmates already seemed to know them. Shortly after learning our letters, we began reading out loud a series of books, sitting on the carpet in small groups around our teacher's rocking chair. I do not remember the plots of the books, but I do remember one title: Mr. Mugs—A Jet Pet. Some of my classmates arrived in kindergarten without proficiency in English, which seemed strange to me at the time. I remember thinking that only old people did not know English.

Learning to read and write through the early years of elementary school continued. I particularly enjoyed when a teacher would read a story to the class, pausing to display the pictures in her book to us. I loved how they read so assuredly, words and sentences flowing in captivating musical rhythms. I especially appreciated rhyming poetry, songs, and prayers, which I could easily memorize and recite at will. I loved how my teachers wrote so neatly on the blackboard, and I imitated their perfectly proportioned letters. They seemed like movie stars at the time, always knowing, never making mistakes. French class began in grade one with my teacher from Africa, Monsieur Antoine; it mostly consisted of repeating words associated with pictures or objects, reciting prayers and poems, or singing songs. I can still recite many of these today. I continued to enjoy primary school and excelled in both English and French, taking pleasure in more analytical activities, such as grammar, but also in more playful ones, like role-playing and dialog writing. I had a strong memory for spelling, poetry, songs, advertising jingles, and dialogs from films or television. Music was also a pleasure for me; I joined our school's choir and band. Sometimes, after school, I would go to my mother's hair salon, which was always humming with activity and women sharing personal stories, gossip, and jokes. Nothing unlocks memories of that time more than walking into a hair salon and smelling perm solution. My Italian, however, remained limited. Although I could always hear it around home, especially with my grandparents, I did not always pay attention to it; it was sometimes like background noise. At times, I think I even distanced myself from the Italian, just in an effort to "fit in." Although, in retrospect, my classmates were from diverse backgrounds, so we were all probably distancing ourselves to some extent from our home cultures in order to fit in with each other, or rather the Anglo-American actors from our favorite television shows.

Beginning high school at the age of 14 was a difficult transition for me. Whereas my primary school had been a stable environment, mostly middle or working class, the high school I attended was located in an area that could be described as having more social problems. I confronted issues I had not previously experienced, such as violence, racial tension, theft, and drugs. Police officers were regular visitors at the school, dealing with theft and violence issues; by the end of my time there, security cameras were installed. While I had felt quite safe and familiar in my primary school, I now often felt scared, especially after becoming the target of bullying. There were times I wished I could attend another school, and I sometimes imagined myself at a school for the arts, even though it was located too far away. I needed to escape the chaos, and I turned to language learning as an outlet. I enrolled in immersion courses in school, where some of my subjects, like social sciences, were offered in French. French was no longer just a regular class, it was something I could feel good at, something I wanted to be part of myself. I began filling my environment with French: books, television, magazines, music, and visits to a French theater. At 14, I took on a part-time job to finance a language course one summer in France when I was 15. Traveling to France was my first time away from North America, away from my family on my own. My parents, particularly my mother, were not enthusiastic about this trip, but I was unyielding. It felt exhilarating and a little scary, like all my efforts to learn French prior had been a rehearsal for this experience. The other students in these French classes were mostly American and Canadian from wealthy families. A few of them mocked that I was from Scarborough, a poorer suburb of Toronto; most of them had never had part-time work like me. My roommates were more interested in getting drunk in the evenings than learning French, so I spent my time with more serious students. Even though I had worked hard to make French a part of me, and I could manage in all situations in France, I was still very aware that to the ears of the French, I was strange or foreign.

Returning to Scarborough felt like drudgery, but I had decided to meet a new goal: learning Italian. I registered for an Italian course that fall at my high school. My classmates were of Italian origin and voiced their surprise about seeing me in that course, given my Anglo-Saxon name. But I was fearless and felt a certain urgency, like I had to make up for lost time. As with French, I charged through my Italian learning with resolute determination. I quickly made connections between standard Italian and my family's dialect, filling in the gaps in my comprehension at home. I was now able to engage in conversation with greater confidence and felt the relationship with my grandparents strengthen as they shared their stories with me. The next year, a cousin and her new husband from Italy came to Canada on a 2-week visit, and I was so enchanted by them. They spoke a crisp, standard Italian, and had little knowledge of English. During those 2 weeks, I rushed to visit them after school, soaking in the music of every sentence, writing down new words and expressions, making grammar lessons from Italian class come alive.

The following summer, I took my first trip to Italy to meet the rest of my Italian family. So much of what I experienced felt at once foreign, yet familiar. All around me, I heard the sounds of a language I had known since childhood. Only now, complete strangers were using this language that previously had remained mostly reserved for the home, heard at family dinners. In some ways, it felt like I should know these strangers by virtue of their language. Sights and architecture were new and stimulating, as were sounds like sirens and phones ringing, but smells from cooking were intensely familiar. The result was at once bewildering and grounding, unknown and known, like discovering a new part of myself, then realizing with shock that this part had always been there. Furthermore, I realized that the Italy I was seeing for the first time was not the same as the one my family had left in the 60s. It was no longer the place of desperate poverty they had fled; the Italy I saw was now a fashion and design capital, complete with luxury boutiques and seaside resorts. I remained diligent about mastering Italian, writing down new words and phrases in a journal every night. Occasionally, my cousins would laugh when I misused an idiomatic expression or word. At times, I was taken aback about small customs I was completely unaware of, like before entering a room or someone's home, one asked *Permesso?* (permission), and the other answered *Avanti!* (forward), even if it had been entirely clear from the beginning that one was expected to walk right in. At times, I felt like this Italian-ness was who I was, but I also realized, sometimes painfully, that to my Italian family and other Italians, I was definitely not Italian—I was *Americano*. Again, like my experience in France, I felt like I could not actually become Italian, yet upon returning to Scarborough, I did not feel complete just in English. I remember at the time describing this feeling like sitting between two chairs: uncomfortable. I even envied how easy it seemed for my Italian cousins: this was where they were from, where their families had always been—they owned it in a way.

Shortly afterwards, I began university and moved to Montreal, choosing a program in translation and literature, followed by a certification in second-language education. I also took courses in German and Spanish, but achieved less proficiency in them than my other languages (particularly German, which now seems like a distant memory. Ich habe alles vergessen?). During my studies, I worked part-time in a shop owned by a couple from the south of France. Marie-Laurence and I shared stories as we worked on window displays, the intricate arrangements she designed told their own beautiful stories. All of my friends from university were bi- or multilingual: Javier from El Salvador, who speaks French, English, Italian, and Spanish; Darren from the Seychelles, who speaks Creole, French, and English; and Natasha, who speaks Russian, French, and English. Rightly or wrongly, it is still with bi/multilingual people or people who have immigrated that I feel most comfortable. Perhaps my perception is that, like me, they have experienced feeling like an insider and outsider simultaneously. Or perhaps I do not trust that I will be understood in just one language, that someone will mistake me for being singular rather than plural, or expect that information like my last name or my place of birth tell a complete story of who I am. From time to time, I am confronted with this, like when I registered for my master's program, the application required that I check one box corresponding to my mother tongue. Which one should I choose? Am I a whole person if I check just one box?

Both during and since university, I have had the chance to visit and live in different places within Canada and Europe. Sometimes the definition of "home" is an elastic one, because I always seem to be missing someone or somewhere. Ultimately, I believe that learning languages has been an empowering tool for me—one that has put me in touch with my own stories and the stories of others; a passport that has given me the freedom to travel deeper within myself, my family, and around the world.

Biography

The following is a summary of four hours of interviews conducted on Saturday, August 6, 2011, Sunday, August 7, 2011, and Tuesday, August 9, 2011. The interviewee is the interviewer's mother, who was born in the mid-1940s and grew up in a small town in north-central Italy, then immigrated to Canada as an adolescent. For the purpose of this paper, we will refer to her as Francesca. The draft of the biography was submitted in writing for Francesca's validation on Sunday, August 7, 2011. Further questions were asked, and the biography was resubmitted for validation on Tuesday, August 9, 2011.

When asked to harken back to her earliest memories, Francesca recalled her grandfather bouncing her on his knees. She was intrigued with the galloping sound he was making and tried to imitate it. She squealed with laughter at how fun both this ride and the noise were. Francesca reckoned that this event took place before the age of 3 in her family's home. She further recollected, "I don't remember being able to speak at this time, and I don't really have memories of my parents before this." She then described her memories of her grandfather's death when she was three and a half. She recalls that there was hushed speech in the home, not intended for children's ears. "I didn't understand what was being said, but knew that something important must be happening because of the way they were talking quickly and whispering." She was taken away from the family home for 3 or 4 days. She deduced that this was likely in order to keep a child away from a funeral and the corpse that had been exposed in the home.

The next episode that she recollected took place around what she reckoned would be age three and a half. She had been elected to present a bishop visiting their village with a bouquet of flowers, accompanied by a poem recital. She knew that someone had written the poem for her, because she could not read or write at the time, but did not know who had written it. She recalls that she rehearsed the poem many times and was directed to stand in a certain way and project her voice, pausing and emphasizing certain phrases. The day of the *vescovo*'s visit felt like a big event, and she wore her best clothes. The mixed bouquet of flowers she held was tied with a white satin ribbon; she liked the texture of the satin between her fingers. Francesca began to recall a few words from the poem: "*Sono contadinella/ Tanto pulita e bella*" (I am a little farmer girl, very clean and pretty). At this point, Francesca claimed she could not recall the rest of the poem, but surmised that it may have contained some lines about Jesus. The poem seemed familiar to me, so I asked Francesca if the following line sounded like something she knew: "*Sono piccolina, tre anni son pochi*" (I am very small, three is not very old). "Yes!" she approved enthusiastically, "How do you know it?" We reconstructed the next lines together, "*Mi piacciono libri e giochi/Tante cose, non le so/Ma ci vuole pazienza/Perché un giorno, crescerò*" (I love books and games/I don't know many things/But be patient/Because I will grow up one day). Francesca could not believe that I could know this poem. We assumed that her mother, my nonna, must have told me it, although I do not remember when. The recital took place in the spring, outside the church; it went well, and the small crowd applauded. The bishop came down and put his hand on her head, making the sign of the cross with his thumb on her forehead. "I remember he looked kind," Francesca added. The event seemed very important, although no one had explained to her who this *vescovo* was.

Francesca's family moved several times, living in different villages in her native region of central Italy, as well as different apartments in Rome. Each time, she felt anxiety about living in a new home and making new friends, and she sometimes could not say good-bye to her friends before moving. The first school in a small village hosted grades 1 to 5 in one room. Francesca began her formal schooling in grade 1, as there was no kindergarten. She remembers learning the alphabet by reciting it in a sing-song way. She recalls that learning to count was fascinating, because once you got to 10, you could just add one to the end, and so on, to arrive at a new number. She enjoyed recognizing these patterns. She remembers that older children would write using a pen that they dipped in an inkwell, sometimes making big blobs on their page. A favorite trick that boys could play was sticking a girl's braid, *la treccia*, in the ink, *l'inchiostro*. She recalls that the Italian spoken at school was different from the local dialect used every day, and sometimes her teacher would correct students on how to speak standard Italian.

She remembers her first major writing project from grade 1. All students were required to write a letter as part of a Christmas Eve tradition by which children placed a letter under their parents dish at the table. In the letter, they asked for forgiveness from their parents if they had behaved badly, promising to try to make them proud in the future. She practiced writing this letter several times in pencil before being allowed to write a good copy on fancy, patterned paper using ink. Since parents had to buy this writing equipment, and money was scarce, children were sure to take good care of these pens and ink tips. She remembers trying to be careful with her pen, and careful with the fine paper and envelope she had been provided for this important activity. She had never seen paper like this before. When asked what Christmas was like in their home, Francesca responded,

> Christmas was religious, we didn't get any presents at Christmas. It was all religious. If we were lucky, we got some sweets. It was all about going to church, going to Christmas Eve mass. Eating fish for that day. We didn't have a Christmas tree, only the nativity. It wasn't until I came to Canada that I actually saw a Christmas tree and Christmas presents. Mainly, it was all around religion and going to church, and we also celebrated New Year's Day. We didn't get anything until the Epiphany; we didn't get presents, we would get oranges, candies, or *torrone*. It was *la Befana* who brought them, not Father Christmas or Santa Claus. We didn't know about that until we came to Canada.

Sometimes, letters would arrive from relatives who had immigrated to Canada. Francesca's grandmother would ask her to read these letters to her, since she could not read. Francesca protested, saying that she did not really understand everything that was written, but her nonna would say, "Just take your time. Tell me the words you know." Hearing what was written in the letters made her nonna happy, sometimes bringing her to tears, and she would often ask her to repeat what was written. Francesca remembers being very young then, and she could not make out all the words, so she would try to sound them out. Letters also arrived via air mail from her father in Canada for her mother. These letters came more frequently than the others, but she was not allowed to read them. She simply knew they were from her father. She recalls one incident when a teacher asked the class what their fathers did, so she explained that hers was in Toronto, Canada. When her teacher asked if she could locate the city on the map of the world, she became nervous, and just pointed anywhere, feeling embarrassed.

Francesca then moved with her mother and younger sister to the big city of Rome, where she completed grades 4 and 5. She recalls that there was somewhat of a class distinction between those who spoke standard Italian and those who spoke dialect. "The dialect speakers were looked down upon as peasants," she explained. One girl from northern Italy was made fun of for speaking a different dialect, and Francesca felt empathy toward her and tried to console her. To avoid being teased herself, Francesca made efforts to speak her "best Italian." She devised roleplaying games for her and her younger sister, choosing pretend, "fancy" names for each other. "*Tu sei signorina Paula!*" By adopting a fancy name and a fancy way of speaking, she not only practiced a more formal, standard Italian, but also succeeded in holding her younger sister's attention long enough to make getting through her chores go more smoothly than if she spoke dialect.

Francesca's teacher in Rome identified her as a good student. If her teacher had to exit the classroom, she appointed Francesca to sit at her desk and write down the names of any misbehavers in a red ballpoint pen. Francesca did not report anyone's behavior to her teacher, because she knew that this would cause problems for her after school, but she does recall that she was fascinated with the pen that could write in red. They did not have any such things in the small villages she had lived before! She also felt honored that her teacher had entrusted her with this responsibility. Francesca felt that she had earned it by having made such progress in standard Italian. In fact, she now spoke it so well that other people could not detect traces of her dialect. She recalls, "It was important to be accepted. You wanted to blend in, otherwise they'd make fun of you. They teased you and called you names and made you feel bad."

Sometime during this period in Rome, Francesca had fallen ill with what she deduced to be the measles. She recalls being kept in a dark bedroom because it was believed that any light or reading would strain her eyes and ruin them. At this time, her friend Pietro's mother bought her a book, *The Wizard of Oz* in Italian. Pietro read the story to her, and she was fascinated. "I was totally mesmerized! I loved the pictures of the flying monkeys, Dorothy's red shoes, and the tin man, the scarecrow, the different characters," she explained. This was the first book that she remembers, since they had workbooks in school (*quaderni*), but not textbooks.

Her second book was purchased for her by her mother when traveling: an Italian version of an American comic book, Charlie Brown. She was thrilled, absorbed by it for days, as she read and reread it. The pictures were in black and white. She remembers that one of the characters had an English name: Lucy. She had never seen the letter "y" before, and asked what it was: "*i-greca*." She remembers this response clearly, because she had not encountered a "y" before, since it is not part of the standard Italian alphabet.

At this point, Francesca remembered moving back to a small village in her native area of central Italy. She was in a small hospital to get her tonsils removed. This procedure was carried out in a chair, without anaesthetic. Francesca recalls this event as being very traumatic, not only because of the excruciating pain, but because the instrument for performing the surgery broke after her first tonsil had been removed. She was brought to lie down on a table as the doctors went to a neighboring village for a replacement tool. The pain was so tremendous that she could not even cry or scream, lest it hurt her throat. When they returned, she had to be strapped into the operating chair with her hands behind her back. "I knew what they were coming back to do, and I didn't want it," she recalled, adding her memory of seeing splatters of blood on the walls. After this, she remained in hospital for several days. Everyone around her seemed very concerned because she would not speak or eat. They even tried to entice her to eat by purchasing ice cream—the first time she had seen ice cream. Francesca claims she was able to speak, but was too angry with the doctors who had inflicted this misery on her, so she used silence to express her anger.

The local village school did not go past grade 6, so she lived in the convent of a larger neighboring village in the care of nuns for the year. She enjoyed living in the convent and found the environment to be orderly and calm. Each morning began with songs in the chapel, which she enjoyed, followed by prayers before breakfast. The nuns accompanied the girls to the village school in the morning. Francesca made friends with a Jewish girl, Stephanie. "I didn't know what Jewish meant at the time; I figured that out later," Francesca explained. Stephanie's mother was also the 6th-grade teacher, *la maestra*, and the two friends sat beside each other. Francesca wanted to make a good impression on her friend's mother, and she did very well in school that year. This was when she also began studying Latin, a language she had already heard in church, where the mass was conducted in Latin. She recalls, "Latin was familiar, but I didn't really know what it meant. I just recited it."

During this year at the convent, Francesca knew that her mother had been waiting for news to be able to immigrate to Canada and join her father. They immigrated in August, traveling by boat, arriving at Pier 21 in Halifax, where they then boarded a train to Toronto. The train ride felt tremendously long. She recalls that other Italians from the boat were on the same train. They were given food during the ride. The bread was white and fluffy, thinly and evenly presliced and so different from what they had known in Italy that they hardly recognized it as bread. Francesca, her mother, and her sister were also given small, individual serving boxes of cereal. She surmised that these must have been Kellogg's Corn Flakes, because she later recognized the rooster on the package in a Canadian grocery store. When they finally arrived in Union Station in Toronto, they could not find her father, who had agreed to meet them there. "There were panicky moments. No one really knew what to do, but no one really understood us. No one was there to interpret. Somehow we got a cab, and nonna had zia Melinde's address." So Francesca and her sister and mother had to get in a taxi and go to a relative's home on their own. As it turns out, her father and uncle had made it to the station, but they could not read the English signage and ended up waiting in the wrong area of the station. "I guess we had left our luggage at the station, because we had too much to put in a taxi. We had a big trunk! In the meantime, they were there, waiting on another platform upstairs. They had brought a truck to drive the luggage back."

Beginning school in Canada was another difficult transition. She was forced to repeat grade 6 due to her lack of proficiency in English. Moreover, she was mocked by Canadian students, particularly boys, who called her stupid, which she understood, or a WOP, which she did not understand, but latter learned stood for With Out Papers, a pejorative term applied to Italian immigrants. "They were really mean," she recalls, "But my teachers never made fun of me." That fall, she remembers taking part in a different Canadian custom: trick or treating. She could not believe that people actually gave candy away to strangers! Halfway through the year, her family moved again, and she began at yet another school. The wife of this school's principal was a kind, older lady. "I knew she was older because wore her hair piled in a bun on her head," Francesca said. She took small groups of students out of their regular class for an hour a day to work on their English skills. In Francesca's group there was a girl from Poland, a boy from Japan, and another boy from Hungary. The principal's wife showed these kids pictures and sounded out words in English. Italian is a fairly transparent language, in which every letter is associated with a sound, but English seemed so confusing because how a word was spelled was not what it sounded like. Moreover, some words had multiple meanings: box was a container and a verb; make up was a verb, but also something you wore on your face. Some sounds in English did not exist in Italian, like the "th" sound, and other sounds were quite different, like the "r" in each language. Francesca remembers that she really learned English at this time through sounds and pictures. She recalls the picture books the principal had them read: Dick and Jane. "Run, dog, run! See Spot run! See Jane run!" She associated the picture with the vocabulary. She also believes that her studies in Latin in Italy helped her to recognize cognates in English.

By grade 8, Francesca had become completely bilingual and was called upon by the principal to help out in the office by calling the parents of other Italian students and translating back to the principal what was said. At this point, she was only speaking Italian at home and used English everywhere else. She recalls trying very hard to imitate the way Canadians spoke and acted, so she would not be the target of teasing again; it was important for her to mask traces of her accent. She asked her family's neighbors from London, England, to attend her parent-teacher conferences, since her own parents would not understand what was being said. By grade 9, she took on a part-time job at a Dominion grocery store on Thursday and Friday nights, and Saturdays. The grocery stores in Canada had many different items all under one roof, whereas in Italy, a butcher only sold meat, and you went to a fishmonger for fish, a bakery for bread. For the first time, her family also began to buy canned food. In Italy, she had never seen olives or tomatoes in cans. Her mother had always made her clothing for her, only in the material shops in Canada, she could choose from many different bolts of fabric. Churches in Canada, however, seemed excessively plain. She also recalls, "In Italy, we never had our own phone, and we didn't have a TV. The only TV I saw was in a community center, but I didn't see it often, maybe four or five times. Everyone in Canada had a TV and a phone in the house. Everyone had a bathroom. We didn't have that in Italy. I was all very different." Francesca recalls many people in Italy writing to her the first few years after arriving in Canada. Her contacts with relatives already in Canada, however, were intermittent, "It was different over here. Even though there were some relatives, we were spread out, it wasn't the same. We were more isolated from our relatives and friends. Things got busier and more spread out. Getting to see them was harder, because we had to take the bus, and we had no car. Nothing was in walking distance. I had cousins and everything over here, but I didn't get too close with them because we were far away, and some of them didn't even speak Italian anymore. It wasn't like the relatives we had in Italy."

With Francesca's fluency in English also came great responsibilities. She now went with her parents on doctor's appointments and translated, she verified bank statements, and filled out forms for them in English. Her responsibilities toward her family soon became financial: she was asked to leave high school at the age of 16 to attend hairdressing school and begin earning wages. Francesca was disappointed. Despite the upheaval of several moves and several school changes, from village to village, then to Rome, and to Canada, she had managed to do well in school and had hoped she could one day become a teacher. She accepted her family's decision, recalling that a girl was not necessarily expected to pursue her studies, and learning a trade, *il mestiere*, was sufficient. Luckily, Francesca did enjoy her hairdressing studies—in fact, she excelled at it—and soon began earning a living at her new trade.

Completing this biography provided me with an ideal opportunity to have more open dialog with my mother about her past. Only recently has my mother been coming to terms with traumatic episodes from childhood and immigration, not all of which have been reported here.

Cross-Cultural Analysis

Rooted in sociocultural and critical literacy theories, the ABC model to cultural understanding and communication makes use of narrative discourse to foster both self-reflection and reflection about others (Schmidt & Finkbeiner, 2006, p. 4). This 3-step process begins with the writing of one's own autobiography (the "A" phase), followed by an interview and biography of another person (the "B" phase), followed by a cross-cultural analysis of the two accounts (the "C" phase). By having pre- or in-service teachers experience this model, it helps them gain insight into issues such as cultural awareness and literacy development, which can then serve to create consciousness-raising experiences in the classroom. The ABC model, based on the maxim "Know thyself, understand others" (Schmidt & Finkbeiner, 2006, p. 4), is adaptable to a variety of settings and ages, and can be used following the autobiography, biography, cross-cultural analysis approach in pairs or groups of three or by having both partners act as biographers or by conducting reciprocal ABCs.

I am currently completing a master's degree in second-language education while working as an ESL instructor to students, mostly Francophone, at a CÉGEP (junior college) in Montreal. In the past, I have also worked as a French teacher at primary and secondary levels in Canada and an ESL teacher abroad. Hence, for the purposes of the autobiography, the self-reflection or "A" portion of the ABC model, I have paid particular attention to experiences related to language and learning. Similarly, the biography or "B" phase of this ABC assignment had the same focus. I acted as biographer to myself in the "A" phase and interviewed my mother for the completion of the biography or "B" phase.

As I stated at the end of my mother's biography, the motivation to have her participate as an interviewee in the ABC assignment was to open a dialog about her personal history that had often been shrouded in silence. This silence and subsequent search for self are common themes in literature written by second-generation immigrants in North America. Two who come immediately to mind are Canada's Nino Ricci in his trilogy *The Lives of the Saints* and the Chinese American author Amy Tan; both write about characters who grapple with what is unspoken, confronting their parents' past and its secrets. I liken this process to a storm that stirs the waters at sea; each wave that comes to shore carries elements that were previously hidden on the sea floor beneath murky waters. What was once invisible or unknown is now available for closer inspection, which can lead to new realizations, associations, memories, and questions, some of which are discussed this paper, the cross-cultural analysis phase of this ABC process.

Commonalities and divergences emerged from these two stories. To describe these biographical episodes in such binary terms, however, would be misleading, for what on the texts' surface seems to be a clear similarity, upon further analysis can turn out to be a difference and vice versa. To illustrate the overlapping and diverging of common themes in these two stories, I will refer to Weaver's iceberg analogy of culture (Weaver, 1993, p. 159). The tip of the iceberg represents what is actually observable from a situation, whereas what is below the surface, the majority of the iceberg, is invisible and includes beliefs, values, and feelings about a situation.

What follows is the cross-cultural analysis of my autobiography and biography. When citing information sourced from my autobiography, I have used the abbreviation "Auto," whereas for information cited from Francesca's biography, I have used "Bio." General commonalities and differences have been displayed on Tables 3.1 and 3.2. Four salient themes from the two stories will be discussed in greater detail. They are organized under the headings phonological awareness, church, media, and choice. I will follow with a critical appraisal of the assignment in the conclusion.

Phonological Awareness

For both participants, the theme of phonological awareness plays a prominent role throughout their language histories, which both begin with early

TABLE 3.1   Iceberg Model of Commonalities and Differences: Above the Surface

	Differences: Francesca	Commonalities	Differences: Troy
Above the surface themes	Female. Period of biography covers mid-1940s to mid-1960s, spans from Italy to Canada. Grew up in more monocultural community. Early years characterized by disruption, moving. Formal schooling ended while in high school. Immigration experience was stressful. Grew up in lower socioeconomic bracket. Assumed role of responsibility toward parents once immigrated.	Both cited early memories in home. Both cited grandparents as nurturers. Both received formal schooling. Both express respect for teachers. Both identify as successful learners. Both began part-time work around age 14. Both have a Europe-Canada connection. Identify as bi/multilinguals. Both experienced teasing/bullying.	Male. Period of biography covers mid-1970s to mid-1990s, mostly in Canada, includes travel episodes to Europe. Grew up in diverse community, hybrid home culture. Early years stable. Formal schooling continued past university undergrad. Travel experience was positive. Grew up in middle socioeconomic bracket.
Above the surface themes discussed in detail.	3. Access to media was limited. 4. Life events characterized by lack of choice.	1. Both aware of playful nature of sound. Phonological Awareness: "Narrowing the gap" between own speech and target speech. 2. Both received education through religious institutions. Early memories of learning include religion. Shared membership in a religion.	3. Access to media was rich. 4. Author of own life choices. Determined.

TABLE 3.2 Iceberg Model of Commonalities and Differences: Below the Surface

	Francesca	Commonalities	Troy
Below the surface themes.	Socioeconomic status positioned her at disadvantaged end of power distance.	Both associated early memories in home with positive feelings. Both valued teachers and schooling. Both felt determined to learn. Both value hard work. Both experienced fear growing up.	Middle socioeconomic status, but from wealthy country with access to education. At advantaged end of power distance.
Below the surface themes discussed in detail.	1. On disadvantaged end of power distance: "Narrowing the gap" was motivated by stigmatization and feelings of inadequacy.		1. Native speaker of English, a lingua franca, which is at the privileged end of power distance. Acquisition of second and heritage languages.
	2. Referred to church and its representatives in positive terms.		2. On disadvantaged end of power distance with church and school community. Association of church with feelings of alienation.
	3.	3.	3. Media reflected bias and power distance.
	4. Grew up in collectivist society.	4. Inequalities between men and women.	4. Grew up in individualist society.

memories of fascination with sound. Common to both childhoods was a depiction of sound's pleasurable, playful qualities, as noted in Francesca's biography when she recalled her grandfather making a galloping sound as he bounced her, "She squealed with laughter at how fun both this ride and the noise were" (Bio). They both enjoyed associating learning with musicality and memory, as illustrated in their remembering of poetry or lists chanted aloud in the classroom: Francesca recalls "learning the alphabet by reciting it in a sing-song way" (Bio); whereas I recall, "I especially appreciated rhyming poetry, songs, and prayers" (Auto). We both describe a desire to narrow the gap between our own linguistic production and more prestigious or standard pronunciations. For Francesca, this meant rehearsing standard Italian in Italy. She then worked on English and all its new sounds once in Canada. I rehearsed "th" sounds in English, as I mention that my brother's teasing had motivated "me to practice my 'th' sounds obsessively until mastery" (Auto). Although not heavily highlighted in my autobiography, I also paid careful attention to imitating both French and Italian, so as not to "stand out" in Europe. I can recall taping my voice on cassette, listening back to it, then repeating the process again in an effort to reduce my accent.

On the surface, we can observe a commonality that seems to support R. W. Schmidt's Noticing Hypothesis in second-language acquisition (1990): once learners notice the gap between their linguistic production and the target production, they will consciously attend to these features.

On closer inspection, however, these two stories are quite different. Francesca refers on several occasions to a sharp desire to adopt the more prestigious Italian variant in order to avoid being stigmatized by peers: "The dialect speakers were looked down upon as peasants . . . You wanted to blend in, otherwise they'd make fun of you. They teased you and called you names, and made you feel bad" (Bio). She even associated the acquisition of the standard Italian variants with rewards, such as being considered a good student, and being entrusted by her teacher with special tasks. She described a desire to acquire English quickly once arriving in Canada to avoid being made the target of bullying: "she was mocked by Canadian students, particularly boys, who called stupid, which she understood, or a WOP, which she did not understand, but latter learned stood for With Out Papers, a pejorative term applied to Italian immigrants" (Bio). Again, becoming bilingual was associated with the reward of completing special tasks in the principal's office. When Francesca and her family first arrived in Canada, a lack of proficiency in English also played a central role in turning what was to be a happy reunion at the train station into panic and chaos (Bio). Without abilities in English, signage was impossible to decipher, and communication with train station officials was also impossible.

In contrast, I had acquired a standard variation of English, the language of instruction in my schooling, before entering kindergarten, and do not describe any limitations related to my dominant language. In my second and heritage languages, I may have been identifiable as a nonnative or seminative speaker, causing me a small degree of embarrassment at times. My situation was different in that I was already a speaker of a lingua franca and from a wealthy country. I described my proficiency in French and Italian in empowering terms. Learning language was about self-fulfillment, since I very well could have chosen to manage as a monolingual with a rudimentary knowledge of French in order to pass the basic requirements of secondary education.

This divergence illustrates Hofstede's notion of power distance (Hofstede, 1997). Power distance refers to the degree of inequality between two people in a given situation. In these episodes, both participants have cited a similar behavior, namely, narrowing the gap between their language production and the target form. Francesca's behavior, however, was fueled by being on the disadvantaged end of a large power distance. The acquisition of prestigious variants was related to access to education and socioeconomic status. Language is therefore not a neutral vehicle for communication; it carries with it a sociocultural context. English has maintained a position of linguistic hegemony for the past 150 years, moving at a juggernaut speed as a lingua franca, placing native speakers of this language in a position of privilege and therefore creating a power distance in relation to other languages. As a native speaker of English, it is important to acknowledge that this power dynamic may be present with speakers of other languages. Moreover, as a language educator, it is essential to be aware of this power distance when relating to students.

Church

Both participants cited the role the church played in their childhoods and education. Early memories for me included reciting prayers in English and French at school (Auto), whereas for Francesca, an early memory included reciting poetry (Bio). Francesca alluded to the church and its representatives in positive terms on several occasions during the interview, referring to the bishop as "kind" (Bio), and the nuns' convent as "orderly" and "calm" (Bio). While for Francesca, the church seemed to be in the foreground of her language and cultural experiences, for me, it moved into the background around secondary school, when I grew critical of the Catholic dogma that was part of religion class at school. I observed that some students used their interpretation of religion to adopt self-righteous, conservative views, and they frequently pointed a condemning finger at gays. I briefly mentioned in my autobiography feeling fearful at school and being bullied in early grades of secondary school. Although I did not recognize myself as gay until later in school, other people had already noticed my difference, which became their excuse to target me during and outside the classroom through homophobic name-calling, threats, and physical abuse. In this case, the homophobia I endured was rooted in institutional and societal factors, including the age and gender identities of the perpetrators, as well as the time period, the late 1980s, which was character-ized by a certain backlash against gays following the mass hysteria surround-ing AIDS in the early 80s. The church's role in condemning homosexuality and how members of the church's community interpreted this role cannot be disentangled from these institutional and societal factors. I felt increasingly alienated by the church; since I attended a Catholic school, I also felt alienated by the school. This time coincided with my strong motivation to acquire other languages and feel part of other communities.

Referring once more to Hofstede's power distance dimensions (1997), I would consider myself to have been on the disadvantaged end of a large power distance. Francesca's text, conversely, only reveals a positive appraisal of her church-related experiences. Using Weaver's iceberg analogy (1993), we can therefore observe that despite shared membership in a religion on the surface, the participants' experiences, values, and feelings toward the church and members of its community diverge. These differences in attitudes are also rooted in time and space: I grew up at a time and in a city where I began to understand that multiple perspectives regarding religion and spiri-tuality were valid, whereas Francesca grew up at a time and in a place where there was one dominant perspective toward religion.

Media

One of the more salient points of divergence in the stories of these stories lies in our respective depictions of access to media. For the purposes of this paper, "media" incorporates press, television, telephony, radio, advertising, and Internet, as well as the people who represent media and the tools used to create it. I recall enjoying rich access to various media on multiple occa-sions, from school supplies in kindergarten onward, to television programs, films, music, books, magazines, and theater in multiple languages. As I men-tion in my autobiography, I grew up in a diverse urban/suburban setting; my school's library was vast, and public libraries housed media in many lan-guages. In contrast, Francesca's descriptions painted a different picture: she took great care of her writing tools, books were rare so they were read and reread, and classrooms were without textbooks (Bio). As well, the two books she cited as memorable were American, *The Wizard of Oz* and Charlie Brown, translated into Italian (Bio). Also, her family did not have a phone or television set in the home (Bio). Moreover, once arriving in Canada, the books used to instruct English as a second language were in fact intended for young mother-tongue learners, not adolescents (Bio). Such differences un-derscore the temporal and geographical distance between the participants, but also a socioeconomic difference. As well, Francesca's memories of read-ing stories imported from America are testament to the cultural power that the country was already attaining around the world.

Although I do recall having access to various media, I would hesitate to qualify this situation as ideal. As I mentioned in my autobiography, I made friends in kindergarten with a girl of Caribbean origin, whom we will call "Rose." I remained friends throughout elementary school with her until we went to different high schools. In grade 4, one of our first assignments was a self-portrait drawing. I sat beside Rose, and I was surprised to see her coloring in her face in the drawing using a light, peachy color. I remember even pointing out to Rose that we should be drawing ourselves. "This is me," she replied. Each pencil crayon's color had a name stamped on it. Rose pointed to the name on the crayon: "Skin." I recall feeling very uncomfortable about this. This may have the first year that color was being sold in pencil crayon packs, because I recall previously using yellow to color in the faces of my family or myself in drawings. I believe the name of the pencil crayon color was changed the following year. Nevertheless, the tool used to mediate the self wore a biased label, implying that Caucasian skin tone was the generic or standard against which others are compared. As Pattnaik points out, it is important "to critically reflect over white privileges and racism in the American society" (Pattnaik, 2006, p. 117). In this case, the tools used by my friend to mediate her self-image were most definitely reflective of white privilege.

Also, I referred in my autobiography to sensing that some of us in school may have been shelving away our home cultures in an effort "to fit in with each other, or rather the Anglo-American actors from our favorite television shows" (Auto). Media was indeed a powerful agent of socialization in my early years in the 1970s and early 1980s. Much television we watched was American programming: The *Six Million Dollar Man*, *Wonder Woman*, *Charlie's Angels*, *The Love Boat*, *Sesame Street*, *The Muppets*, *Diff'rent Strokes*, *The Facts of Life*, *Little House on the Prairie*, The *Brady Bunch*. These programs featured mostly white and sometimes Afro-American characters, but rarely or never Caribbean, East or South Asian, First Nations, bicultural, or biracial characters. Gay and lesbian characters were either nonexistent or someone to make jokes about or, worse, monsters to be feared. Not until the mid-1980s do I recall seeing Canadian television that reflected a reality more familiar to me, such as that depicted on *Degrassi Junior High*. In essence, access to media is not synonymous with access to fair media. Again here, media offered an incomplete or inaccurate portrayal of society. By granting more prestigious visibility to certain segments of society, media attributed power to those already on the privileged end of the power gap. As Leftwich and Madden assert, "School had not taught us to question and to think against the grain or status quo" (Leftwich & Madden, 2006, p. 79). Similarly, although access to media had granted me media literacy, it had not necessarily granted me critical media literacy. Without cultivating critical awareness, one can mistake media as an accurate depiction of reality, or a reality to be imitated, rather than one that is constructed through a biased lens. To develop this critical awareness of cultural dimensions that are not readily observable, we need to develop strategies "in order to be more precise and more successful in orienting and locating ourselves in a network of possible places, premises and sites" (Finkbeiner, 2009, p. 153). Finkbeiner aptly likens this process to employing "human GPS." Not only does it require turning on our awareness (the "GPS"), it requires receiving and processing information from multiple perspectives ("GPS satellites") (2009, pp. 154–155).

Choice

Choice, or lack thereof, is a central theme in each participant's life story. I refer to myself as the agent of many of the determining events in my life: learning French and Italian, travel, courses in secondary school, university location and course of study. Francesca, conversely, seemed to be at the mercy of much of her life's circumstances, as illustrated by several family moves and school changes, which entailed the loss of friendships and stability each time (Bio). Her early experiences with learning, the recital of the poem, and the writing topic were performances of imposed topics (Bio). Ownership of learning was external. Immigration and the choice of her own career studies were also not under her control. The image she gave of having her tonsils removed, strapped in an operating chair, hands bound, speechless, powerless, and in pain is a very fitting one (Bio), and perhaps not at all coincidental.

The lack of choice available to Francesca can be explained by multiple factors. One essential factor is socioeconomics, but other explanations are rooted in historical, geographical, and societal factors. Referring once again to Hofstede's (1997) theories of cultural dimensions, societies can be more collectivist or individualist, masculine or feminine. In a collectivist society, family often consists of extended members. Children who grow up in collectivist societies "learn to think of themselves as part of a 'we' group, a relationship that is not voluntary but is given by nature" (p. 75). In contrast, the child who grows up in the individualist society thinks of him or herself more as an individual, and his or her preferences are not shaped by group membership but by personal interests (p. 75). Societies that are more "masculine" are characterized by, among other things, having distinct gender roles, whereas in more "feminine" societies, gender roles overlap (p. 120). The Italy of the 1950s and 1960s in which Francesca grew up was more on the collectivist pole of the cultural dimension. Francesca actually grieves the loss of close extended family after arriving in Canada: "Even though there were some relatives, we were spread out, it wasn't the same. We were more isolated from our relatives and friends.... It wasn't like the relatives we had in Italy" (Bio). In addition, Italy in the '50s and '60s had clearly defined roles for men and women. It stands to reason that Francesca's lack of choice was related to growing up in a collectivist, masculine society. In contrast, Canada in the '80s and '90s was a more individualist society, although there was probably a wide continuum between individualist and collectivist dimensions from family to family. Even though I was raised in a hybrid Italian-English home, I could take ownership in a number of areas in my life based on personal interest. Whether or not Canada was/is a masculine or feminine society remains open to debate. On the one hand, we have historically focused on collective well-being through universal health care and affordable education, policies that promote official bilingualism, as well as multiculturalism rather than assimilation of newcomers, all areas that are more typically feminine (p. 157). To assert, however, that Canadian society is more feminine according to Hofstede's dimensions, however, would be rather simplistic. To illustrate this, it is important to bear in mind that Canadians witnessed horrifying acts of terror committed against women in between 1989 and 1992, which brought to the surface inequalities between men and women in Canadian society. In Montreal in 1989, a mad gunman, Marc Lépine, singled out 14 young women studying engineering at the École polytechnique, shooting them dead before turning the gun on himself. Beginning around the same time in Scarborough, Paul Bernardo inflicted unspeakable sexual violence on young women, killing several of them. Moreover, these acts of violence were not just passing news stories for me: although not proven in court, one of these young women may have been the sister of my high school classmate. While it is important to note that these acts of violence were committed by crazed individuals, they also gave impetus for discussion and reflection on the status of women in Canadian society in general, bringing to light issues of gender inequality.

CONCLUSION

While my initial motivation for carrying out the ABCs was to open dialog with my mother and situate myself within a family history, I believe the experience has also been an exercise in locating myself within much wider geographical, historical, and cultural dimensions. The information collected during the self-reflection and the interview phases of the project served as jumping-off points to identifying a host of factors that shaped both participants' critical life experiences. I have made reference to Hofstede's cultural dimensions on several occasions in this paper: power distance as a measure of inequality, collectivist vs. individualist societies, and masculine vs. feminine societies. Indeed, the world in which we navigate is never a neutral, static one, but a dynamic one being shaped by the values, beliefs, and experiences of those around us. As a language teacher, I believe this model has contributed to fostering a more reflective practice: Where have I failed to acknowledge and diffuse power distances? To what extent are the values and beliefs of my students taken into account in my classroom and in the institution in which I teach? How does my teaching honor multiple perspectives? How does the ministry of education's curriculum honor multiples perspectives?

Much of this cross-cultural analysis has focused on issues relating to power dynamics. During this ABC experience, I felt that, as the interviewer in the process, there was a power distance between my interviewee and me due to the fact that the interviewee filtered her life story through me, whereas I was the author of my own autobiography. I feel that a more equitable process could have been achieved by having us both act as biographers to each other. Moreover, we each could have had the experience of understanding another person and seeing ourselves through someone else's lens.

REFERENCES

Finkbeiner, C. (2009). Using "human global positioning system" as a navigation tool to the hidden dimension of culture. In A. Feng, M. Byram, & M. Fleming (Eds.), *Becoming interculturally competent through training and education* (pp. 151–173). Tonowanda, NY: Multilingual Matters.

Hofstede, G. (1997). *Cultures and organizations: Software of the mind. Intercultural cooperation and its importance for survival.* New York, NY: McGraw-Hill.

Leftwich, S., & Madden, M. E. (2006). "Doing" the ABCs: An introspective look at process. In P. R. Schmidt & C. Finkbeiner (Eds.), *The ABC"s of cultural understanding and communication: National and international adaptations* (pp. 73–92). Greenwich, CT: Information Age.

Pattnaik, J. (2006). Revealing and revisiting "self" in relation to the culturally different "other": Multicultural teacher education and the ABCs model. In P. R. Schmidt & C. Finkbeiner (Eds.), *The ABCs of cultural understanding and communication: National and international adaptations* (pp. 111–142). Greenwich, CT: Information Age.

Ruggiano Schmidt, P., & Finkbeiner, C. (2006). Introduction: What is the ABCs of cultural understanding and communication? In P. R. Schmidt & C. Finkbeiner (Eds.), *The ABC's of cultural understanding and communication: National and international adaptations* (pp. 1–18). Greenwich, CT: Information Age.

Schmidt, R. W. (1990). The role of consciousness in second language learning. *Applied Linguistics, 11*, 129–158.

Weaver, G. R. (1993). Understanding and coping with cross-cultural adjustment stress. In R. M. Paige (Ed.), *Education for the intercultural experience.* Yarmouth, ME.: Intercultural Press.

CHAPTER 4

THE ABCs MODEL

A Foundation
for Culturally Responsive Teaching

Jane L. Neer and William J. Neer

INTRODUCTION

For several years, Ruggiano Schmidt's ABCs model of Cultural Understanding and Communication (Ruggiano Schmidt, 2001; Ruggiano Schmidt & Finkbeiner, 2006) has been incorporated into a required literacy course for preservice teachers working toward secondary certification in New York State. Students involved in this undertaking are usually in their third year of college and are preparing for a student-teaching internship during their fourth year. The ABCs model additionally is an integral part of a graduate-level course in a master's program designed for students who have completed a bachelor's degree in a content area but have had no undergraduate coursework in either foundations of education or pedagogy. The vast majority of these students have had limited access to diversity training or experiences or diversity education. The inclusion of the ABCs in both programs is designed to build an awareness of and appreciation for the wide spectrum of student diversity found in American schools and

Getting to Know Ourselves and Others Through the ABCs, pages 71–83
Copyright © 2015 by Information Age Publishing
All rights of reproduction in any form reserved.

in their families and communities. Such awareness lays the foundation for preservice teachers to consider and develop culturally responsive teaching strategies. In this chapter we will look at how the ABCs model is incorporated into the preservice teacher education core curriculum at a small Jesuit college in New York State. Discussion will include how students write an autobiography, biography, cross-cultural analysis, a cultural self-analysis of differences, and communication plans for connecting the home, school, and community for literacy learning (Ruggiano Schmidt, 2001; Ruggiano Schmidt & Finkbeiner, 2006).

Sociocultural Context and Setting

The ABC's of Cultural Understanding and Communication (Ruggiano Schmidt & Finkbeiner, 2006) is required as part of the undergraduate (and graduate) programs for preservice teachers who will be teaching at the secondary level, that is, grades 7 through 12. These preservice teaching students attend a small liberal arts college in New York State and must complete a course of study within a content area such as mathematics, history, English language arts, foreign languages, and any of the sciences that are taught in New York State public schools, including earth science, biology, chemistry, and physics. As part of their preparation, they must also successfully complete a series of courses in foundations of education and pedagogy. The pedagogical coursework includes studies in literacy, planning, classroom management, special education, and methods. Their course of study also requires two student-teaching internship assignments, which place these preservice teachers in two different public or private school environments. These assigned internships most often include one at the middle school level and the other at a high school. Additionally, such placements are mixed to introduce the preservice teacher to an urban, a suburban and/or a rural environment. Such preservice experiences hopefully will provide the student with various environments in which they may work with students from diverse backgrounds (NYSED.gov).

The Educational System

The educational system in the United States is controlled and managed by each individual state. In the case of New York State, students come from a wide spectrum of diversity, which includes many different and varying socioeconomic, cultural, ethnic, racial and religious, and multilingual backgrounds. Additionally, family structure varies from one household to the next with children being raised in wide-ranging circumstances. New York has many students who come from immigrant and/or refugee families, many of whom speak a language other than English in the home. Although the majority of families fit the traditional definition of parents and children, there is diversity in many family structures that may include or simply consist of grandparents, adult siblings, foster parents, adoptive parents, or diverse constructs in which adults are raising children. As we design programs for preservice teacher education and for professional development of those already in the field, we need to consider these points from *Learning to Be Literacy Teachers in Urban Schools: Stories of Growth and Change* (Lazar, 2004).

> [We] realize that teachers needed to do a better job of adjusting literacy instruction to match the needs of children in high-poverty communities, whose ways of using language and print do not always match school expectations. [We] also must realize that teachers need much more support to inquire about children's ways of using language and print, to teach in culturally congruent ways, and to identify and challenge the policies and practices interfering with literacy learning. (p. 29)

Therefore, the *ABC's of Cultural Understanding and Communication* (Ruggiano Schmidt & Finkbeiner, 2006) will help to meet this challenge by encouraging preservice teachers to appreciate and empower the wide diversity among students in their future classrooms.

Autobiography

The autobiography, as an essential portion of the ABCs, is a requirement nearly every student has not previously considered. This is the beginning of the process to help students fully grasp that attitudes often are socially constructed. By writing an autobiography, the student traces his or her personal "history relative to particular communities of people, exposing the critical experiences that have influenced who" (Lazar, 2004, p. 24) he or she is and how he or she perceives others. Each student needs to gain the awareness that a person's life experiences will influence how that person interacts with others and will influence the dynamics of such interaction. On occasion, a student may have attempted an autobiography, for instance, as a middle/high school assignment, but never at the depth required for the ABCs course project. In her ABCs model, Ruggiano Schmidt (2001) elaborates on this activity "The assignment is meant to be rigorous, but should not make one miserable or uncomfortable . . . [it is made] clear that life stories, with the greatest of detail, are the most helpful for cultural analysis assignments" (p. 428).

Students are to consider this as the beginning of their family history. They are to consider this as an integral and crucial start to understanding themselves and building an appreciation for their background. Students are asked to write a minimum of ten pages to produce an in-depth discussion of who they are and the influences and environments that have shaped them as a person. For confidentiality issues, no one but the student and the professor will ever see this document. Students are strongly encouraged to consider honors, triumphs, disasters, family, traditions, customs, languages, religion, political thought, personal relationships, and whatever else each student personally considers to be important factors in his or her development as a human being and as a preservice teacher. Students know that whatever they write about is completely confidential and that no one, except each one of them, will be aware of what is left out. What appears in the autobiography is totally left to the discretion of the individual author.

Amazing results have occurred over the span of years during which the ABCs project has been part of the required course of study in the education program. Profound examples appear every year. A few of these students have experienced serious and traumatic events in their lives yet are so open and willing to relate their situations in this confidential setting. For some, it seems to be a cathartic process. There are stories of tragedy, of sadness, divorce, death, loneliness, yet immeasurable strength, resilience, and optimism. For the professors involved in this study, it has been a thrilling experience to read such autobiographies and to see the students in light of such grace, optimism, and hope for their future as well as for their future students. An incredible discovery is that many of these individuals have made insightful statements about what they have learned from their own joys and successes as well as the pain and suffering in their lives. They see themselves transformed from these experiences with a new depth of understanding that may help them to be more empathetic of their future students. As these students analyze and write about their own personal past, they seem to develop a deeper understanding of and appreciation for the backgrounds of others. One such example was expressed by an ESL teacher:

> I have made it a priority to go out of my way to get to know my students and their families on a personal level and learn first hand about their cultures, experiences, fears, hopes and dreams...I [now] plan my instruction and selection of materials and literature so that it is relevant and meaningful to their lives. (Ruggiano Schmidt & Finkbeiner, 2006)

Additionally, there are many stories from those students who come from privilege, not necessarily the privilege of wealth, but the privilege of strong family relationships, of support, love, and encouragement. Such students confess to a broader appreciation for their parents and siblings and the effects their respective families have had in their lives.

Many of our students are white, from suburban middle-class homes, and have never been introduced to the world of diversity that they may encounter as teachers (Ruggiano Schmidt, 2001). Yet their appreciation of their families, their traditions, their ethnicities, cultures, and religions play such a central role in their lives. Many admit that the autobiography assignment is the first time they have taken the opportunity to examine the importance of their backgrounds. A common experience for many is that each sees for the first time how influential one's family heritage and personal background have been in one's development. What is crucial to this assignment is each student's realization of how one's family and background have played such an influential role in who one ultimately becomes as an adult—of how one may view his or her surroundings—and of how each individual sees his or her future students. It's an awakening of compassion, of understanding, of appreciation, or at the very least, a conscious discomfort about differences that might never have occurred if the student had not made such an in-depth study of one's self.

Concerning the writing of the autobiography, Lazar (2004) states,

> It is continually evolving, it is difficult and risky; it requires personal motivation fueled by a desire for social justice; and it is nurtured through external means (people, programs, settings). The significance of this last point is huge... teacher education and professional development hold so much promise for those who have not yet committed themselves to see teaching as an act of social justice. (p. 37)

It becomes an eye-opening experience that bursts upon one's conscious in ways that are difficult to explain or capture in words. Suddenly, each student has a whole new appreciation for who he or she is as well as an appreciation for one's varied background and family. It is at this point each begins to realize the importance of understanding others. It is at this point that most students begin to realize and to rationalize the importance of knowing their future students—of truly appreciating the culture, the background, and the lives of each of the children they will encounter in their classrooms.

Biography

Students involved in the ABCs project, after completing their autobiographies, begin a biography of another person who is culturally different along at least two of the following three dimensions: class, race, and language. The majority of students in this program are white, middle-class, and Christian. Often, subjects of the biographies are persons who trace their background to Asia, Latin America, or Africa. Sometimes two students within the same class interview each other, if such differences exist. The result of such pairing has often led to strong bonding experiences between the students.

Students will often find subjects of the biographies from coworkers, friends, friends of their parents or siblings, other students on campus, professors, and in some cases, family members. We have had a few especially enlightening examples from students who select an in-law with whom they previously had not had the opportunity to discuss such matters as cultural diversity, heritage, customs, and traditions that may be different from the student's nuclear family focus. This was due to geographical distance between these family members, such as an aunt or uncle who marries into a family but lives far away in another state. This most often results in a closeness and bonding with the in-law that was missing before the interview process. Through the process, a new level of respect for the other often is acknowledged in the students' reflections.

Biographies very often result in a bonding between the participants through a meal, possibly a religious ceremony or celebration, or some other event that the interviewer might have never otherwise experienced. Students have built closer relationships with these people, especially when the biography subject is a family member, childhood friend, coworker, or college acquaintance. During all the semesters of doing the ABCs, a negative situation has never been revealed as a result of this process. More often than not, a new friendship develops and, at the very least, a sincere appreciation for the other. Ruggiano Schmidt (2001) states: "Teachers, after writing their autobiographies, seem to gain the confidence needed to share portions of their own stories with interviewees. This stimulates the interviewees to share in kind" (p. 428).

Many interesting situations have evolved in the process of completing the biography. Once, a student who was challenged in locating an interviewee for the biography, decided to approach a homeless person. He offered the man lunch and a small remuneration if he would spend the afternoon at a popular fast food restaurant and relate his life's story. It was a one-time situation that did not create a lasting friendship; however, the student learned more from that experience than he might otherwise have gained from a casual discussion with someone else. By embracing the challenge to reach beyond his known experiences, he was able to relate to a decidedly different experience than those that he had encountered within the prior scope of his life experiences.

Although anonymity is crucial in the interview process as well as in writing the document as part of the project, students do share the basics of their subjects in a class seminar. The breadth and the depth of some of these biographies are astounding. There have been many emotional and touching situations during which the students gain so much awareness from the sheer scope of diversity that exists just in their class. They realize that the task before them, as future teachers, is one in which they will need the compassion, empathy, and understanding necessary to work collectively with students who will potentially represent every corner of the globe, as well as every philosophy of religion, government, and family structure. They will have students who represent many different languages, customs, holidays, family traditions, as well as traditional and nontraditional lifestyles. This realization is critical for preservice teachers before they are placed before future students. To teach fairly, equitably, and successfully, they will need to embrace diversity. The process of writing the biography also develops awareness among these preservice teachers of how best to relate to their future students' family members, to learn about their lives, and to develop the "cultural sensitivity necessary to analyze similarities and differences between life stories" (Ruggiano Schmidt & Finkbeiner, 2006, p. 5).

Cross-Cultural Analyses of Similarities and Differences

The next portion of the project for our students is to do an in-depth analysis of the similarities and differences between one's autobiography and the biography. To focus this analysis, each student prepares some type of graphic organizer that visually represents similarities and differences between the two. Students often create very interesting and visually appealing representations in some form of a graphic, but often a simple Venn diagram or inverted "T" organizer serves very nicely to organize each student's discoveries as he or she prepares the analysis. However, others have suggested that the Venn diagram only relates surface differences and similarities. It may prove more enlightening to use the "Venn Iceberg," in which the student will delve more deeply, below the surface, to discuss similarities and differences (Finkbeiner, 2009).

Following this activity, the students must compose a written analysis of the ABCs. It is at this point they are encouraged to use depth of thought and consideration not only to the product of the ABCs but, very importantly, to the process. In what ways did this project enlighten their thinking, lead to open discussion, and foster appreciation and respect for the diversity of others? Often, a great deal of self-analysis comes to the fore as each student realizes his or her own preconceived thoughts on diversity and the influence of one's personal background in creating mental constructs of what cultural differences exist and the impact of such differences on one's perceived views of others. It is at this point in the project when many of the students begin to understand and articulate the consequences of their involvement in the ABCs process. They begin to understand their own ideas on diversity and how some of these ideas have influenced their thinking and appreciation of others. Many express a deeper understanding of themselves and their own perceptions about others. Additionally, the students are encouraged to discuss in their analyses the problems they experienced with the project. Did they begin to acquire insights about others and develop a sense of their own ethnocentricity? (Ruggiano Schmidt & Finkbeiner, 2006). Many students have never discussed moments from their upbringing with anyone outside the family. Some students begin to understand how fortunate they have been with parents, siblings, friends, and significant others. Other students examine the conditions that may have led to uncomfortable, harmful, or hurtful events in their past. They have the opportunity, through the ABCs, to begin to understand their family's problems, whether such problems include divorce, substance abuse, physical or mental abuse, gender inequities, poverty, or any number of issues that may plague families. Although students do not always find solutions to these problems, they do report feelings of understanding and empathy for those they interviewed. Others begin to realize at this point that their backgrounds and upbringings have been with privilege, that is, strong family ties, economic security, and positive support and encouragement as they matured into young adults.

Another part of this analysis is the discussion of the biography and the process by which the student found and interviewed a subject. Results of the process often indicate an appreciation of their interviewees. Students often discuss the difficulties they encountered in broaching sensitive subjects that they may never have discussed with someone before. Frequently, students express their discomfort discussing topics such as race, gender, sexual orientation, or abuse. Sometimes they overcome their discomfort and simply enter the discussion. Other times the student is relieved to have the interviewee initiate such discussion, and yet others dare not approach certain topics but explain how this person has made them more sympathetic to the difficulties others may face in their lives. An important observation is that the vast majority of biography subjects are quite open and willing to discuss these issues, even when our students completing the ABCs tend toward reluctance in asking such personal questions. We often conclude this part of the ABCs with a full class discussion of the positives and negatives of the process, and not of the individuals involved.

Home-School-Communication Design

At this point, students begin relating and applying what they have gleaned from the process of the ABCs model into meaningful ideas, activities, and lesson plan concepts that are intended to encourage communication and understanding among the school, the home environment, and the community. Students work in cooperative small groups to design multiple ways in which they must accomplish the following objectives:

- Identify the varying cultural, ethnic, and social diversifying characteristics among the children assigned to their classroom.

- Develop methods, lessons, and creative activities that enable the teacher as well as the students to learn about one another and to build an appreciation and understanding of others.
- Cultivate ways in which the teacher may communicate and recognize the diversity that exists in the child's home, neighborhood, and community.
- Generate ideas for incorporating the child's caregivers into the school community and to participate in the educational process.
- Establish methods of communication with caregivers for children who speak a language other than English.
- Involve the community in the educational process by bringing community members into the classroom and creating situations in which the students experience the community firsthand.
- Involve other teachers within the school environment to participate in these activities promoting communication and understanding with the home and community.
- Develop an appreciation for and understanding of those cultural and ethnic differences that enrich the educational setting.

The collaborative effort implied by the home-school-communication design promotes a team approach to working with diversity in the classroom. Participants' inventiveness and creativity surface as they design activities and lessons that will incorporate diversity understanding among their students. At the same time, they are creating interactive possibilities for involving the home, the child's caregivers, and the community in the educational process. Common among these designs are simple ideas that reappear frequently in various ways, allowing teachers to close the gap among school, the home, and the community. The following list includes ideas that are culturally responsive:

- Have students create the "Where I'm From" poem, as designed by George Ella Lyon (2011).
- Create age-appropriate variations of the ABCs for students.
- Have students design acrostics, make illustrations, and/or create bulletin boards that showcase the ethnic and cultural diversity of the classroom.
- Plan lessons that involve parents or any significant other within the home.
- Plan lessons that may involve a neighbor or community member.
- Incorporate the first language of all students into learning experiences for all class members.

- Encourage and appreciate the diversity of customs and traditions by inviting parents into the classroom to share special ones that relate well to different holiday times and celebrations.
- Attend school events, including sports, plays, musicals, or other events, to connect with students while they participate in nonclassroom activities.
- Host events for families that bring them into the school environment.
- Meet with parents and caregivers at community places outside of school.
- Invite community members into the classroom.
- Make home visits when appropriate.
- Work with students in nonacademic venues.
- Provide parents or caregivers clear school goals and objectives.
- Encourage parents to call with questions, concerns, and suggestions.
- Create newsletters for parents and community members that contain information about school and classroom activities.
- Call home with positive compliments rather than just concerns.
- Offer invitations to parents to witness student performances in the classroom, school, or community setting.
- Engage students in community events.
- Involve students in community projects.

This list contains just some of the creative and clever ideas that preservice teachers attempt to provide in their home-school-communication designs. The important goal of the project is to stimulate the preservice teacher's mindset regarding how to connect with the great diversity of the homes and community that exists beyond the environment of the four walls of the classroom and school setting. It is only when teachers can fully understand their students, their backgrounds, and their needs, both academic and personal, that they can best begin to provide an educational environment that incorporates the best of both the school and the home. The critical importance of involving the home and the community into the educational setting cannot be overemphasized. This allows for the optimum in creating an educational system that is capable of providing what each individual child really needs for reaching his or her potential in the classroom.

Culturally Relevant Teaching

The discussion can now be focused on the importance of culturally relevant teaching within and beyond the American school system. It is imperative that educators realize the need for communication and understanding with and among their students and their students' homes and communities.

It is also important that the teacher helps to bring each student as well as his or her cultural background into the classroom and the school community, fostering an appreciation among all students and the individuals who are stakeholders in the school community. Without this emphasis, cultural differences among students and between students and teachers may create gaps of misunderstanding (Soto-Hinman & Hetzel, 2009). Teachers need to learn about the many cultural differences within a single class and spend time making sure students value their differences (Beers, 2003). Educational programs for preservice teachers and professional development workshops that incorporate the ABCs model promote these objectives.

A great deal of educational research currently deals with cultural literacy and culturally responsive teaching. This research supports the research that has already been done on the ABCs model, highlighting the importance of gaining a better understanding of the self in order to gain greater understanding of, and empathy for, the other. This was confirmed when we looked at the feedback of preservice teachers who participated in the ABCs model. They were given pre- and postpolarity polls that included ten statements that dealt with the students' understanding of and experiences with people from diverse backgrounds.

Additionally, some of these students volunteered for a one-on-one personal interview concerning the process. The qualitative data from these polls and interviews suggests strongly that many of these students, both undergraduate and graduate, expressed a sincere growth process in terms of gaining a greater awareness of and appreciation for other cultures. Many of the students confessed to having made prior judgments about certain communities based on stereotypical information that they had been exposed to during their formative years. A major conclusion drawn by many of the teacher candidates was that they felt that they had been sensitive to diverse populations, but that now upon examination, they felt that some of their assumptions about other cultures had been narrow and condescending and were based on preconceived notions or information that had no factual or personal basis. These students expressed that they were appreciative of the ABCs process and that they would be more careful about being culturally sensitive in the future. Many expressed that they felt better equipped to be culturally sensitive because of participation in the ABCs model. This cultural sensitivity was evident in most of the home-school-community project designs. Some students wrote (anonomously):

> The ABCs made me realize that reaching students who are of different cultural or ethnic backgrounds is easier once we get to know ourselves and our own literacy backgrounds.

> The ABCs assignment made me realize that to reach every student on every level we must be able to differentiate instruction accordingly.

It [the ABCs] helped me to understand the differences and yet similarities that many cultures have. It opened my eyes to the diversity within my neighborhood and my school and my friendships.

CONCLUSION

This is a first step in helping future educators build a mindset to enable them to become culturally responsive teachers. As Ruggiano Schmidt and Finkbeiner (2006) purport in their book *The ABC's of Cultural Understanding and Communication,* the process is "an important step toward effective communication that results in collaborative learning among diverse populations in our classrooms, school, community, nation, and world" (p. 14). Much of the qualitative data gathered from the reflections of these preservice teachers engaged in the ABCs process indicates that, for them, this has held true. The importance of bridging the space between home, school, and individual student's cultures leads to better student connectedness with the classroom and learning and also brings with it the climate of acceptance that sets the stage for individual students to meet with success within that school environment (Ruan & Gomez, 2011; Salamone, 2011). Research shows that when a student feels a part of the fabric of the community that he or she then can embrace the social and academic opportunities that exist in that community.

In many American schools, opportunities to learn are not equally offered to all when teachers are not culturally responsive (Lazar, 2011). To better balance the playing field, future educators must embrace and develop strategies and teaching models that will enhance students' experiences through culturally responsive teaching. Such practices are needed for today's youth to meet with success both as students and as lifelong learners who will engage and communicate effectively with others as part of a globally aware society. Using the ABCs model in teacher preparation programs lays the foundation for culturally relevant teaching.

REFERENCES

Beers, K. (2003). *When kids can't read, what teachers can do: A guide for teachers 6–12.* Portsmouth, NH: Heinemann

Finkbeiner, C. (2009) "Using human global positioning system" as a navigation tool to the hidden dimension of culture. In A. Feng, M. Byran, & M. Fleming (Eds.), *Becoming interculturally competent through education and training* (pp. 151–173). Bristol, UK: Multilingual Matters.

Lazar, A. (2004). *Learning to be literacy teachers in urban schools: Stories of growth and change.* Newark, DE: International Reading Association.

Lazar, A. (2011). Access to excellence: Serving today's students through culturally responsive literacy teaching. In P. Ruggiano Schmidt & A. M. Lazar (Eds.), *Practicing what we teach* (pp. 3–21). New York, NY: Teachers College Press.

Lyon, G. E. (2011). *Where I'm from.* Retrieved from http://www.georgeellalyon.com/where.html

Ruan, J. & Gomez, G. (2011). Becoming a teacher for all children: A teacher's story. In P. Ruggiano Schmidt & A. M. Lazar (Eds.), *Practicing what we teach* (pp. 250–262). New York, NY: Teachers College Press.

Salamone, K. (2011). From pasta to poets: Creating a classroom community through cultural sharing. In P. Ruggiano Schmidt & A. M. Lazar (Eds.), *Practicing what we teach* (pp. 110–120). New York, NY: Teachers College Press.

Ruggiano Schmidt, P. (2001). The power to empower. In P. Ruggiano Schmidt & P. B. Mosenthal (Eds.), *Reconceptualizing literacy in the new age of multiculturalism and pluralism.* Greenwich, CT: Information Age.

Ruggiano Schmidt, P., & Finkbeiner, C. (Eds.). (2006). *ABC's of cultural understandingand communication: National and international adaptations.* Greenwich, CT: Information Age.

Soto-Hinman, I., & Hetzel, J. (2009). *The literacy gaps: Bridge-building strategies for English language learners and standard English learners.* Thousand Oaks, CA: Corwin.

CHAPTER 5

PUTTING A FACE ON POWER AND INEQUALITY THROUGH THE ABCs PROJECT

Althier M. Lazar

INTRODUCTION

Much has been written about the ways the Ruggiano Schmidt's ABCs Model of Cultural Understanding and Communication enhances our ability to understand others and ourselves through the lens of culture (Ruggiano Schmidt & Finkbeiner, 2006). A significant part of culture is how we are privileged and subordinated across various cultural attributes such as race, class, gender, or language ability (Nieto, 1999). Equally important to literacy educators like myself is how we are privileged and subordinated in our access to the literacies and languages that are valued in school, as these abilities are also part of who we are culturally. The question I explore in this chapter is the usefulness of the ABCs project for helping teachers understand and respond to discoveries about power and inequality.

The ABCs project was used with teachers in a graduate literacy course that focused on relationships between race, class, culture language, literacy, and social inequality. I will look at how the experience of producing an autobiography, interviewing and writing about another person's life and

Getting to Know Ourselves and Others Through the ABCs, pages 85–99
Copyright © 2015 by Information Age Publishing

experiences, and comparing these documents, provided teachers with personalized evidence to reflect on issues of inequality, including those related to literacy and language. I will also examine the implications for using the ABCs project in teacher education programs.

Background

The ABCs project was conceived to help educators understand cultural differences so they may be better able to serve a growing population of culturally and linguistically diverse students. Through writing autobiographies, interviewing others and learning about their life stories, and conducting cross-cultural analyses, teachers throughout the United States and beyond have learned firsthand about the beliefs, values, and practices of those who are culturally different from themselves (Ruggiano Schmidt & Finkbeiner, 2006). Teachers' understanding of culture and appreciation of cultural diversity is a necessary foundation for culturally responsive teaching.

A complex construct, culture encompasses socially shared beliefs, values, and practices, which are all influenced by power relationships and are constantly changing (Gutierrez & Lee, 2009). Therefore, culture is more than socially agreed-upon ways of behaving, thinking, and valuing. It is also about power and the ways in which we are all privileged and subordinated across various domains such as race, class, gender, age, language ability, citizenship, religion, and sexuality (Nieto, 1999). Relative to the culturally marginalized students that occupy many classrooms today, teachers are privileged along lines of class and often race, and these privileges can translate to institutional advantages in access to education, housing, health care, and so on. Yet they may see their privileged positions as a consequence of their own merits and work habits, a trend that has been established among mainstream preservice teachers (Castro, 2010).

Research also finds that those who are raised in "mainstream" homes are socialized into literacy and language practices that match those valued in school (Heath, 1983; Purcell-Gates, 1995). Alternatively, those in communities outside of the mainstream may use language and print in ways that differ from school ways, but these ways are nonetheless purposeful and legitimate. Yet, because these ways of using language and print are different from those valued in school, teachers may view them from a deficit perspective.

The ABCs project has the potential to reveal how race, class, language ability, and other dimensions of culture can work to one's advantage or disadvantage. Comparing one's own life story with another's may expose the varied factors that subordinate children and their families and prevent their access to quality educational experiences and/or the literacy and language practices that are valued in school. In particular, I wondered whether the ABCs project could help teachers recognize "systems of failure embedded in institutional practices that disfavor and disenfranchise minority groups" (Castro, 2010, p. 207). Understanding these historical, political, and sociological factors that impact literacy may help teachers question deficit perspectives about culturally marginalized children and families. These discoveries may also help them see their own responsibility to change the status quo through teaching.

Method

Participants and Course

Set in an urban-based Jesuit university in the mid-Atlantic region, 48 teachers (28 in 2009; 20 in 2010) participated in the ABCs project as part a course that focused on issues of race, class, literacy, language, and social equity. Some 43 identified as white; 3 as African Americans, 1 as a Pakistani American, and 1 identified as Trinidadian. The majority of the participants were women ($n = 47$). About two thirds were certified teachers who had enrolled in a "fifth-year" master's degree program leading to reading specialist certification. The rest had taught for fewer than 10 years.

The course involved reading and responding to research on the following topics: the complexity of culture, issues related to social inequality, institutional racism, poverty, white privilege and racial identity, literacy as a culturally situated practice, language variation and identity, and culturally responsive instruction (see Appendix for a list of course reading assignments). Teachers wrote reflectively about these topics and shared their insights in small and whole group discussions.

At the beginning of the semester, teachers were asked to write an autobiography from the perspectives of the topics addressed in the course. The autobiographies were to include information about family, beliefs, values, traditions, racial/ethnic identity, and key life events that affected them either positively or negatively. One modification to the originally conceived ABCs project was that I asked teachers to reflect on their ways of being privileged or subordinated based on race, class, gender, or other kinds of affiliations. I also asked them to discuss their literacy and language practices while growing up and whether they believed they were either privileged or subordinated in their access to school-valued literacy and language practices.

At the midpoint of the semester, teachers interviewed a person they considered different from themselves based on at least two of the following attributes: race, class, religion, or native language. Teachers were invited to ask interviewees about key life events, similar to those addressed in their own autobiographies. They were also invited to address any of the topics related to culture, power, or privilege that they add addressed in their own autobiographies, based on their level of comfort in discussing these issues with interviewees. In other words, they were not *required* to delve into discussions of power or privilege with those they interviewed. In class, I modeled open-ended questions to prompt interviewees to provide details about their lives: "Please tell me more about your earliest memories;" "Please tell me about growing up in your town or village." Next, teachers were asked to produce a biography of their interviewee based on the information they gathered during the interview. Finally, teachers were asked to allow the interviewee to read this document and make any necessary corrections or revisions to enhance its accuracy.

For the cross-cultural analysis, I asked teachers to compare their autobiographies to the biographies and generate a list of similarities and differences between themselves and the person they interviewed. Following this, they were asked to comment on their personal discomfort or admiration with each cultural difference they found. They were not directed to write specifically at issues of power, privilege, or social inequality. Teachers later developed lesson plans based on their expanded understandings about culture through the project.

Following their participation in the course, I asked teachers to write about the significance of the ABCs project for developing their cultural awareness and for preparing them to serve students in culturally and linguistically nondominant communities. I focused my study on these statements as well as the cross-cultural analysis papers.

Data Analysis

Data analysis involved reading and coding the cross-cultural analysis papers and their statements about the significance of the ABCs project. I looked at both papers to see whether, and to what extent, teachers focused on (a) issues of power, privilege, and social equity and (b) their one's responsibility to address issues of social inequality through teaching. I categorized the ways that teachers discussed power and social equity, and these related to issues of race and class (or both), gender, literacy, and language. I read and coded the statements of significance to examine any language that specifically linked teachers' involvement in the ABCs project to their approaches to instruction. I formed assertions about the significance of the ABCs project based on the themes that surfaced across the papers and the relationship between the cross-cultural analysis papers and teachers' statements about the significance of the ABCs project.

Findings

The majority of teachers (83%) recognized power relationships in their cross-cultural analysis papers. Power differences related to race, class, gender, and language surfaced in teachers' descriptions, and those related to race and class were most prominent.

White Teachers: Race and Class

Most white and middle-class teachers acknowledged their own race and class privileges. They frequently indicated discomfort in learning about institutionalized racism that surfaced in the narratives of people of color. This was especially the case when interviewees reminded them of their white privilege, as with Leslie who interviewed an African American man named Leon with whom she worked:

> Despite having a great credit score, Leon was denied when he went to purchase his first car because of the color of his skin—I was uncomfortable talking to Leon about this topic, because it was another part of the conversation when I felt a disconnect between us. I know that I have never been discriminated against because of the color of my skin, and Leon made this known during the conversation. He wasn't blaming me, but it felt as if he showed a little anger towards the fact that I have so much going for me because I am white.

Among those who wrote about racial advantage/disadvantage, many focused on institutional racism in education and particularly the lack of cultural representation in the curriculum for people of color. Claire, for instance, interviewed an African American woman named Ellen, whose heritage was not well represented in the schools she attended:

> I experienced strong feelings of discomfort when I realized the difference between the amount of attention given to my culture in the media, school, etc. versus that given to Ellen's culture. I never really thought about the fact that most of the faces in my history books and on posters in my classrooms were white. I cannot imagine what it must feel like to grow up without feeling represented in one's own school. Ellen also mentioned that as a child, she grew up thinking that only white people and African American celebrities had expensive things. It was not until she went to college that she realized being African American did not automatically mean that someone was working class. These realizations were upsetting to me as I began to understand that many of the privileges I previously took for granted are connected to my race and culture.

It is important to review Claire's phrasing here: "as I began to understand that many of the privileges I previously took for granted are connected to my race and culture." This kind of language—"I am beginning to understand," "I am starting to learn"—was typical among the white teachers. It suggests that they had not realized these things before and therefore discovered the realities of race-based advantages/disadvantages through the ABCs project. What is noteworthy about this choice of wording is that the course began with an in-depth study of institutional racism, yet these teachers' statements suggested that they were first learning this concept through their interviews with people of color, which took place several weeks after the module on racism. This suggests that the ABCs project was instrumental in helping teachers understand systems of race-based advantage/disadvantage.

In some papers, reflecting on racial privilege led to an analysis of racism as a historical-structural problem in U.S. society. The life story of a Brazilian man, Jose, prompted Richard to reflect on this problem and his own culpability in it:

> I find myself a bit uncomfortable when I compare Jose's Brazilian society with my own. Here, people are more separate, segregated, and compartmentalized. There is a sense of unfinished business between the races, here. Race has always been a glaring issue in America and racial mixing has historically been regarded as undesirable, even taboo. And the way we have marginalized, persecuted or shunned people, on the basis of race, is disgraceful. I think we get a failing grade in this respect, compared with Jose's society. So, I feel a sense of guilt about, not just what my country has failed to do about racial equality, but for my white privilege. I did not have to struggle, as Jose has done since he has been here, simply because he was not a member of the "in-group."

As his comments show, Richard's critique of racial advantage in society led to acknowledging his own complicity in racism. Further, racial privilege was frequently conflated with class privilege, and teachers like Richard tended to link racial/ethnic subordination to reduced economic opportunities. Often these statements included teachers' recognition that they benefited from inherited wealth. Statements such as these following were common among these teachers:

> When Jose moved to the U.S., as an ethnic minority, he lost his privilege. It took years of hard work to lift himself further up the "ladder" in this country. In addition to earning my own income, I inherited the fruits of my father's labor. (Richard)

> Mufeng worked extremely hard to stay afloat in the educational realm in China where your success in school determines your success in life. I pretty much had the world at my fingertips when I graduated high school as I was assured that I could attend any university I wanted to attend in any geographic loca-

tion because my parents were willing and able to provide the monetary support needed to make this possible. The fact is that my socioeconomic status and even my race helped me to make it to where I am today. (Ashley)

Teachers of Color, Privilege, and Subordination

Three teachers of color interviewed people who had emigrated to the United States within the last 10 years. They described these interviewees as either "poor" or "working class" who were English learners as adults. These teachers commented on their own class and language privileges but connected culturally with their interviewees in the area of racial subjugation. After reflecting on the differences between herself a woman from Ethiopia (Obah), Shonyelle wrote the following:

I felt uncomfortable that both Obah and myself experienced overt racism, her in Africa and I in America. Racism is so prevalent in the world yet we often as a society try to pretend that we live in a raceless society. I think that it is important to see how race plays out all across the world not just in America. It is important for all students to learn about how race affects our society and begin to critically think about the many ways our society supports racism. Students need to learn that they can challenge racist thoughts and ideas but first they must understand racism so that it can be recognized because it is often masked.

One of the African American teachers, Derrick, interviewed his white friend, Edward. Derrick, who was raised in an upper-middle-class home, found that Edward maintained certain stereotypes about the poor and did not take into account the history of racial and class subjugation in this country. Like most of the other teachers, Derrick conflated race with poverty in his criticism of Edward's point of view:

I have discomfort with Edward's view overall of race and money. There was one statement he made in his interview that he stated that basically, if you go to a rich person's house for a charity, they would rarely give money. And, if you go to a poor person's house they would give money. This is indicative of his perceptions about the poor. He is of the belief that poor people are poor because they are not good with money. And, contrarily the rich are rich because they save and work hard for their money. This view fails to account for historical, institutional, and social reasons behind socio-economic stratification. I would imagine that this view translates into views on education and intelligence. There is usually a strong correlation between these views.

Note how Derrick critiques Edward for not considering the "historical, institutional, and social reasons behind socio-economic stratification." Just as Richard interpreted Jose's story through the lens of white privilege and structural racism, Derrick's understandings about social inequality were a filter through which he made sense of Edward's stereotypes about the poor. These quotes show how the ABCs project allowed teachers to put a "face" on their growing conceptual understandings about race and class.

Gender

Learning about gender subordination was disturbing for teachers who interviewed women from Ecuador, Malaysia, Ethiopia, and Pakistan, and how these women were expected to maintain subordinated roles in the United States. Most connected with these women's stories of subordination but concluded that their own opportunities growing up female in the United States had not been nearly as compromised as those they interviewed. For instance, Anne interviewed a young Ecuadorian woman named Tany, who was expected to maintain very traditional female roles:

> In Tany's culture, the role of women is clearly established. Women are expected to stay home to cook, clean, and do household chores while the boys are free to go out with friends and practice a lifestyle filled with more freedom and less restriction. I found it to be extremely unfair when Tany spoke of her brothers' ability to go out with friends and basically do whatever they wanted while Tany was expected to stay home and tend to household things. While I respect her acceptance of what she believes to be her family responsibility, I would be extremely distraught if I was treated so much differently due to the fact that I am a female. Upon graduation from high school, my brother was given permission from my parents to attend an unsupervised, co-ed trip to the Bahamas. I was informed that I would not be able to do the same, as "it is different for girls." While this is one of my only explicit memories of inequality by my parents regarding gender, it seems as though Tany has numerous examples and her experiences with inequality due to gender are much greater. In terms of domestic aspects, I have always done more around the house in the forms of cooking, cleaning, baking, etc., than my brother. However, I never felt enslaved or subordinated because of it, and was still allowed to go out with my friends basically as much as my brother was. For the most part, my siblings and I were given the same privileges and restrictions, regardless of our gender.

Anne's statement suggests that as she commented on Tany's domestic roles, she generated more examples of her own duties in the home. But while she provided specific instances where she was given less freedom to take a trip, and was expected to do more household tasks than her brother, she resisted the notion that these practices enslaved or subordinated her. For the most part, teachers did not reflect nearly as much about issues of gender inequality than they did on race or class inequality. Yet three of the teachers related the women they interviewed to the teenager named Hanh in Guofang Li's (2007) book *Culturally Contested Literacies*. A first-generation Vietnamese American, Hanh was highly restricted in her ability to leave her home after school and was expected to take on most of the domestic chores within the home as well as tutor her younger brother.

Literacy and Language Privileges

The ABCs project also helped teachers understand power differences in accessing the literacies and languages that are valued in school. One of the white teachers, Sarah, interviewed her friend Athena who affiliated as a first generation Greek American. Here, Sarah comments on her feelings of discomfort when she compared her own access to a variety of books to Athena's limited access to books:

> I feel discomfort that Athena had a limited exposure to books in her home as a child. There were no children's books, but she was sometimes read to from the Bible or her father's Greek books. I admire her parents for utilizing the resources that they had and still taught Athena about literacy. Her mother developed a picture dictionary from magazine pictures and Athena learned Greek through her father's books. I was privileged by growing up in a literacy-filled environment. I know that not everyone has the capabilities to provide multiple children's texts, but Athena's parents developed literacy in the home using the Bible and other available resources. I admire the importance of education in the home, being a conscious effort that influenced Athena in the early grades.

Although Sarah framed Athena's access to books as being more limited than her own, she also recognized the presence of literacy in Athena's home. This statement not only acknowledges privileges in the teacher's access to school-based literacies, it also suggests Sarah's acceptance of different kinds of literacy practices, a theme that was promoted in the graduate course.

Other cross-cultural analyses involved discussions about language. Julia interviewed a woman named Melanie, a Puerto Rican American whose father required her to speak only English in the home. Through reflecting on Melanie's story, Julia made discoveries about the dominance of English, her own privilege in not having to learn another language (and her own misgivings about this), and the relationship between language and cultural identity. These discoveries led her to embrace language difference in the classroom:

> I feel a sense of discomfort at the fact that Melanie's father denied her of the privilege to be bilingual and denied her an important part of her culture.

Growing up in the dominant culture, I never realized the importance of using a language other than English. "Everyone speaks English" was my mentality. Living abroad, I felt naïve and shameful not being able to speak a language other than English. I now know the importance languages are to a person's self-concept and the value it has in general. As a future educator, I will value every language that my student brings into the classroom. It is my job to teach students from non-dominant cultures that their language is valued, not silenced, and to change the curriculum so that they can see themselves and their language within their learning.

Collectively, these teachers' statements reveal the ways the ABCs project helped them recognize power, privilege, and inequality in areas of race, class, gender, literacy and language ability. Next, I will discuss how recognizing the element of power in culture shaped their instructional plans and perceptions of themselves as teachers.

Impact of the ABCs Project: Deeping Relationships— Transforming Practice

About two thirds of the teachers (32/48) who participated in the ABCs project discussed how it motivated them to change their instructional approaches. For instance, when Jennifer interviewed an African American woman named Kiaya, she realized how privileged she was to have been in a school that honored her own cultural heritage. This prompted her to ensure that her students' culture was reflected in her curriculum and instruction:

My teachers, even though I did not realize it at the time, were always doing language arts lessons with materials based on my culture. They did science and history lessons that were rooted in stories and achievements of people of my culture. My schools were warm and welcoming and safe. The teachers wanted us to succeed. I do not see this as being the case with Kiaya. This made me extremely uncomfortable, to think that I am entering a profession which includes teachers like this. It makes me that much more determined to make sure my students never experience what Kiaya did in school, and that it does not take my students until graduate school to be proud of their accomplishments, to believe in themselves, and to see the purpose of what they are learning.

Translating understandings about privilege to their own responsibility to construct a more inclusive curriculum was a theme that surfaced in many of the papers, as indicated by these teachers' comments:

Prior to taking this course I had not thought about all of the unearned privileges that I am able to use simply because of the color of my skin. I naively believed that I did not play a part in racism. I think my level of discomfort in hearing about Ellen's life is beneficial to me because it allows me to understand and recognize the injustices that still exist. Creating multicultural lessons has given me an opportunity to think about ways that I can start to dismantle social injustices by empowering students within my own classroom as a teacher. (Claire)

Hearing Adam talk about his shame, hurt, and discomfort during school culture projects really pushed me to think about how to modify instruction and include students like Adam in the curriculum. (Cynthia)

Other teachers translated their understandings about racial privilege to the realization that they need to confront color blindness in the classroom. Michele discussed how the various perspectives introduced in the course helped her to better understand Jovan, the African American man she interviewed, and how her understandings of white privilege means that she can no longer deny the significance of race in the classroom:

I feel a sense of discomfort and almost shock that I have lived most of my life unaware of race and culture, specifically in terms of society defining privilege and disadvantage based on race. Through the different aspects of this class I have learned to identify and recognize in my life the many privileges that I have because of being white. I feel guilty knowing that Jovan from a young age has identified not only being an African American male, but has learned to deal with and accept what he calls "living in a white world." From this standpoint, I see the importance as an educator to not be "color blind" but instead acknowledge the different cultures within my classroom and provide opportunities for all students to see themselves expressed in the curriculum to draw on their knowledge and skills they bring with them in order for them to experience success.

For Leslie, reflecting on the power differences between her and Leon was pivotal in helping her recognize the importance of getting to know her students:

Interviewing Leon was an enlightening experience for me. I am now able to think critically and analyze the many different experiences in my lifetime where I have been privileged due to the color of my skin, subordinated due to my womanhood, and granted opportunities because of my hard work and determination. It has also given me a better understanding of the African American heritage as well as the struggles that are faced by African Americans on a daily basis. I never sat down to talk to someone of a different race and culture about such deep personal experiences. Although Leon and I were very close before this interview, I feel that we have established a new level of trust and understanding in our relationship. As a teacher, this just makes me realize how important it is to get to know and understand your students.

A few teachers, like Rachel, decided that it is not enough to infuse culture into the classroom. What they really needed to do was help their students understand cultural differences in terms of privilege and to help them question the status quo:

> As an educator I need to demonstrate how children can critically question ideas of difference and acceptance and find ways to integrate in my teaching the knowledge that each individual has been privileged in different ways. It is important for children to feel a sense of self worth in their life and their community.

Similarly, Michele attributed her involvement with the ABCs project to her emerging identity as a social activist:

> The ABCs project helped me understand the need for social action/reformation in the classroom by thinking about ways in which Jovan was impacted by racism in society and school. It also allowed me to acknowledge the role I played in perpetuating racism—creating a need to stop it and change it in society through classroom instruction (the most powerful means I will have available for social action in the future).

These findings reveal the impact of the ABCs model for influencing teachers' plans to construct a more culturally inclusive curriculum, make issues of race/ethnicity explicit, improve relationships with students, and to help students become more critically conscious. Next, I will discuss these findings and why they matter in helping us evolve as educators for social equity.

Implications

This study revealed the potential of the ABCs model to help teachers understand how certain cultural attributes work to either privilege or disenfranchise people. It also showed that acknowledging power differences prompted teachers to think about how they might create more culturally responsive classrooms. In some cases, I provided evidence that the project influenced teachers to identify as activists.

This study suggests that the ABCs model can help to broaden educators' understandings of culture to include power relationships. This is an important point given that most schools often frame culture superficially, focusing on the foods or holidays of particular ethnic groups. In this kind of "heroes and holidays" approach, culture is conflated with ethnicity (Cinco De Mayo Day) or race (Black History Month). These kinds of "Culture Days" rarely address the more complicated dimensions of culture that reveal power differences between people. Unless educators expand their definitions of culture, we will continue to see these kinds of superficial celebrations in schools. Understanding the significance of power within culture can help educators shift the school climate as one that helps students understand themselves and others, and one that addresses social equities in school and beyond.

This study also affirms that teachers' understandings about the role of power in culture were enhanced through course readings and discussions, but reinforced and made concrete through the ABCs project. This suggests that the ABCs model needs to be completed in the context of thoughtful studies of issues such as race, class, gender, language, literacy, and social equity. Applying these lenses to the ABCs project will help teachers go beyond superficial observances of culture.

While the ABCs model can increase cultural awareness, interviewing one person provides limited exposure to diversity; it does not reveal the full range of diversity that is reflected in society. To deepen teachers' understandings of culture and cross-cultural differences, it is possible to extend the project by reading and comparing the cultural comparison papers. As an extra assignment, I invited teachers in the 2010 course to do a meta-analysis of the cross-cultural comparison papers in class, a project I call ABCs-Meta. After they had completed the ABCs project, I asked teachers to read the cross-cultural analysis papers of each person in their group and discuss the typical and atypical themes that were addressed in these papers. Teachers then were asked to write about their discoveries discuss them with their peers. Preliminary analysis of these papers suggests that sharing and writing about the cross-cultural analysis papers expanded teachers' awareness of culture.

Finally, many teachers who included an analysis of power in their descriptions of cultural difference tended to establish very specific goals for transforming their own teaching practices. Only a few teachers, however, discussed their responsibility to teach students to question and change the status quo in their cross-cultural analysis papers. It is possible that additional study of critical pedagogy (Freire, 1985; Lankshear & McLaren, 1993) and critical literacy (McDaniel, 2006) would help ABCs participants see their responsibility to enhance students' critical consciousness. These pedagogies address the significance of joining with students to interrogate power relationships in society and take an active role in confronting social inequalities. Critical literacy looks specifically at the need to scrutinize texts from a variety of perspectives: an author's purpose and political stance, what the author chose to include or exclude in the text, power relationships of story characters, and instances of social dominance and oppression (McDaniel, 2006). This is an important area of teacher development if we want students to be politically active citizens. According to Ladson-Billings (1995), developing students' critical consciousness is a major component of culturally relevant teaching:

Beyond those individual characteristics of individual achievement and cultural competence, students must develop a broader sociopolitical consciousness that allows them to critique the cultural norms, values, mores, and institutions that produce and maintain social inequities. If school is about preparing students for active citizenship, what better citizenship tool than the ability to critically analyze the society? (p. 162)

Studying critical pedagogy/literacy would help teachers translate the social inequalities they discover through the ABCs model to instructional practices that help develop students' critical consciousness. This is where we need to be going as educators if we are to truly empower students.

CONCLUSION

Culture is complex and shaped by power. Findings from this study show that the ABCs model helped to make the cultural attributes of privilege, subordination, and social equity real for most of the teachers in the course. After identifying elements of privilege and subordination in their own and others' life stories, many teachers were able to generate statements about their discomfort with the social inequalities that surfaced in these papers. Many acknowledged their own responsibility to challenge the social inequalities they discovered, especially inequalities in education, through teaching. Although much of the research to date has focused on the role of the ABCs project to challenge stereotypes and enhance cultural awareness, this study reveals another significant project outcome—to help us understand cultural differences from the perspective of power. This is a necessary foundation for creating socially conscious teachers and students.

APPENDIX

Course Reading Assignments

Compton-Lilly, C. (2007). *Re-reading families: The literate lives of urban children.* New York, NY: Teachers College Press.

Delpit. D. (2002). *The skin that we speak: Thoughts on language and culture in the classroom.* New York, NY: New Press.

Gonzalez, N. E., Moll, L., & Amanti, C. (Eds). (2005). *Funds of knowledge: Theorizing Practices in Households and Classrooms* (selected chapters).

Lazar, A. (2004). *Learning to be literacy teachers in urban schools: Stories of growth and change.* Newark, DE: International Reading Association.

Additional Articles and Chapters

Heath, S. B. (1983). *Ways with words: Language, life, and work in communities and class-rooms.* New York, NY: Cambridge University Press.

McDaniel, C. (2006). *Critical literacy: A way of thinking, a way of life.* New York, NY: Peter Lang.

Nieto, S. (1999). *The light in their eyes: Creating multicultural communities.* New York: Teacher's College Press.

REFERENCES

Castro, A. J. (2010). Themes in the research on preservice teachers' views of cultural diversity: Implications for researching millennial preservice teachers. *Educational Researcher, 39*(3), 198–210.

Freire, P. (1985). *The politics of education: Culture, power, and liberation.* South Hadley, MA: Bergin & Garvey.

Gutierrez, K., & Lee, C. D. (2009). *Robust informal learning environments for youth from nondominant groups: Implications for literacy learning in formal schooling.* In L. Morrow, R. Rueda, & D. Lapp (Eds.), *Handbook of research on literacy and diversity* (pp. 216–232). New York, NY: Guilford.

Heath, S. B. (1983). *Ways with words: Language, life, and work in communities and class-rooms.* New York, NY: Cambridge University Press.

Ladson-Billings, G. (1995). But that's just good teaching! The case for culturally relevant pedagogy. *Theory Into Practice, 34,* 159–165.

Lankshear, C., & McLaren, P. (1993). *Critical literacy: Politics, praxis and the postmodern.* Albany: State University of New York Press.

Li, G. (2008). *Culturally contested literacies: America's "rainbow underclass" and urban schools.* New York, NY: Routledge.

McDaniel, C. A. (2006). *Critical literacy: A way of thinking, a way of life.* New York, NY: Peter Lang.

Nieto, S. (1999). *The light in their eyes: Creating multicultural learning communities.* New York: Teachers College Press.

Purcell-Gates, V. (1995). *Other people's words: The cycle of low literacy.* Cambridge, MA: Harvard University Press.

Ruggiano Schmidt, P., & Finkbeiner, C. (Eds.). (2006). *The ABC's of cultural understanding and communication: National and international adaptations.* Greenwich, CT: Information Age.

CHAPTER 6

OTHERIZATION AND NONOTHERIZATION STRATEGIES IN THE ABCs MODEL

Josep M. Cots

INTRODUCTION

The focus of this chapter is on Step C of the ABCs method proposed by Ruggiano Schmidt and Finkbeiner (2006); that is, on the stage in which students are asked to reflect upon the differences they have found between themselves and their partners. The aim of the study is to explore the discursive activity of a woman describing another woman by approaching it as a process of "otherization" (Holliday, Hyde, & Kullman, 2004), which I interpret as a discursive activity of presenting somebody as culturally different. After introducing the notion of "otherization strategy" and the particular academic context in which the ABCs was implemented, I will analyze the discourses constructed by three adult female participants in their attempt to represent another woman from a different cultural origin. More specifically, the analysis will focus on the students' adoption of particular discourse strategies through which they construct their interlocutor as somebody "different."

Getting to Know Ourselves and Others Through the ABCs, pages 101–115
Copyright © 2015 by Information Age Publishing
101

Two different analytical frameworks will be introduced and exemplified: factors affecting intercultural communication (Scollon & Scollon, 1995) and politeness theory (Brown & Levinson, 1987). The analysis of the data will show, in the first place, what aspects of the other person's culture are brought to the fore by the ABCs students and, secondly, their efforts to display face-saving strategies to attenuate the process of otherization intrinsic to the activity.

Otherization Strategies and the C Stage of the ABCs

The concept of "otherization" has been used by Holliday et al. (2004, p. 3) to refer to the process of "imagining someone as alien and different to 'us' in such a 'way' that 'they' are excluded from 'our' 'normal,' 'superior' and 'civilized' group." The series of oppositions that form part of the process of otherization, such as "us vs. them," "normal vs. strange," "superior vs. inferior," "civilised vs. uncivilised," is very much connected with an essentialist view of culture, according to which a culture is a physical entity with geographical boundaries; it has a country and a language (although it may form part of larger religious or ethnic cultures and include subcultures); people in one culture are essentially different from people in another culture; people's behavior is fairly homogeneous within a culture; and a culture can be summarized into a series characteristics or stereotypes. In front of this view of culture, there is a nonessentialist view of culture whose definition includes the following elements: it is a social force that is not always relevant in the everyday life of an individual; it has to do with sets of values and perspectives as much as with a language; it is not a stable entity but changeable; people can belong to different cultures, and their behavior is not always consistent with one culture; and the complexity and variability of a culture make it impossible to reduce it to a series of defining traits or stereotypes.

The ABCs, as it was implemented by the instructor, could sometimes be seen as a learning activity that forced the students to engage in a process of otherization from the very beginning, since the instruction that was given to them in the assignment presupposed the notion of "different cultural background" in asking them to "select and interview a previously unacquainted person from a different cultural background." This same presupposition is made by Ruggiano Schmidt and Finkbeiner (2006, p. 4) when they describe the B (biography) stage as involving "several in-depth, audiotaped, unstructured or semi-structured interviews . . . of a person who is culturally different." In both cases, the assumption is made that the students will easily be able to define culture and identify someone who does not belong to their cultural group. The "risk" for the ABCs project to become an act of otherization by the students is increased in the third stage when students are asked to reflect upon visible and invisible differences and similarities between themselves and their interviewee.

I agree with Duszak (2002, p. 2) when she talks about the "impossibility of non-othering," since categorization is an intrinsic aspect of human nature in its attempts to organize experience. However, the author also claims that "social identities tend to be indeterminate, situational rather than permanent, dynamic and interactively constructed." This point of view is shared by Piller (2007) for whom culture should not be seen *a priori* as a variable in explaining social interaction, and what is sometimes considered as cultural misunderstanding is not the result of a different worldview but rather of linguistic misunderstanding and a relationship of inequality and injustice.

ANALYTICAL PERSPECTIVES ON OTHERIZATION AND NONOTHERIZATION DISCOURSE STRATEGIES

This section presents the two analytical perspectives with which I have approached the texts produced by the students during the C stage of the ABCs. I look at the data as the result of the individual's choice of particular discourse strategies with the aim of reaching a balance between what they may interpret as a demand for constructing what is in part an otherizing text and their efforts to nonotherize their interlocutor. Following Cots (2005), discourse strategies are defined as linguistic moves that competent language users make, from several possible choices, in order to achieve their aim in what they consider to be the most efficient, effective, and appropriate way. These choices involve aspects related to content and form, and they are constrained, among other factors, by the need to preserve the addressor's face as well as that of the addressee or a third person involved in the communicative event.

The first analytical framework adopted for the analysis of the data focuses on the otherization strategies displayed by the ABCs student which are based on content and, more specifically, on the particular attributes of the individual described associated with their social life. This framework is based on Scollon and Scollon's (1995, p. 127ff) proposal involving four major factors in intercultural communication:

- Ideology: including beliefs, values and religion (history and worldview)
- Social organization: including kinship, the concept of self, in-group vs. out-group relations, and definition of social structure
- Forms of discourse: functions of language and resources for nonverbal communication.

- Socialization (or culture learning): education vs. enculturation, primary vs. secondary socialization, theories of the person and of learning.

The second analytical framework is based on Brown and Levinson's (1987) study on universals in politeness, and it centers on a series of nonotherization strategies through which the ABCs student makes use of face-saving strategies in order to protect the face of the person they are describing, thereby presenting themselves not only as considerate of the other but also as culturally respectful. In this case, I approach the discursive act of "describing difference" as a face-threatening act, which requires the addressor to activate a series of strategies to protect the negative and the positive face of the other person. Brown and Levinson define face as "the public self-image that every member wants to claim for himself" (p. 61). The authors also suggest that face consists of two related aspects: negative face, which they define as "the want of 'every competent adult member' that his actions be unimpeded by others," and positive face, which refers to "the want of every member that his wants be desirable to at least some others" (p. 62).

In the rest of this chapter, I will first provide some contextual information about the academic context in which the ABCs methodology was implemented and from which the data analyzed were obtained. This section will be followed by the analysis of the data, through which I will attempt to answer the following questions: What aspects of culture do the students resort to in order to construct their discourses of otherization? What face-saving strategies are employed by the students in order to downplay their discourse of otherization implicitly required by the task? In trying to answer these questions, my aim is to explore the applicability of two theoretically based analytical frameworks for the analysis of discursive productions derived from the application of the ABCs method. These frameworks can be used both by researchers interested in intercultural communication and by ABC practitioners (including teachers and students) to reflect on interculturality as a process of discourse construction, in which individuals make use of specific discursive strategies to accomplish their goals.

Context of Data Collection

The data that I will analyze in this chapter were part of the coursework required in a course module entitled Intercultural Communication, which I taught in the academic year 2009–2010. This module forms part of an MA program in Applied Languages at the University of Lleida (Catalonia, Spain), and it basically aims at making students aware of the relevance of the intercultural communication component in the learning of a second/

foreign language and the need to reflect upon the most appropriate cultural aspects and teaching resources. The syllabus for the module is divided into two parts, intercultural discourse and teaching language and culture, and it is during the development of the first part that students became familiar with the ABCs method, as they were asked to apply it to carry out the first of two projects for the module. The project was carried out by the students over a period of 9 weeks, and it was divided into three stages of 3 weeks each, which correspond to the three stages of the ABCs method: autobiography, biography, and contrast. For the autobiography stage, students were asked to "write an autobiography intended to be read by someone from another culture" in a minimum of 1,500 and a maximum of 2,000 words. The text should include key life events related to topics like childhood, education, family, religious tradition, recreation, and such. In the biography stage, the students were instructed to select and interview (between two and three times) a previously unacquainted individual from a different cultural background in order to discover his/her cultural background and write his/her biography in an essay of the same length as their autobiography and, if possible, using the same topics. The third stage, contrastive analysis and intercultural awareness, included three tasks: (a) identify similarities and differences between themselves and their respective interviewee; (b) analyze, in between 1,200 and 1,500 words, the differences by responding to the questions "Why am I feeling uncomfortable about this difference?" and "Why do I admire this difference?"; and (c) suggest a minimum of five "culturally responsive ideas" that they thought they could implement in their present or future professional task.

In this study I focus on the productions for the second activity of the third stage of the ABCs of three students who were enrolled in the MA module Intercultural Communication. The specific instruction they were given was as follows:

> Analyze the differences between yourself and your partner. Here the student explains how he or she feels about those differences, i.e., "Why am I feeling uncomfortable about this difference?" and "Why do I admire this difference?" (min. 1,200—max. 1,500 words).

Previous to this, the students had tried to identify similarities and differences between themselves and their partner and classify them into whether they were visible or invisible. They did this following Weaver's (1993) metaphor of culture as an iceberg, in which only one seventh of the whole is visible. The three students selected had been born in Spain and had spent most of their lives in this country, with the exception of one of them, who had worked as a teacher of Spanish in Thailand. Two of them were in their 30s and one was in her 50s. Each of them chose a female partner in order to carry out their ABCs assignment. These three women were from Morocco, Ecuador, and Nigeria and had lived in Spain for a few years when the interviews took place.

Findings

For the analysis of otherization strategies in the textual productions of the students, I use Scollon and Scollon's (1995) four major factors having an impact on intercultural communication: ideology, social organization, forms of discourse, and socialization. Table 6.1 is a schematic summary of what each of the three students mentioned in their attempt to present their partner as different from themselves.

TABLE 6.1 Summary of Students' Descriptions of Partners

Factors	Moroccan interviewee	Ecuadorian interviewee	Nigerian interviewee
Ideology	• Comes from a country occupied by another country. • Educated in the Muslim religion and continues to practice.	• Comes from a high-power distance culture.	• Religion is key aspect of her life. • Does not like sports nor pets; she watches church programs on TV.
Socialization	• Has lived in four different countries: Sahara, Mauritania, Algeria,and Spain. • Has been educated by the family of an aunt. • Has had a brief and fragmented schooling because she has spent part of her life in the desert.	• Has been separated from her family for a long time, raised by her grandmother, and with little contact with her mother, who was living in another country. • "Has got more intercultural competence than me." In Spain she has become acquainted with a different culture and language (Catalan) and she has adapted quite well.	• Went to school away from home, in the city; many pupils in the classroom; physical punishment. • Migrated to Spain illegally in a boat. • She depends economically on her husband. • Distant and strict relationship with her mother. • Childhood holidays spent in the house of a relative.

(continued)

TABLE 6.1 Summary of Students' Descriptions of Partners (cont.)

Factors	Moroccan interviewee	Ecuadorian interviewee	Nigerian interviewee
Social organization	• At 37, she already feels quite old. • Believes that it is important to acknowledge the prominent position of the man of the house (e.g., with guests, he serves tea and leads the conversation). • Housework and taking care of an ill sister make sense as a contribution to the welfare of the family. • Polygamous father.	• The "family" includes cousins, aunts and uncles, grandparents as well other more distant relatives. • Age is associated with authority and respect.	• Two Christian names: one in English and another one in her native language. • Adopts her husband's surname. • Comes from large family (10 brothers and sisters). • As a child, her family shared a large house with other families. • Polygamous grandparents. • Her family would not allow her to marry someone from a different country but accepts marriage between different tribes. • She feels she belongs to the husband's family.
Forms of discourse	• Not mentioned in report	• In her culture, one needs to behave respectfully, sympathetically, and appropriately at all times. • Importance of avoiding interpersonal conflict. • Projects a kind personality when speaking. She speaks without rushing; "I speak very fast, going quickly from one thought to another."	• Not mentioned in report

In Table 6.1 we can see how the students' comments on their partner are distributed among the four factors. From the point of view of the "ideology" factor, religion and the sociopolitical situation of the country of origin are mentioned by two of the students. Within the "socialization" factor, we find that the three students comment on their partners' migratory experience and on their family upbringing, which in the three cases is characterized by their separation from their parents; two students refer to the secondary socialization of their partners by commenting on the length and methods of schooling. In connection with the "social organization" factor, the three students consider worth mentioning issues related to family structure and responsibilities; here we include topics such as the definition of family (nuclear vs. extended), the roles of men and women, and polygamy. Finally, we can observe that only one of the students makes reference to the "forms of discourse" factor to comment on the interactional style of her partner.

By approaching the students' productions in this way, we can begin to have an idea of the relevance that each factor has in the students' construction of a discourse of otherization. In this way, we can learn not only about the specific topics that are mentioned within each of the four factors but also the frequency with which each topic appears in the discourse. Thus, with the three students selected for this study, Table 6.2 shows the results. The numbers in parentheses refer to the number of students that made a reference to the topic. This can give us an idea of the predominance of a specific topic across the students. By looking at the number of topics and the students that refer to them, we can attempt to measure in quantitative terms the relevance of each of the four types. Thus, we can see that socialization and organization are the factors on which the students tend to focus.

Findings: Nonotherization Strategies

As I have mentioned above, I consider otherization as a potential face-threatening act both for the ABCs students and for the individuals with

TABLE 6.2   Factors and Frequencies of Partner Descriptions

Factor	Topic
Ideology	Religion (2), sociopolitical situation of country of origin (2)
Socialization	Life mobility: migration (3), primary socialization: mother (3), secondary socialization: length/type of schooling (2)
Social organization	Definition of family: nuclear vs. extended (3), family responsibilities: spouse, elderly, spouse's family, etc. (3)
Form of discourse	Social behavior (1), discourse style (1)

whom they are comparing themselves. Following Brown and Levinson (1987), a face-threatening act can be classified into two main types depending on whether it threatens the negative or positive face of addressor, addressee, or, as is the case in this study, a third person. In order to avoid the potential threat, the speaker/writer needs to undertake some redressive action, which takes the form of negative or positive politeness, depending on whether it is aimed at compensating for a negative or a positive face-threatening act:

- Negative politeness: the efforts made by the students to save or protect their partners' face want for freedom of action.
- Positive politeness: the efforts made by the students to save or protect their partners' face want for their actions to be approved, and save or protect their own face want for their actions (in our case, the analysis that they are making of their partner) to be approved and be seen as respectful with the other and as contributing to social harmony.

Negative Politeness

Within negative politeness, we include those utterances through which the ABCs students project the idea that they respect their partners' lifestyle and they do not want to impose their views or suggest that they are better than their partners. Among the different strategies proposed by Brown and Levinson (1987) for negative politeness, I have found examples of hedging and of admitting the potential impingement on their partner's negative face.

A hedge can be defined as a particle, word, or expression that qualifies the immediate contextual reference of an utterance and, at the same time, contributes to establishing interpersonal relationships of affinity or solidarity by diminishing the assertive force of the utterance of which it forms part (Kreutz & Harres, 1997). For Brown and Levinson (1987, p. 145), the main function of hedging is that of diminishing the "potential threats to cooperative interaction" that appear in the course of ordinary communication.

A great deal of hedging appears in the student productions for Step C of the ABCs when they attempt to respond to the question "Why am I feeling uncomfortable about this difference?" The choice of the expression "feeling uncomfortable" (instead of, for instance, a more face-threatening verb like "dislike") for the question is a very good example of the kind of hedging that is used by the students to refer to aspects of their partner's biography. In extract 1, the student employs the adjectival expression "somewhat shocking" (*algo chocante*) to refer to the cultural traits of wearing a wig or braids associated with women in Nigerian society:

(1) I find it somewhat shocking, because for me comfort and simplicity in external appearance are more important than what others think.

(Spanish original) *Me resulta algo chocante, pues para mí es más importante la comodidad y la sencillez, en el aspecto exterior, más que lo que piensen los demás.*

Later on, the same student comments on another aspect of Nigerian women's dressing style. In this case, the comment is related with the fact of wearing shoes of a smaller size than the one they actually need, so that their feet look smaller. In extract 2, we can see how the student resorts to presenting this fact as "inconsistent" with her principle of comfort in dressing:

(2) Something similar happens with the shoes; I think that in order to hide their very large feet they often use a smaller size than they need, which to me is an inconsistency since it must be very uncomfortable.

(Spanish original) *Algo parecido sucede con los zapatos; creo que para disimular que tienen los pies muy grandes suelen usar un número menos del que necesitarían, lo cual para mi es una incongruencia puesto que debe ser muy incómodo.*

In the next extract, (3), another student refers to the polygamist structure of her partner's family and avoids expressing a direct disagreement or rejection by saying that it is an aspect of family life in front of which it is most difficult not to take a stance and that, for her, monogamy is a basic social norm:

(3) The aspect of Fatima's family life that is more difficult not to judge is her father's polygamy.... For me, monogamy is a basic norm for my relationships and those of the people around me.

(Catalan original) *L'aspecte de la vida familiar de la Fatima que resulta més difícil de no jutjar és la poligàmia del pare de la Nina. . . . Per a mi, la monogàmia és una norma bàsica per a les meves relacions i les de les persones que m'envolten.*

One last example of hedging appears in extract 4, which follows a student's comment on the subservient role of women in Moroccan society in relation to men. The situations used by the student to prove her point are the following: the husband serves tea and leads the conversation; when having a guest, the wife stays in another room in order to leave all the protagonism to the husband; the wife must give up whatever she is doing to take care of her husband when he is ill. After these examples, instead of passing a clear judgment of disapproval of the situation, the student makes the following comment:

(4) In my opinion there is a certain imbalance between the sexes that would be hard for me to accept in my house.

(Catalan original) *Per a mi hi ha certs desequilibris entre sexes que em costarien de viure a casa.*

We can see here how hedging is realized by means of the noun "imbalance" and the subjectivization of the judgment restricting it to herself—"for me."

The second strategy for saving the negative face of the addressee or of a third person is defined by Brown and Levinson (1987) as "admit the impingement." The authors consider the action by S (speaker) of indicating that he or she is aware of H's (hearer) negative face not wanting to be impinged on as a strategy for saving H's negative face. According to the authors, there are two ways of implementing this strategy: apologize and manifest explicitly S's wish not to impose their point of view on H. In the data analyzed in this chapter, all of the examples that have been found belong to the second case, and this is probably because we are dealing with a situation in which the addressee of the student's text (the university instructor who will read the analysis) is not the person whose negative face may feel attacked by the student's words.

Extract 5 is an example in which a student, after pointing out certain characteristics of the external appearance of her partner, explicitly appeals to the right of an individual to freely decide on her physical appearance:

(5) I do not admire nor feel uncomfortable about the differences in the physical appearance of my interlocutor, since I understand that we are all free to choose the image we want to show the world.

(Spanish original) *Ni admiro ni me siento incómoda ante las diferencias de aspecto de mi interlocutora, puesto que entiendo que todos somos libres para elegir la imagen que queremos mostrar al mundo.*

In Extract 6 the student acknowledges that in expressing her disapproval of the practice of migrating illegally and leaving one's children with a relative, she is also aware of the fact that sometimes people are forced by the circumstances to do things that they do not want to do:

(6) The third argument, although I must respect it because I understand that sometimes people are forced to make tough decisions in life, I find it a bit awkward.

(Spanish original) *El tercer argumento, aunque debo respetarlo porque entiendo que a veces las personas se ven obligadas a tomar decisiones drásticas en la vida, me resulta un poco incómodo.*

Positive Politeness

Positive politeness includes those actions by the addressor to make the addressee feel that their actions are desirable. Brown and Levinson (1987,

p. 101) define positive politeness as "the appreciation of alter's wants in general" or "the expression of similarity between ego's and alter's wants." One of the strategies that the authors mention as instrumental to accomplish these goals, which we can find in the students' productions, is "exaggerate (interest, approval, sympathy with Hearer)." In the data analyzed, this strategy is realized by the students through mentioning particular positive features of their partner connected with the way they dress, their personality, or their values. Extract 7 includes two examples related to the partner's physical appearance and personality, respectively:

(7) Fatima wears very colorful and cheerful clothes.

(Catalan original) *Fatima porta roba molt acolorida i alegre.*

She is much simpler and less greedy in this respect.

(Catalan original) *Ella és molt més senzilla i menys cobdiciosa en aquest sentit.*

Another way in which the ABCs students work on positive politeness is by claiming common ground with their interlocutor and adopting a strategy that Brown and Levinson (1987, p. 113) define as "avoiding disagreement." This is effected by diminishing the relevance of a difference that the student has just mentioned. In Extract 8, the student comments on the fact that her interviewee dresses in a particular way:

(8) Fatima comes from the Sahara, an area in the Maghreb where women tend to wear a robe and veil and they have dark skin due to their life in the desert. **However, this is not an important difference between her and me,** and I neither like nor dislike it especially.... **It's a very superficial difference.** (my emphasis)

(Catalan original) *La Fatima procedeix del Sàhara, una àrea del Magreb on les dones se solen vestir amb túnica i vel i tenen la pell més morena per la vida al desert.* **No obstant, aquesta no és una diferència important entre ella i jo,** *i no m'inquieta ni m'agrada especialment....* **És una diferència molt superficial.**

When the difference is an important one for the ABCs student, such as is the case of the polygamist structure of her interviewee's family, she may be not able to tone down the relevance of the issue by saying that she does not consider it important, as in the previous example. Thus, in Extract 9 we see that the avoidance of disagreement is achieved by adding a comment in which it is said that this particular feature is not important for her partner.

(9) It [polygamy] is a tradition in the Muslim religion that I find difficult to live with, **but Nina does not consider it very important, first, because she does not remember it as a personal experience because she was very**

young and, second, because she point outs that it is not a common situation nowadays. (my emphasis)

(Catalan original) *És un costum procedent de la religió musulmana amb què em resultaria difícil conviure,* **però la Nina no li dóna massa importància, rimer perquè no se'n recorda com a experiència personal perquè encara era molt petita i en segon lloc perquè destaca que actualmen, és una situació rara.**

DISCUSSION

In this chaptrer I have looked at the C stage of the ABCs model as a discursive activity in which students construct a culturally different identity. I look at this activity as a process of "otherization," which involves the presentation of somebody as different from the speaker/writer. I have suggested that this process is implicit in the instructions given in the task, in which students are asked, in Step B, to select and interview a person "from a different cultural background" and, in Step C, to "analyze the differences" between themselves and their respective partner. I have also shown the writer's efforts to balance this process of otherization by adopting a series of nonotherization strategies aimed at reducing the impression of cultural distance between herself and her partner.

The analysis presented is based on a combination of two analytical frameworks. On the one hand, otherization has been analyzed in terms of the writer's choice of topics related to Scollon and Scollon's (1995) four main aspects of culture which have been shown to be the major factors influencing intercultural communication: ideology, social organization, forms of discourse and socialization. From this point of view, we have seen that topics related to social organization and socialization tend to be preferred by the student-writer to construct their partner's "different" identity. The explanation for the lower presence in the students' discourse of references to ideology and forms of discourse would require further research, possibly involving a recall interview focusing on the text. One possible explanation could be that they are seen as less salient aspects of cultural contrast. However, I would like to hypothesize that in the case of ideology, the students may have felt that with two or three encounters, they had not been able to get to know their interviewee well enough and gather enough evidence to express their views about their partner's way of thinking without putting their own and their partner's face at risk (A. Lazar, personal communication, 2012). In the case of forms of discourse, we should take into account that the interviews were held in Spanish and that the interviewees had lived in Spain for a few years; therefore, they might have been able to accommodate to the discourse styles of the students, which might have made it less noticeable.

On the other hand, the student-writers' nonotherization efforts have been described through Brown and Levinson's (1987) politeness theory, and it has been shown how these efforts include the adoption of both positive and negative face-saving strategies.

CONCLUSION

This chapter is by no means intended to reach any particular conclusion in terms of facts, such as the specific topics or face-saving strategies preferred by women to describe difference in other women. The type of data analyzed and the qualitative approach adopted makes the issue of "counting" and "generalizing" from the data difficult; although, as I have tried to show, it is not impossible to attempt a quantification of the topics selected by the students. I believe that the main contribution of this study is to suggest and exemplify two analytical perspectives from which both intercultural communication researchers and teachers and students following the ABCs can approach part of the textual data resulting from it. In combining the two perspectives, we can see how the ABCs is ultimately a process of social interaction in which the social actors fluctuate between two opposite impulses in intercultural communication: otherization and nonotherization.

The analysis of the ABCs as social interaction represents an initial move toward an alternative view of the interview (Mann, 2011; Talmy, 2011) as a research tool for extracting information from an individual, focusing exclusively on the referential contents of the interviewee's responses. In this new perspective, researchers need to consider the interview as social practice and focus not only on the content of the interviewee's responses but also on the negotiation of both meanings and social relationships between interviewer and interviewee. The exploratory study reported in this chapter represents the two perspectives. Thus, the analysis of "otherization strategies" is influenced by the perspective of the interview as a research instrument for extracting information. On the other hand, the approach adopted in the description of "nonotherization strategies," focusing on the sociality of the encounter between two previously unacquainted individuals, represents the view of the interview as social practice.

NOTE

All the extracts included in this chapter have been translated from either Catalan or Spanish, the languages in which they were originally written. In each case, I include the English translation first and the original version immediately below and in italics.

REFERENCES

Brown, P., & Levinson, S. (1987) *Politeness: Some universals in language usage.* Cambridge, UK: Cambridge University Press.

Cots, J. M. (2005) Discourse strategies. In P. Strazny (Ed.), *Encyclopedia of linguistics* (pp. 271–272). New York, NY: Fitzroy Dearborn.

Duszak, A. (2002). Us and others: An introduction. In A. Duszak (Ed.), *Us and others: Social identities across languages, discourses, and cultures* (pp. 1–28). Amsterdam, The Netherlands: John Benjamins.

Holliday, A., Hyde, M., & Kullman, J. (2004). *Intercultural communication: An advanced resource book.* London, UK: Routledge.

Kreutz, H., &. Harres, A. (1997). Some observations on the distribution and function of hedging in German and English academic writing. In A. Duszak (Ed.), *Culture and styles of academic discourse* (pp. 181–202). Berlin, Germany: Walter de Gruyter.

Mann, S. (2011). A critical review of qualitative interviews in applied linguistics. *Applied Linguistics, 32*(1), 6–24.

Piller, I. (2007). Linguistics and intercultural communication. *Compass, 1*(3). doi:10.1111/j.1749–818x.2007.00012.x, 208–226

Ruggiano Schmidt, P., & Finkbeiner, C. (2006). *ABC's of cultural understanding and communication: National and international adaptations.* Greenwich, CT: Information Age.

Scollon, R., & Scollon, S. (1995). *Intercultural communication.* Oxford, UK: Blackwell.

Talmy, S. (2011). The interview as collaborative achievement: Interaction, identity, and ideology in a speech event. *Applied Linguistics, 32*(1) 25–42.

Weaver, J. (1993). Understanding and coping with cross-cultural adjustment stress. In M. Paige, (Ed.), *Education for the intercultural experience* (pp. 137–16).Yarmouth, ME: Intercultural.

CHAPTER 7

CONSTRUCTING IDENTITY THROUGH THE ABCs OF CULTURAL UNDERSTANDING AND COMMUNICATION

Sylvia Fehling

This chapter focuses on Step A of the ABCs of Cultural Understanding and Communication (Finkbeiner & Koplin, 2002; Ruggiano Schmidt, 1998; Ruggiano Schmidt & Finkbeiner, 2006), which includes writing an auto-biography about important aspects of one's life such as family, religion, and education. Writing one's autobiography while reading the ABC's of Cultural Understanding and Communication has the purpose of looking at oneself before learning about others. This process is supposed to "build awareness of personal beliefs and attitudes that form the traditions and values of cultural autobiographies" (Ruggiano Schmidt & Finkbeiner, 2006, p. 4). Furthermore, it is supposed to trigger awareness of our own cultural development and therefore it opens up the following Steps B and C. What indicators of personal beliefs, attitudes, traditions, and values can be found in autobiographies? In addition, how is identity constructed through Step A of the ABCs model? To answer these questions, a sample autobiography

Getting to Know Ourselves and Others Through the ABCs, pages 117–128
Copyright © 2015 by Information Age Publishing
117

of a graduate student from a German university participating in the international research project *TRANSABCs: Dissemination and Adaptation of the ABCs of Cultural Understanding and Communication* (Finkbeiner & Lazar, this volume) is analyzed and conclusions are drawn.

INTRODUCTION

Writing an autobiography as the first step of the ABCs model is an important tool for identity construction. It also provides valuable data and insights into understanding which factors might influence one's notion of identity. To understand the processes involved in identity construction in the context of the ABCs model, it is necessary to have a closer look at identity first, since it is a very complex and ambiguous term. Therefore, in the first part of the following chapter, an overview of the concept of identity is given and connections between the ABCs and identity are shown. In the next section, the sociocultural context and setting of the study is described, which was conducted in connection with the project TRANSABCs. Furthermore, one sample autobiography of this study is analyzed and topics are identified that can be found in connection with identity building. Finally, the main results are summarized and further perspectives are given.

Identity

Identity is a concept used in a wide range of disciplines from sociology, psychology, pedagogy, philosophy, literary studies to applied linguistics, as data bank research has shown. Among the results are numerous publications on some of the following topics:

- identity and migration (e.g., Raths, 2009)
- identity and religion (e.g., Hunner-Kreisel & Andresen, 2010)
- identity and language (e.g., Abali, 2000; Erol, 2009)
- identity and developmental psychology (e.g., Wilkening, Freund, & Martin, 2009)
- identity and politics (e.g., Kuhn, 2001)
- professional identity (e.g., Dervin, 2011; Sigel, 2009)
- identity and foreign language teaching and learning (e.g., Finkbeiner & Fehling, 2006; Hu, 2003; Wilden, 2008)
- identity and interculturality (e.g., Finkbeiner, 2006; Finkbeiner & Koplin, 2001; Fischer, Athemeliotis, & Griese, 2009; Pattnaik, 2006; Ruggiano Schmidt, 1998; Ruggiano Schmidt & Finkbeiner, 2006)

Furthermore, the concept of identity is considered to be "one of the pivotal concepts of our times" (Dervin & Risager, 2011). Nevertheless, some critics argue that identity "tends to mean too much (when understood in a strong sense), too little (when understood in a weak sense), or nothing at all (because of its sheer ambiguity)" (Brubaker & Cooper, 2000, p. 1).

Despite the fact that this term is ambiguous, it has been used by numerous authors in various fields in a complex and differentiated way (Straub, 2004). In addition, identity is of main importance in the context of cultural studies, and it plays an important role in the context of the ABCs model. Therefore, it is necessary to have a closer look at this term and to understand its main features. Since the concept of identity is complex, I will address only those aspects that are relevant to the ABCs model.

Approaching the Concept of Identity

Straub (2004, p. 278) differentiates between *personal* and *collective identity*. *Personal identity* refers to an aspired and imagined identity, which influences a person's behavior and motivation. Furthermore, identity can be seen as a standard, which an individual claims for oneself and others, knowing that this standard may not be fulfilled (p. 279).

Collective identity is more widely used in research, as can be seen in numerous publications on issues such as identity and religion, political identity, gender and identity, and so on. It refers to identities of groups of various sizes, such as couples, linguistic communities, cultures, genders, and such (Straub, 2004, p. 291). These collectives share similar expectations, experiences, values, goals, and orientations, and depend on the identification of each single individual. Members of a collective possess a tacit knowledge, which influences and structures their thoughts, feelings, and deeds (Straub, 2004, p. 300).

Besides differentiating between a personal and collective identity, it is also important to consider the following aspect of the term identity: Ivanič (1998) argues that the singular form of this word is misleading, since it does not capture "the idea of people identifying simultaneously with a variety of social groups" (p. 11). She mentions that people usually possess a multitude of *identities* simultaneously, which might be either contradictory or interrelated. Despite this dilemma, she prefers the term *identity* as "general-purpose word" (p. 11) because "it is the everyday word for people's sense of who they are" (p. 10). Nevertheless, one has to keep in mind that the term *identity* might indicate diverse and complex identities.

Furthermore, Ivanič focuses on *writer identity*, which is especially relevant in the context of the ABCs model. The author differentiates three types of writer identities that are closely linked and that influence each other:

- Autobiographical self
- Discoursal self
- Self as author

The *autobiographical self* focuses on the way a writer portrays herself or himself in a text and is shaped by a person's sociocultural background (Ivanič, 1998, p. 24). This aspect of identity is not fixed and can change as a consequence of a changing life history. According to Ivanič (1998), "the term also captures the idea that it is not only the events in people's lives, but also their way of representing these experiences to themselves which constitutes their current way of being" (p. 24).

A writer's *discoursal self* is formed through the discourse characteristics of texts, such as values, beliefs, and power relations (Ivanič, 1998, p. 25). Consequently, social and ideological aspects play an important role on how the text is written and how identity is constructed in a text. Ivanič (1998) emphasizes that the discoursal self "is concerned with the writer's voice in the sense of the way they want to sound, rather than in the sense of the stance they are taking" (p. 25). The aspect *self as author* focuses on writers' positions, opinions, and beliefs and the authorial presence they construct in their writing. It is strongly influenced by the *autobiographical self* as Ivanič illustrates: "The writer's life-history may or may not have generated ideas to express, and may or may not have engendered in the writer enough of a sense of self-worth to write with authority, to establish an authorial presence" (p. 26).

Another important aspect influencing identity construction is "the perspective of the self and the perspective of the other" in social interaction (Finkbeiner, 2006, p. 35). Finkbeiner differentiates between three levels of perspectives: The *actual*, the *hypothetical* and the *desired level*. While the *actual level* can be based on previous experiences, the *hypothetical level* refers to an assumption about oneself without having experienced this assumption. The *desired level* is what a person wishes to be. These three levels can also be found in respect to the perspective of the other. As Finkbeiner (2006) makes clear, "the 'other' can be a part of oneself in an inner dialogue or it can be another person one is having a dialogue with" (p. 35)

Finally, *memory* can be seen as an essential factor of identity construction, as Hume (1964, pp. 239–247, as cited in Glomb, 1997, p. 16) clarifies:

> [We] are nothing but a bundle or collection of different perceptions, which succeed each other with an inconceivable rapidity, and are in a perpetual flux and movement. . . . As memory alone acquaints us with the continuance and extent of this succession of perceptions, it is to be considered, upon that account chiefly, as the source of personal identity.

Though memories have an impact on one's identity construction, memories are also influenced by one's identity and individual factors, such as one's current mood, wishes, requirements, situation, and such. In addition, individuals might manipulate or censor their memories subconsciously according to their current identity in order to create a coherent and positive self-image (Glomb, 1997, p. 21).

These perspectives show that identity construction is a very complex and dynamic lifelong process influenced by a multitude of factors involving sociocultural background, social interactions, and memories. While some of these aspects are transparent and can be easily captured and understood, other factors are very tacit and hidden in the subconscious. In the next section, the relevance of identity-construction theories in the ABCs model will be described.

Identity and the ABCs of Cultural Understanding and Communication

Writing an autobiography is the first step of the ABCs model. Thus, students should focus on relevant aspects and events of their lives to establish images of themselves in terms of their cultural and ethnic values, beliefs, and attitudes (Finkbeiner, 2009; Ruggiano Schmidt & Finkbeiner, 2006). This writing also helps to organize the students' ideas and emotions and fosters their understanding of identity (Osetek, 2006, p. 47).

In addition, Step A is the necessary preparation for the cross-cultural analysis (Step C) of the ABCs model, which is the comparison of one's own experiences with those of a culturally different partner. The comparison enables "students to realize the influence of culture in their own and that of their interviewee's beliefs, values, and experiences and to accept diversity and difference as resources of learning" (Pattnaik, 2006, p. 117).

These aspects emphasize the relevant role that identity plays in connection with the ABCs model and intercultural learning. I therefore decided to analyze the data gathered in the *TRANSABCs* with a special focus on identity construction. The data were collected in three seminars on the ABCs, which I taught at a German university. To get an understanding of the sociocultural context and setting of these seminars, I will provide further details in the next section.

Sociocultural Context and Setting of the Study

The students participating in the seminar were all graduate students, mainly in the field of teacher education. In addition, some students focused on English and American Studies as well as English and American Culture and Business Studies. Furthermore, international students from Turkey and Spain attended my seminars on the ABCs model. The average age of the students varied between 21 and 25. Since the seminars were part of the international TRANSABCs Project, where English was used as the working language, the different steps of the ABCs were written in English. Consequently, all autobiographies were written in English, though the first language of most students participating in the project was German. Other languages learned as the L1 were Polish, Serbian, Russian, Turkish, Spanish, Icelandic, Farsi, and Macedonian.

In the next section, I will focus on one autobiography written by a student attending my seminar. I refer to this single case because it contains interesting and different dimensions of identity. This enables me to consider issues on identity much more deeply.

Since the personal data of the participant must be held confidential, I will refer to the student who composed the sample autobiography as Participant A. Quotes taken from the autobiography will be marked with quotation marks.

Analysis of a Sample Autobiography

The data analysis is based on a qualitative approach. With the help of an expert group, categories were developed in a bottom-up and top-down process (Finkbeiner & Koplin, 2001; Mayring, 2003; Scollon & Scollon, 2005; Wilden, 2008). The autobiography was written by a female graduate student of English and American Culture and Business Studies. She was born and grew up in Poland with her parents, grandparents, and in close contact with many other relatives. She visited Germany during her childhood regularly with her family and finally moved to Germany after finishing school. Her parents had already migrated to Germany before her, so for some time she had stayed in Poland without her parents until she graduated from school.

The following categories were found in the data analysis and therefore will be elaborated on in more detail:

- Sociopolitical events
- Critical incidents
- Challenges and difficulties
- Family
- Education
- Friends

In her autobiography, the student refers to various *sociopolitical events* that had an important influence on her family and herself: Thus, she refers to World War II, which had a great impact on her family and forced them to move all around the world. In addition, this incident also influenced her own life and her own perception concerning nationality and patriotism, as follows:

> The great impact on my family structure was World War II. This spread my whole family around the world beginning from Australia, through Israel, Eastern Europe, France, Italy, Germany and America. Therefore, I have never felt only Polish or very patriotic, that is why I would rather call myself cosmopolitan.

In addition, the fact that some part of her family had moved to Germany made her and her family visit some German cities such as Berlin many times during her childhood, so she called Berlin her "second home" during this time. Finally, her parents migrated to Germany, and then later she herself did as well. Furthermore, she refers to the political events in the 1980s in Poland, claiming that her childhood was not affected by the aftermath of a "socialistic system or civil war." The student draws parallels between her own life and the history of her country: "The years passed as I grew up, my attitudes have changed and my life got full of ups and downs as drastic and rapid as the constantly changing social, political and economical situation in Poland."

As a consequence of different *sociopolitical events*, the student names *critical incidents* (Finkbeiner & Koplin, 2002, p. 8) that had an enormous impact. One of these events was her parents migrating to Germany without her one year before her graduation. Another *critical incident* was when she migrated to Germany after her graduation. As a consequence of these *critical incidents, challenges* and *difficulties* had to be faced and overcome, such as managing the house on her own, having to adapt to a foreign culture, and being unable to speak the language proficiently when moving to Germany. *Family* and the relationship with her family also play an important part in this autobiography: It seems relevant to mention that the student's concept of the family includes parents and grandparents, and also more distant relatives, whom she feels herself obliged to support. Furthermore, *education* is an important factor for this person. She calls herself an "always ambitious" and hard-working person with clear goals. This is evident when she refers to learning the German language:

> With 12 hours per day and uncountable hours of self-study, I have put myself through the mill, but I have no regrets because that was a great milestone to further my career but also a tryout of my strong will and determination for achieving my designated goals in life.

Participant A also discussed the importance of friends in her life, especially meeting international friends when moving to Germany and having a boyfriend who was not German. She believed these relationships broadened her cultural experience. On the other hand, this new experience in Germany caused other *critical incidents* as she was alienated from her old home:

> Nevertheless, changing the place of living has adversely affected my relations with my relatives and friends from my home country. Some of them did not want to have contact with me anymore and my relatives accuse me of being an egoistic person just because I did not stay in Poland to help my relatives in their household duties, babysitting, etc.

In addition, she had to deal with stereotypes about the Polish culture:

> More than once I had to run the gauntlet because of my nationality and associated prejudices. At the beginning I felt a little bit offended but in the course of time I learned how to deal with it, by making jokes about my nationality by myself.

In conclusion, it can be said that Participant A constructs her identity as that of a strong-willed, open-minded and successful person. In addition, it is pointed out that many *challenges* and *difficulties* had to be overcome with strong will and hard work. This is emphasized by repeating expressions such as "struggle" and "challenge" in this autobiography. Furthermore, the student finishes her autobiography with the following statement: "My turbulent experiences showed me that if you really want to achieve your targeted objectives a strong will and determination are the first steps to succeed."

Finally, the student structures her autobiography chronologically and coherently mainly through her family history, as well as experiences of acculturation and enculturation (Finkbeiner, 2006; Scollon & Scollon, 2005).

This sample also shows interesting facets of identity construction as already explained (Straub, 2004). Thus, the aspect of *personal identity* seems to play an important aspect in this autobiography: As pointed out, *personal identity* refers to an aspired-to and imagined identity, which can influence a person's behavior and motivation. In the sample autobiography, the person describes herself as very hard-working and ambitious. This helped her to solve various problems in her life and enabled her to reach her goals. Consequently, the aspect of education and reaching explicit goals seems to be a driving factor in this person's life and a crucial part of her personal identity. Aspects of *collective identity* (Straub, 2004) can also be found: In the sample autobiography, the student refers to herself as feeling not "only Polish" or "very patriotic," but rather calls herself "cosmopolitan." Thus, she identifies with one group, while distancing herself from another group. This example also contains aspects of the *autobiographical self* (Ivanič, 1998), since the person's sociocultural background and her changing life-history has an immense influence on constructing her identity.

The analysis and interpretation of this autobiography can be supported by Step B and Step C: The student verifies the construction of herself in Step C by emphasizing again that she is an "ambitious and energetic" person who has "fixed plans for the future" and "who never lost [her] priorities."

This becomes even more evident, as her interview partner in Step B is described as the exact opposite, a person who is "chaotic, lazy, disorganized and waits with important decisions until the last moment." Consequently, the ABCs process seems to confirm the construction of the participant's identity found in Step A.

CONCLUSION AND FURTHER PERSPECTIVES

As could be shown, autobiographies present rewarding research material in terms of identity construction. The autobiography presented in this article reveals some very unique aspects of identity construction, such as *personal identity, collective identity,* and the *autobiographical self.* In a next step, it might be interesting to analyze and compare a range of autobiographies to gain a more diversified picture of the ways personal and cultural factors manifest themselves in the process of identity construction. These cross-cultural analyses (Finkbeiner & Koplin, 2001, p. 121) could focus on further criteria, such as narrative aspects, forms of discourse, or cultural aspects such as ideology and aspects of socialization (Scollon & Scollon, 2005). Thus, some consistent patterns of these manifestations typical for different cultures may be revealed.

Furthermore, the analysis of the autobiography could be used within the ABCs model to raise awareness about factors of identity construction to follow the underlying principle of the *ABC's of Cultural Understanding and Communication:* "Know thyself and understand others" (Ruggiano Schmidt, 1999). In this context, it would also be very interesting to see what influence the ABCs model has on the construction of one's identity by comparing the findings of Step A with the findings of Step B and Step C.

Autobiographical research and research on identity are key factors in the scientific debate on interculturality and intercultural learning (Dervin & Risager, 2011; Ruggiano Schmidt & Finkbeiner, 2006). Nevertheless, there are still many questions about the extent to which autobiographical factors contribute to intercultural learning. Therefore, more empirical research is needed to deepen an understanding of the processes and factors involved in identity construction in the context of intercultural learning. Further research in this field might give important impetus to theoretical and methodological considerations of teaching culture within the field of foreign language teaching, as pointed out by Hallet and Surkamp (2011):

> A theory and methodology of teaching culture ("*Kulturdidaktik*") has not yet been fully established within the field of foreign language teaching. "*Kulturdidaktik*" includes several concepts of teaching, representing and understanding communicative interaction with cultures of other languages or with individual members or products of these cultures.... Recent approaches of

teaching culture regard learners as cultural subjects who are participating in social and cultural developments and processes. However, considering the vastness of the entire domain of culture as the object of research and the variety of the related fields of research involved, many open questions remain. These concern several aspects:... the competences required of the learners as cultural agents as well as the didactical and cultural expertise required in the foreign language teacher enabling them to design and teach up-to-date culture classes.

NOTE

I want to thank Prof. Dr. Claudia Finkbeiner (University of Kassel, Germany), Prof. Dr. Althier Lazar (Saint Joseph's University, Philadelphia, Pennsylvania) and Prof. Dr. Jiening Ruan (University of Oklahoma, Norman) for their advice in analyzing the data.

REFERENCES

Abali, Ü. (2000). Kulturelle Identität und Sprache—Türkische Schülerinnen und Schüler in Deutschland. Eine empirische Untersuchung. *Deutsch Lernen, 25*(4), 310–331.

Brubaker, R., & Cooper, F. (2000). Beyond "identity." *Theory and Society, 29,* 1–47. Retrieved October 1, 2011, from http://www.sscnet.ucla.edu/soc/faculty/brubaker/Publications/18_Beyond_Identity.pdf

Dervin, F. (Ed.). (2011). *Analyzing the consequences of academic mobility andmigration.* Cambridge, UK: Cambridge Scholars Publishing.

Dervin, F., & Risager, K. (2011, July 4–8). *International doctoral summer school: Identity and interculturality: Research methods—Roskilde University, Denmark.* Retrieved October 1, 2011, from http://magenta.ruc.dk/upload/application/pdf/29d3a50c/Summer%20School%20Description%20Webpage%20feb%202011.pdf

Erol, R. (2009). *Türkische Jugendliche in Deutschland—kulturelle Orientierung und Zweisprachigkeit.* Dissertation. Universität Köln.

Finkbeiner, C. (2006). Constructing third space: The principles of reciprocity and cooperation. In P. R. Schmidt & C. Finkbeiner (Eds.), *ABC's of cultural understanding and communication: National and international adaptations* (pp. 19–192). Greenwich, CT: Information Age.

Finkbeiner, C. (2009). Using "human global positioning system" as a navigation tool to the hidden dimension of culture. In A. Feng, M. Byram, & M. Fleming (Eds.), *Becoming interculturally competent through training and education* (pp. 151–173). Bristol, UK: Multilingual Matters.

Finkbeiner, C., & Fehling, S. (2006). Investigating the role of awareness and multiple perspectives in intercultural education. In P. Ruggiano Schmidt & C. Finkbeiner (Eds.), *ABC's of cultural understanding and communication: National and international adaptation* (pp. 93–110). Greenwich, CT: Information Age.

Finkbeiner, C., & Koplin, C. (2001). Fremdverstehensprozesse und interkulturelle Prozesse als Forschungsgegenstand. In A. Müller-Hartmann & M. Schocker-v. Ditfurth (Eds.), *Qualitative Forschungsansätze im Bereich Fremdsprachen lehren und lernen* (pp. 114–136). Tübingen, Germany: Gunter Narr.

Finkbeiner, C., & Koplin, C. (2002). A cooperative approach for facilitating intercultural education. *Reading Online, 6*(3). Retrieved March 3, 2012, from http://www.readingonline.org/newliteracies/lit_index.asp?HREF=finkbeiner/

Fischer, C., Athemeliotis, A., & Griese, H. M. (2009). *Jugend—Migration—Sozialisation-Bildung Festschrift zum 65. Geburtstag von Hartmut M. Griese.* Münster, Germany: LIT-Verlag.

Glomb, S. (1997). *Erinnerung und Identität im britischen Gegenwartsdrama.* Tübingen, Germany: Gunter Narr.

Hallet, W., & Surkamp, C. (2011). *Panel 5: Teaching culture ('kulturdidaktik'): Concepts and ways of learning in the foreign language class.* 24th Conference of the German Society of Foreign Language Research—28th September to 1st October 2011 at the University of Hamburg. Retrieved April 3, 2012, from http://kongress.dgff.de/en/sections/panel-5.html

Hu, A. (2003). *Schulischer Fremdsprachenunterricht und migrationsbedingte Mehrsprachigkeit.* Tübingen, Germany: Gunter Narr.

Hume, D. (1964). *A treatise of human nature.* London, UK: Oxford University Press. (Original work published 1739)

Hunner-Kreisel, C., & Andresen, S. (Eds.). (2010). *Kindheit und Jugend in muslimischen Lebenswelten: Aufwachsen und Bildung in deutscher und internationaler Perspektive.* Wiesbaden, Germany: VS Verlag für Sozialwissenschaften.

Ivanič, R. (1998). *Writing and identity. The discoursal construction of identity in academic writing.* Amsterdam, The Netherlands; Philadelphia, PA: John Benjamins.

Kuhn, H. P. (2001). Mediennutzung und politische Identitätsbildung in der Adoleszenz. In K. Richter & T. Trautmann (Eds.), *Kindsein in der Mediengesellschaft* (pp. 163–183). Weinheim, Basel: Beltz Verlag.

Mayring, P. (2003). *Einführung in die qualitative Sozialforschung. Eine Anleitung zu qualitativem Denken* (4th ed.). Weinheim, Germany: Psychologie Verlags Union.

Osetek, J. M. (2006). The ABCs: A journey toward making a positive difference. In P. Ruggiano Schmidt & C. Finkbeiner (Eds.), *ABC's of cultural understanding and communication: National and international adaptations* (pp. 43–72). Greenwich, CT: Information Age.

Pattnaik, J. (2006). Revealing and revisiting "self" in relation to the culturally different "other": Multicultural teacher education and the ABCs model. In P. Ruggiano Schmidt & C. Finkbeiner (Eds.), *ABC's of cultural understanding and communication: National and international adaptations* (pp. 111–141). Greenwich, CT: Information Age.

Raths, A. H. (2009). *Türkische Jugendkulturen in Deutschland. Die dritte Generation auf der Suche nach Identität.* Marburg, Germany: Tectum-Verlag.

Ruggiano Schmidt, P. (1998). The ABCs of cultural understanding and communication. *Equity and Excellence, 31*(2), 28–38.

Ruggiano Schmidt, P. (1999). Focus on research: Know thyself and understand others. *Language Arts, 76*(4), 332–340.

Ruggiano Schmidt, P., & Finkbeiner, C. (2006). Introduction: What is the ABCs of cultural understanding and communication? In P. R. Schmidt & C. Finkbeiner (Eds.), *ABC's of cultural understanding and communication: National and international adaptations* (pp. 1–18). Greenwich, CT: Information Age.

Scollon, R., & Scollon, S. W. (2005). *Intercultural communication. A discourse approach* (2nd ed.). Malden, MA: Blackwell.

Sigel, J. (2009). Berufliche Identität von Polizisten mit Migrationshintergrund. In K. Liebl (Ed.), *Polizei und Fremde—Fremde in der Polizei* (pp. 105–151). Wiesbaden, Germany: VS Verlag für Sozialwissenschaften.

Straub, J. (2004). Identität. In F. Jaeger & B. Liebsch (Eds.), *Handbuch der Kulturwissenschaften. Grundlagen und Schlüsselbegriffe* (pp. 277–308). Stuttgart, Germany: Metzler Verlag.

Wilden, E. (2008). *Selbst- und Fremdwahrnehmung in der interkulturellen Onlinekommunikation. Das Modell der ABCs of Cultural Understanding and Communication Online. Eine qualitative Studie.* Frankfurt, Germany: Peter Lang.

Wilkening, F., Freund, A. M., & Martin, M. (2009). *Entwicklungspsychologie. Kompakt.* Weinheim, Germany: Beltz, PVU.

CHAPTER 8

LEARNING TO READ AND READING TO LEARN THROUGH LITERACY MEMORIES

An Implementation of the ABCs Model in a Reading Methods Course

Shelley Hong Xu

INTRODUCTION

The focus of preparing teacher candidates (i.e., candidates) for culturally responsive teaching is not new to teacher preparation programs across the United States (e.g., Cochran-Smith, Davis, & Fries, 2004; Ladson-Billings, 2004; Sleeter, 2001). It is common for candidates to take a course on diversity before taking methods courses. Early studies have shown that candidates' writing up their own literacy experiences and interviewing a peer nudge them to become aware of their own and others' cultural and linguistic experiences (e.g., Finkbeiner, 2006; Ruggiano Schmidt & Finkbeiner, 2006). However, little is known about how candidates would translate their

Getting to Know Ourselves and Others Through the ABCs, pages 129–145
Copyright © 2015 by Information Age Publishing

awareness of diversity issues into their teaching in a subject area, for instance, reading instruction. This study would address this gap in research by replicating a similar study (Xu, 2006) with predominantly Caucasian teacher candidates. The participants in this study reflected a richer layer of linguistic and cultural diversity.

In this chapter, I will first describe the sociocultural context and setting of this study, including a detailed presentation of the implementation of the *ABC's of Cultural Understanding and Communication* (i.e., ABCs Model; Ruggiano Schmidt & Finkbeiner, 2006). Next, I will offer an explanation of the educational system of public schools in California and of the teacher education program for the participants of this study and present a discussion of relevant research studies. The remainder of this chapter will focus on specific setting, data collection and analysis, results, discussions, and implications of this study.

Social-Cultural Context and Setting

In this study, I guided candidates through a series of activities related to the ABCs model (Ruggiano Schmidt, 1999, 2001, 2005) which has been implemented by teacher educators in various countries (e.g., Finkbeiner & Ruggiano Schmidt, 2006; Wilden, 2006; Xu, 2006). Specifically, in activity 1, candidates completed (a) a presurvey about their understanding of cultural and linguistic awareness (Gay, 2000; Ruggiano Schmidt & Finkbeiner, 2006); and (b) a prepolarity profile (about reactions to the ABCs model) developed by Finkbeiner (2005). In activity 2, each candidate wrote his or her autobiography about his or her literacy memories in response to the guiding questions (see Appendix). In activity 3, each candidate interviewed a peer and wrote his or her biography about literacy memories. In activity 4, two candidates listed and discussed areas of similarities and differences in the autobiographies and biographies. Based on the discussion, each candidate wrote about an analysis of the differences and their implications for literacy learning and teaching. In activity 5, each candidate formulated five culturally responsive ideas for teaching reading. In activity 6, each candidate completed a postsurvey about his or her understanding of cultural and linguistic awareness and a postpolarity profile (Finkbeiner, 2005). Three candidates were interviewed one year after their participation in all the activities. The interview questions included (a) Please tell me what you remember about the ABCs of Cultural Understanding and Communication, (b) What types of diversity do you see in your classroom? (c) Tell me about the culturally responsive lessons or units you have created in your classrooms, (d) Please tell me about one of your most successful lessons. Why was it so successful? (e) How do you talk to students who are English language learners? (f) How do you help students stay interested in learning? (g) How do you learn about your students' cultural and linguistic heritage? (h) Why do you think teaching is difficult and rewarding? and (i) How would you define culturally responsive teaching?

Relevant Research Studies

Two bodies of literature have guided this study. One body relates to the importance of preparing candidates for working with students in diverse settings. In a call to "Restore Our Schools," Darling-Hammond (2010) strongly advocated "building an infrastructure that ensures high quality preparation for all educators and ensures that well-trained teachers are available to all students in all communities" (p. 19). Darling-Hammond's advocacy for diverse students' equal access to high quality education presents a broad context about the urgency of preparing candidates for diversity in schools.

While there has been a growing number of studies about preparing candidates for diversity (e.g., Guo, Arthur, & Lund, 2009; Jared, 2010), a limited number of studies focused on candidates' applying their diversity knowledge to working with diverse children in a specific content area. In a work by Atwater, Freeman, Butler, and Draper-Morris (2010), two white teacher candidates, Anna King and Katie Smith, viewed that "culture and ethnicity might be important sometimes" (p. 305). Such a view was reflected in how they worked with diverse students. For example, Anna responded to one Asian student's needs during teaching, but not to other English language learners. Similarly, Karen structured her lessons based on the academic levels of her students, not on their backgrounds and prior knowledge. To some extent, both Anna and Karen's ability to deliver culturally responsive teaching was limited. The researchers concluded with these questions: "What experiences are necessary for teacher candidates whose lives have been very different from the Other's students, to be committed to and have the knowledge and skills to teach these students?" (p. 308). This study was prompted by a need for teacher candidates to expand their often limited knowledge about culturally different Others.

The other body of literature, mainly studies on the implementation of the ABCs model across the United States and the world, directly impacts this study. For example, Ruggiano Schmidt (1999, 2001, 2005) has constantly reminded teacher educators that culturally responsive teaching began with candidates' exploring first their own cultural and linguistic backgrounds and then learning and understanding those of others who were different from themselves. The ABCs model has effectively engaged candidates in critically analyzing similarities and differences in their own cultural and family experiences, and cultural values and beliefs as well as applying such enhanced awareness in making home-school connection in teaching diverse students.

Other scholars' work that built on Ruggiano Schmidt's ABCs model has offered additional insights. For instance, Izzo and Ruggiano Schmidt (2006) presented a powerful model of professional development for teaching diverse students, suggesting that learning to teach in a culturally responsive way itself was a learning process for classroom teachers and that the ABCs model provided a structure for such professional development. In a study with a focus on a MOBIDIC project with Content and Language Integrated Learning classes in Poland, France, Germany, and England, Finkbeiner and Fehling (2006) found that the biography part of the ABCs model particularly played an important role for teachers to understand the perspectives and linguistic interpretations of the word *migration* by the students from different parts of the European Union. Finkbeiner and Fehling highlighted the purpose of the ABCs model in their future work as "a vehicle for facilitating understanding and creating awareness for different perspectives" (p. 108). Such a purpose is resonant with the one for this study with candidates enrolled in a reading methods course.

Educational System

This study was conducted with candidates enrolled in a Multiple Subject Credentialing Program (MSCP) (K–8) in a state university in California. Candidates usually have taken a prerequisite course on diversity before taking five field-based methods courses (i.e., reading, language arts, social studies, science, and math). During methods courses, candidates are required to observe the teaching of a subject area, teach lessons, and work with children. After completing all the methods courses, student candidates teach for one semester in a primary grade (K–3rd grade) and in an upper grade (4th–8th grade). The public school system in California includes elementary schools (K–6th or K–5th), middle schools (7th–8th or 6th–8th), and high schools (9th–12th).

THIS STUDY

The Participants and Time Frame

This qualitative study was conducted with 71 candidates from three sections of a reading methods course. The participants were predominantly Caucasians, Latinos, some Asians, African Americans, and Middle Easterners. The languages spoken by the participants include Chinese, French, Korean, Japanese, Hawaiian, Hebrew, Khmer, Spanish, Tagalog, Vietnamese, and Yiddish. The age of the participants ranged from early 20s to early 60s, and about 11% were males. All the ABCs model activities as described in the foregoing section were integrated into the course assignments. Each candidate taught one phonics/phonemic awareness lesson and one comprehension lesson.

Specific Implementation of the Study (Data Collection and Analysis)

The participants completed six activities in sequence. The data sources included presurvey, prepolarity profile; autobiography; interview and biography; list and analysis of similarities and differences; five culturally responsive lesson ideas for teaching reading; postsurvey, and postpolarity profile. Three candidates participated in an interview one year after they had completed all the activities.

The pre-and postsurveys and the pre- and postpolarity profiles were analyzed quantitatively. I analyzed qualitatively the autobiographies, biographies, lists and analyses of similarities and differences, and the transcribed interview data by identifying emerging themes (Miles & Huberman, 1994; Silverman, 2005). The data of five culturally responsive lesson ideas for teaching reading were analyzed quantitatively and qualitatively. Specifically, each candidate's five lesson ideas were evaluated based on a rubric with a 3-point scale, regarding (a) detailed idea for multicultural literacy lessons in a specific content area; (b) connecting home, school, and community; (c) literacy learning; (d) level of variety and engagement; and (e) organization, appearance, and editing. Qualitative analysis of the ideas centered on identifying emerging categories.

Results

The concept of learning to read and reading to learn is used to structure my presentation of the results. The participants learned to read, beyond just literacy-related events listed in their autobiographies and biographies, their own and their peers' literacy memories that were shaped by their respective unique linguistic and cultural backgrounds. This process was intertwined with reading to learn as participants acquired knowledge about their peers' literacy experiences. The participants' process of learning to read and reading to learn continued through their discussions with peers about the similarities and differences in their literacy memories and their respective formulation of lesson ideas for culturally responsive teaching of reading. Due to space limits, the results presented were mainly drawn from participants' autobiographies, biographies, lesson ideas, and three interviews.

LEARNING TO READ DIVERSITY ISSUES AND THEIR RELATIONSHIP TO LITERACY EXPERIENCES

Cultural and Linguistic Heritages

From autobiographies and biographies, candidates became aware of their own and their peers' cultural heritages, including Cambodian,

Canadian, Cherokee Indian, Chinese, English, Filipino, French, German, Hungarian, Irish, Italian, Japanese, Korean, Mexican, Norwegian, Nicaraguan, Portuguese, Russian, Scandinavian, Scottish, Swedish, and Vietnamese. Candidates, representing close to two dozens of ethnic backgrounds, were shocked to learn that they could speak fewer than a dozen languages: English, Spanish, Japanese, Khmer, Vietnamese, Hawaiian, French, Yiddish, Hebrew, Korean, and Tagalog. As Daisy put it, "I spoke only English so I didn't have any issues linguistically. Culturally I was Japanese, but very much Americanized. It's shameful, but I truly do not know a lot about my culture [and the Japanese language]." Daisy's enhanced awareness fully corresponded with the experience of Celyan, who was a language learner of three languages: "German as a second language, Turkish as a mother tongue and English as a foreign language (Finkbeiner, 2009, p. 161).

Home Support for Literacy

Another discovery through the ABCs activities challenged candidates' views about home support for literacy experience. Stepparents, siblings, librarians, grandparents, aunts and uncles, friends, neighbors, and tutors provided different forms of support in candidates' journey of learning to read and reading to learn. These people also served as literacy role models for candidates when they were young. However, some candidates identified limited support from their parents and other adults because parents did not understand the U.S. educational system or they were too busy with working to pay attention to their children's education. Furthermore, candidates came to understand various forms of home support for their literacy development, ranging from trips to educational institutions (e.g., a library) to extracurricular classes (e.g., a concert) to reading and discussing a book.

Home–School Connections

Many candidates had vivid memories about how home-school connections occurred or did not occur during their schooling. Candidates shared school projects or activities that promoted a connection between school learning and students' cultural and linguistic backgrounds. For example, Betty talked about how one teacher linked her school learning to her linguistic background.

> Mrs. Fischer [pseudonym] taught us songs in Spanish, read Spanish/English books to us. She knew I spoke Spanish, so she would speak to me in Spanish at

times, and she was the only teacher who ever pronounced my name correctly by rolling the "r."

Home-school connection was further evidenced in various text genres that candidates were encouraged to read in and outside schools, including fiction, nonfiction, poetry, newspapers, magazines, TV shows, Japanese animes, video game manuals, song lyrics, comics, and the Bible. By contrast, some candidates recalled painful memories of their schooling where their cultural and linguistic backgrounds were devalued or not capitalized on in their learning. Nancy, with a Filipino heritage, recounted her experience of home-school disconnect.

> My primary language is English so this was of course supported within my classrooms. I did not feel there was any attention or value placed on my cultural heritage. I am full Filipino and my culture was never mentioned. It was simply lumped together with other Asian cultures but the Filipino culture and history is vastly different, and this in a way was kind of disrespectful.

Incorporating Other Cultures

Many candidates recalled their experiences with learning about other cultures during their schooling and/or at a community college or university, including class projects (e.g., family histories), community cultural festivals (e.g., Diversity Week), and learning another language. Simply working with diverse children and teachers at schools and peers in university classes has been an eye-opening experience for learning about other cultures. One Caucasian candidate, Cathy, described her exposure to Latino literature during high school and the impact of such exposure on her understanding of diversity.

> The next was my first exposure to literature written by a Latina author. I immediately fell in love with Latino literature and the way many Latino authors write. This fueled my desire to continue learning about different cultures and the experiences of people from these cultures.

Becoming Aware of Issues Beyond Ethnicity

Writing an autobiography and a biography and discussing similarities and differences between their own and their peers' literacy memories offered candidates unique opportunities to become aware of and explore diversity issues that might be overlooked, if such opportunities would be otherwise unavailable. For example, Fanny developed a deeper understanding of the impact of linguistic, cultural, social, and economic capital on quality of life and education and in particular, literacy experiences.

> I was definitely in an ideal position to have access to a quality education. Linguistically, my mom and other teachers increased my understanding of the language and they encouraged reading on a daily basis. Culturally, I belonged to a middle class white family. People from this group tend to assist their children in whatever ways they can. They feel that knowledge is the key to success and being born into this sort of family definitely predisposed me to a quality education. Socially, I believe that learning and seeking knowledge was always encouraged from the people I engaged with every day. Economically, I am from a middle class family. [Despite] some rough patches, for the most part I always had access to materials, books, and resources.

The other candidate, Vicky, spoke about her family's lack of economic capital:

> My family's low socioeconomic status has hindered my access to a quality education. My family was very poor and we did not own a single book except an Encyclopedia for the letter T. My parents allowed us to make several trips to our neighborhood library whenever possible. These trips became a very memorable pastime for my sibling because it was a way for us to become better readers. My parents encouraged us to complete the library program and made it possible for us to love reading.

Candidates' growing knowledge about availability of economic and social capital and its impact nudged them to explore their own misconceptions and biases and prejudices. For example, one Spanish-English bilingual candidate, Dottie, reflected,

> My experiences helped me see that different cultures have different ways to view and go about education. Parents are always being supportive of their child's education no matter what their background is. From my experience my parents always cared, but due to the language barrier they felt pointless for them to go to the events.

Another issue that became visible to candidates was how a social environment surrounding them motivated or discouraged them to learn a native language. For example, Olivia detailed her limited experience with learning Tagalog.

> Born and raised in California, I was surrounded by an English-speaking community. The language I became much familiarized with was English and I was strongly encouraged to make English my dominant language. However, my mother, who is Filipina, wanted her children to also become dominant in Ta-

galog. Yet, my siblings and I did not get the chance to learn Tagalog because my father discouraged it.

Such social environment impacted children even at a very young age. Peter, who constantly encouraged his prekindergarten students to speak their native language, was shocked to hear a 4-year-old boy tell him, "I do not like speaking Spanish. It is scary." He could not believe that a 4-year-old boy could develop such a stigma for speaking his native language.

Lessons Learned From Selves and Peers

Interacting with peers created a live cultural and linguistic experience for candidates. They expressed their appreciation about gaining knowledge about another culture and language, developed enhanced sensitivity to peers' cultural values and beliefs that might be different from or even contradictory to their own, and realized their own privileged life and experiences. Such enhanced awareness led candidates to contemplate on their work with diverse students. Frank remarked,

> Although I grew up in a white middle class family and had access to adequate literacy experiences in school, reading was not a priority in my home. . . . I did not have the benefit of living in a text-rich environment. My experience has shown me that every student is an individual and has a different literacy background. Although a student may struggle with the English language, they may have a great deal of experience with reading at home in their native language, and this experience can be built upon in the classroom.

One of the most important lessons that candidates learned from the ABCs activities was the human spirit evidenced across the life and literacy experiences of selves and peers within different cultural and linguistic settings. The examples of perseverance, resilience, aspiration, hardwork, and kindness were seen throughout many autobiographies and biographies. Vicky spoke of her motivation to learn:

> My parents only spoke Khmer at home and all my homework was in English. My parent would always encourage me to study, but I had to motivate myself when it came to completing homework assignments. I remember spending hours and hours on certain writing assignment at time because I did not know where to begin.

She further reflected on her experiences and its relation to her becoming a teacher of diverse students.

My family and I traveled to America in hopes of taking refuge in the land of the free. Being a 1.5-generation Asian American has allowed me to connect to my Cambodian roots and still develop an American lifestyle of my own. I want to become an advocate for education. As teachers, we should help students understand our differences and similarities while cultivating our own individuality. I am a motivated individual who can enrich not only the children's educational experience, but also their lives. If a child walks out of my classroom with motivation and confidence to pursue their dreams, I have accomplished my goal.

READING TO LEARN ABOUT CULTURALLY RESPONSIVE TEACHING IN LESSON IDEAS AND WORKING WITH DIVERSE CHILDREN

Lesson Ideas for Culturally Responsive Teaching of Reading

Exploring their own and their peers' literacy memories through a lens of culture and language and discussing with peers about their experiences prepared candidates to become aware of culturally responsive teaching. As evidenced in their writing of autobiographies and biographies, many candidates considered the followings as important components of culturally responsive teaching: understand and value children's cultural and linguistic heritage, provide students with rich multicultural world experiences, set higher expectations, encourage motivation, offer encouragement, and never give up on students regardless of their backgrounds and experiences. Among 355 lesson ideas candidates wrote, a majority reflected that candidates advocated integrating multicultural literature, inviting students to share their cultural and linguistic experiences related to lesson content being taught and engaging students in active participation of lesson activities.

As shown in Figure 8.1, candidates paid special attention to these three areas: home, school, and community connections; literacy learning; and level of variety and engagement (see Table 8.1 for a sample lesson idea). The idea illustrated ways to incorporate a discussion or an appreciation of cultural and linguistic diversity in reading/language arts lessons.

Working With Diverse Children

Working directly with diverse children in classrooms provided candidates with other types of experiences, ones where they directly applied their understanding of diversity issues and explored additional diversity issues. Three candidates I interviewed were two Caucasian females, Sandy and

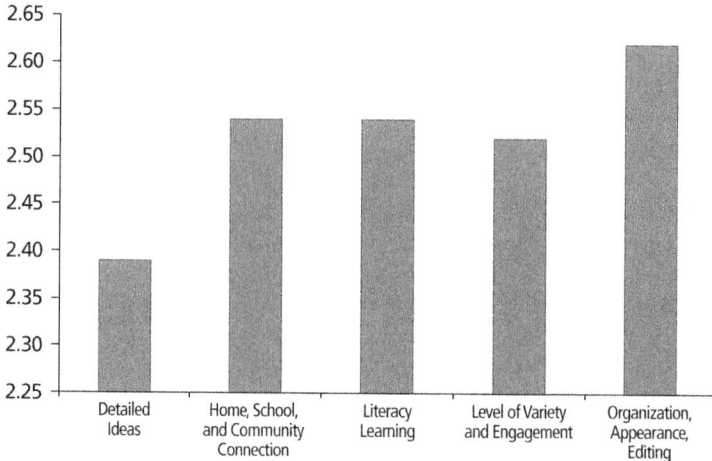

Figure 8.1 Means for different categories on the evaluation rubric for lesson ideas.

Nancy, and one Asian male, Peter. At the time of the interview, Sandy had finished her student teaching at a 3rd-grade and was in a 5th-grade classroom. Nancy continued taking her methods courses (math and science). Peter had already graduated and was working as a teacher in a federally

TABLE 8.1 A Lesson Idea

Lesson Idea	Discussion about Students' Similarities and Differences
Grade Level	3rd Grade
Reading Language Arts Standard	2.2. Ask questions and support answers by connecting prior knowledge with literal information found in, and inferred from, the text
Materials	People by Peter Spier (big book edition), chart paper, paper, pencils, and crayons.
Procedure	Conduct a book walk with the students, in which they must make predictions about the book based on the front and some pictures inside. I will give the students feedback on their predictions. Then, I will read the book aloud to the students. Next, I will lead a class discussion by asking the students various aesthetic questions, such as "What do you think of the book?" "How are people unique?" I will then ask the students, "What is unique about our class and finally, "What is unique about each student." All the students' responses will be recorded on chart paper. Then, individually, each student will draw a picture and write a caption about something that is unique about him or her on a piece of paper. When all the students have completed their drawing and writing, it will be put up in the classroom as a bulletin board to represent all the unique students in the class.

funded migrant education program for 2nd graders on Saturdays and as a substitute teacher in 1st–12th settings.

The lessons of culturally responsive teaching that Sandy, Nancy, and Peter felt successful were those that provided students with hands-on activities and related well to students' prior cultural, linguistic, and academic knowledge and experiences. For a telescope unit for her 3rd-grade students with predominantly Hispanics and Vietnamese, Sandy engaged students not only in reading texts about telescopes, but also in participating in various hands-on activities. She showed a video clip about Galileo and discussed with the class about him, brought to class her own telescope to share with the class, and invited students to share what they have learned on a stargazing night a few days prior to the unit. Additionally, Sandy had her students use art to demonstrate their understanding of visibility of stars during the night time and invisibility of stars during the day time. Finally, the class made a telescope. On reflecting her unit on telescope, Sandy believed in the importance of accessibility:

> Some kids may not have the language skills. So it [the unit] will be more accessible. For those kids who maybe learn better by doing, the *kinesthetic* learners, that was a good activity for them. The kids remember the most is the actual doing.

Similar to Sandy, Peter strived to engage his students in his lessons. Peter's lessons with 2nd graders in the migrant education program focused on academic language. To help his students develop English academic language within a context of Hispanic culture, he chose a book with Spanish phrases, *Skippyjon Jones* (Schachner, 2005). He had his students act out the verbs used in the book and pointed out pictures that represented nouns. As a cumulative activity, each student made a bumblebee out of a construction paper. Students wrote down nouns on the left side of the bee's wing and verbs on the right side of the bee's wing. Peter valued the student learning beyond the classroom, as he encouraged his students to practice using nouns and verbs from the bumblebee's wings outside school.

Like Peter, who incorporated a book to which his students can easily related, Nancy shared her experience of using a multicultural book, *Babies Can't Eat Kimchee* (Patz & Roth, 2002) with four Caucasion students, and one Chinese boy in a kindergarten classroom:

> One little white girl in the group, she loves kimchi and was very excited about the book. The Chinese boy liked to see the image of Asian children. It was not just about being a Korean or anything like that. It is about a little girl who likes fun and annoying her little sister. So the kids ended up talking about their little brothers and sisters, or themselves...they wrote about something they cared, whatever they loved.

Despite the differences in lesson content and grade levels, all three candidates shared some commonalities in terms of culturally responsive teaching: respecting students' prior experience with their culture and language, engaging students in active participation of the lesson activities, and extending the lessons beyond what's required in the curriculum. These commonalities were further reflected in how they defined culturally responsive teaching. Sandy stated, "It is the matter of considering your students' background. It also includes your students' socioeconomic status, and students are not just the ethnicity issue. You have to understand where they come from." She further stressed the importance of valuing other cultures: "Try to bring in a sense of pride of their culture, recognizing their culture is just as valuable." Sandy offered suggestions for other teachers to practice culturally responsive teaching:

> I grew up in a really bad neighborhood. Teachers who do not have this type of experience had a hard time. They do not know how to handle poverty. The only way to make themselves more open to the families [is by] hearing people. I think home surveys are good. Talking to parents is good. Make yourself aware of the community. Go to PTA meetings. Go to parent meetings. Hear about the issues they are dealing with.

Similar to Sandy, Peter placed a heavy emphasis on promoting native and other cultures in his teaching. He explained,

> Culturally responsive teaching is being culturally responsive towards students' cultures. When there is an opportunity, I try to make sure to incorporate every culture and display it in a positive way. Because I believe, number 1 it makes the lesson more interesting. In the classes, I make sure I told my students, one day, you want to visit Mexico, if you take this opportunity to learn about the culture and to appreciate the culture, it is going to be beneficial to you in the long run. And so, in every lesson, I make big efforts try to teach my kids to appreciate their own cultures at the same time.

Unlike Sandy and Peter, Nancy stressed an important role of respecting others' perspectives in culturally responsive teaching. She stated,

> Being culturally responsive means that you do not just stand from one perspective, and then do your lesson planning from the materials. But gauge what your students believe and materials that your kids would enjoy. Also think about developing your kids as global citizens. People need to understand that they have a viewpoint, and other people have viewpoints.

In discussing culturally responsive teaching, Nancy also identified some classroom practices she observed that did not reflect culturally responsive teaching. For example, in a 1st-grade class, the teacher did not allow students to have books on the desk. Nor did the teacher encourage students to make a connection between what they were learning about Native American tribes and the characters they read from the books. Nancy explained,

> They are learning about each tribe [of Native Americans] as people with special abilities to do certain things. They are reading Harry Potter books. There are so many things they were looking at in that class [that] could be related to history or even the language arts in general. I think she does not expect them to connect to what they are reading.

DISCUSSION

In this study, the activities in the ABCs model have enabled candidates to expand and extend what they have learned from a diversity course. Gaining knowledge about others' cultures, languages, experiences, and perspectives *directly* through listening to the firsthand accounts by others (i.e., autobiographies, biographies, and discussions and analyses of similarities and differences) is qualitatively different from learning about diversity from books and lectures. The former provides candidates with concrete, interactive, and reflective experiences. Furthermore, the context of working directly with children and of delivering reading instruction is essential for candidates to explore how diversity issues play various roles in students' learning to read and reading to learn. In such a context, what's a more valuable outcome for candidates is an enhanced aware of various diversity issues beyond what is visible, such as ethnicity and skin color. For example, candidates have now come to understand better how access to or a lack of access to cultural, linguistic, social, and economic capital affects the quality of life and literacy experience.

The ABCs model further bridges candidates' conceptual knowledge about diversity learned from their diversity course and from their peers, and actual teaching reading to diverse students. A series of activities before the candidates formulate their lesson ideas has laid a foundation for them to take into consideration a wide range of diversity issues during planning lesson ideas and working with diverse students. For example, in their lesson ideas, candidates often went beyond just incorporating multicultural literature; they integrated students' prior cultural and linguistic experiences, considered home-school connections, encouraged varied levels of engagement, and offered students opportunities to practice multiple aspects of literacy (e.g., reading, writing, speaking, listening, and arts). In essence, these lesson ideas have been contextualized to capitalize on diverse students' experiences.

Finally, the ABCs model serves as a vehicle for candidates to explore diversity issues within the context of teaching diverse students. The interview data indicate that the more experiences of working with diverse students a candidate has had, the deeper understanding of diversity issues and teaching reading to diverse students the candidate has developed. This finding leads to one instructional implication of this study. It would be beneficial for candidates to experience the ABCs model from the beginning to the end of their teacher preparation program. Such experience would enable candidates to continue expanding and extending their understanding of diversity through fieldwork in different classrooms and developing their ability to teach diverse students in one specific content area. Research with a focus on this type of implementation of the ABCs model is also needed. Some research questions to explore may include (a) How can the implementation of the ABCs model at the different stages of a teacher preparation program benefit candidates? (b) How might such implementation at different stages affect candidates' developing knowledge about diversity and ability to teach? (c) What might be the similarities and differences in the experiences for teacher candidates who are from different ethnic and linguistic backgrounds (e.g., Caucasian candidates vs. Hispanic candidates)?

ACKNOWLEDGEMENT

My deepest gratitude goes to Dr. Patricia Ruggiano Schmidt, Le Moyne College, Syracuse, NY and Dr. Claudia Finkbeiner, University of Kassel, Germany, co-directors of FIPSE-Atlantis Program—*Policy Project on ABCs of Cultural Understanding and Communications*. I thank them for challenging me to explore at a deeper level cultural understanding and communications in my courses and for providing me with valuable opportunities to interact with scholars from the United States and the European Union. I also want to express my appreciation to teacher candidates in this study who helped me gain insights into their perspectives on linguistic, cultural, socioeconomic, and academic diversity and into their developing ability to teach reading in a culturally responsive way. Because of them, I have grown as a literacy teacher educator.

APPENDIX
Guiding Questions for a Literacy Memory

1. When did my literacy experiences occur and where—in or out of school?
2. How did my classroom teachers value and support or did not value and support my cultural heritage and primary language?
3. How was my learning at school connected to my learning out of school?
4. Identify significant positive and negative events. Why were these events positive or negative?
5. Who participated in my literacy development?
6. How did my linguistic, cultural, social, and economic capital allow me to have access to quality education or deny my access to quality education?
7. How did these experiences shape my motivations and goal at the time they occurred?
8. How did my previous experiences influence my understanding of a relationship between cultural and linguistic diversity and literacy development?
9. How did my experiences influence my views on learning and teaching literacy to children with culturally, linguistically, and socioeconomically diverse backgrounds?

REFERENCES

Atwater, M. M., Freeman, T. B., Butler, M. B., & Draper-Morris, J. (2010). A case study of science teacher candidates' understandings and actions related to the culturally responsive teaching of "other" students. *International Journal of Environmental & Science Education, 5,* 287–318.

Cochran-Smith, M., Davis, D., & Fries, M. K. (2004). Multicultural teacher education: Research, practice and policy. In J. A. Banks (Ed.), *Handbook of research on multicultural education* (pp. 931–978). San Francisco, CA: Jossey-Bass.

Darling-Hammond, L. (2010, June 14). Restoring our schools. *Nation,* 14–20.

Finkbeiner, C. (2005). *Interessen und Strategien beim fremdsprachlichen Lesen. Wie Schülerinnen und Schüler englische Texte lesen und verstehen.* Tübingen, Germany: Narr.

Finkbeiner, C. (2006). Constructing third space: The principles of reciprocity and cooperation. In P. Ruggiano Schmidt & C. Finkbeiner (Eds.), *The ABC's of cultural understanding and communication: National and international adaptations* (pp. 19–42). Greenwich, CT: Information Age.

Finkbeiner, C. (2009). Using "human global positioning system" as a navigation tool to the hidden dimension of culture. In A. Feng, M. Byram, & M. Fleming (Eds.), *Becoming interculturally competent through education and training* (pp. 151–173). Bristol, UK: Multilingual Matters.

Finkbeiner, C., & Fehling, S. (2006). Investigating the role of awareness and multiple perspectives for intercultural education. In P. Ruggiano Schmidt & C. Finkbeiner (Eds.), *The ABC's of cultural understanding and communication: National and international adaptations* (pp. 93–110). Greenwich, CT: Information Age.

Gay, G. (2000). *Culturally responsive teaching: Theory, research, and practice.* New York, NY: Teachers College Press.

Guo, Y., Arthur, N., & Lund, D. (2009). Intercultural inquiry with pre-service teachers. *Intercultural Education, 20,* 565–577.

Izzo, A., & Ruggiano Schmidt, P. (2006). A successful ABCs in-service project. In P. R. Schmidt & C. Finkbeiner (Eds.), *The ABC's of cultural understanding and communication: National and international adaptations* (pp. 161–187). Greenwich, CT: Information Age.

Jared, K. (2010). Fostering cross cultural competence in preservice teachers through multicultural education experiences. *Early Childhood Education Journal, 38,* 197–204.

Ladson-Billings, G. (2004). New directions in multicultural education: Complexities, boundaries, and critical race theory. In J. A. Banks & C. A. M. Banks (Eds.), *Handbook of research on multicultural education* (pp. 50–68). San Francisco, CA: Jossey-Bass.

Miles, M. & Huberman, A. (1994). *Qualitative data analysis* (2nd ed.). London, UK: Sage.

Patz, N., & Roth, S. (2006). *Babies can't eat kimchee.* New York, NY: Bloomsbury USA Children's Books.

Ruggiano Schmidt, P. (1999). Know thyself and understand others. *Language Arts, 76,* 332–340.

Ruggiano Schmidt, P. (2001). The power to empower: Creating home/school relationships with the ABCs of cultural understanding and communication. In P. Ruggiano Schmidt & P. B. Mosenthal (Eds.), *Reconceptualizing literacy in the new age of multiculturalism and pluralism* (pp. 389–433). Greenwich, CT: Information Age.

Ruggiano Schmidt, P. (2005). *Preparing educators to communicate and connect with families and communities.* Greenwich, CT: Information Age.

Ruggiano Schmidt, P. & Finkbeiner, C. (Eds.). (2006). *The ABC's of cultural understanding and communication: National and international adaptations.* Greenwich, CT: Information Age.

Schachner, J. (2005). *Skippyjon Jones.* London, UK: Puffin.

Silverman, D. (2006). *Interpreting qualitative data: Methods for analyzing talk, text, and interaction.* Thousand Oaks, CA: SAGE.

Sleeter, C. C. (2001). Preparing teachers for culturally diverse schools: Research and the overwhelming presence of whiteness. *Journal of Teacher Education, 52,* 94–106.

Wilden, E. (2006). The ABCs online: Using voice chats in a trans-national foreign language teacher exchange. In P. Ruggiano Schmidt & C. Finkbeiner (Eds.), *The ABC's of cultural understanding and communication: National and international adaptations* (pp. 189–221). Greenwich, CT: Information Age.

Xu, S. H. (2006). The complexity and multiplicity of pre-service teachers exploring diversity issues. In P. Ruggiano Schmidt & C. Finkbeiner (Eds.), *The ABC's of cultural understanding and communication: National and international adaptations* (pp. 143–160). Greenwich, CT: Information Age.

CHAPTER 9

ABCs AS A TOOL FOR ACTION IN THE WORLD

Ulla Lundgren

INTRODUCTION

How shall I teach intercultural competence in my future classroom?

A core issue for many student teachers who get introduced to a new theoretical concept would be the potential practical implementation of what they are learning at the university. As their instructors, we meet the constant challenge of turning theory into practice. We are reluctant to do it the easy way, that is, to give our students ready-made solutions, because we want them to develop their own ability to critically design their activities and lesson ideas to achieve *action competence* (Jank & Meyer, 2002). Acting is here used in a prescriptive sense and means a politically and pedagogically responsible practice of instructional actions (Jank & Meyer, 2002).

In a short undergraduate course like the one described below there will not be opportunities for students to actually show this competence in a classroom. However, they may be alerted to a prestage progressing the actual classroom practice, the readiness to take pedagogical action. What is referred to in this context is the intentional planning of how to implement *intercultural competence* and *world citizenship* theories with the aim of developing their own

Getting to Know Ourselves and Others Through the ABCs, pages 147–161
Copyright © 2015 by Information Age Publishing
147

students' mindset, which I here call *action readiness* and would like to extend a step further to political *readiness for action in the world.*

In the case of intercultural competence (Byram, 1997, 2008; Stier, 2006), student teachers are not only supposed to develop certain attitudes, knowledge, and skills to be able to act interculturally, they are also expected to find ways to transform their own competences into deliberate pedagogical actions in their future classrooms with the aim of promoting interculturally competent children and young adults. Intercultural competence "is a potential for taking action, for mediating and reflecting the values, beliefs and behaviors of one group to another—and the opportunity for reflexivity, i.e., to critically analyze one's own beliefs and behaviors" (Byram, 2008, p. 228). However, the personal development of intercultural competence is not enough. For a teacher, it should be followed up by professional development leading to action. And true professional development is not possible without personal development.

In this chapter, I will highlight world citizenship education. The concept by no means excludes national citizenship but extends that to include a belonging to the world. This is an old idea already cultivated by the Stoics. It is part of a broad field of adjoining concepts named differently in different contexts and related to liberal arts in the United States (Burrows, 2004; Nussbaum, 1994), intercultural citizenship (Byram, 2008), cosmopolitan citizenship (Osler & Starkey, 2003), internationalization (Stier, 2006), intercultural education, global education and peace education, and so on. (For a discussion of terminology, see Trotta Tuomi, Jacott, & Lundgren, 2008). The aim of world citizenship education is to promote a willingness and capability to act in the world and may be described as follows:

> Students should argue and think critically, take an active role and contribute to the communities in which they participate, recognize the importance of resolving conflicts in a constructive and peaceful way, develop a critical attitude against unequal distribution of development, take into account different perspectives when analyzing and explaining situations and events, understand the world as an interconnected global community and evaluate the possible effects of some actions and decisions taken can have at different levels. (Trotta Tuomi et al., 2008, p. 8)

Readiness for action in the world in this context is closely dependent on the teacher's critical awareness of her own pedagogical objectives, her understanding of why she is using a specific activity/idea in a specific learning situation. Northern European teacher educators argue that *didactic awareness* is vital. The three main questions of Didactics are What? Why? and How? As teacher educators, our mission is to help our students realize that the "How" question could not be answered unless you have answers to the other two. The three questions are inseparable. I am trying to make my students take the initial question of this chapter further to include the following: "What does it imply to teach intercultural competence and extend it to world citizenship?" and "Why should I teach intercultural competence?"

I also want students to be aware of the different discourses underlying these questions. The ABCs model (Ruggiano Schmidt & Finkbeiner, 2006) has been used as a tool to make these issues understandable to a group of student teachers. The model consists of three steps: an autobiography (A) biography (B) and cross-cultural analysis (C 1–2) of your own values and those of the interviewee. In addition to writing your own story and that of a partner followed by an analysis of similarities and differences and reflecting upon your own reactions to these, the students are required to produce lesson activities or ideas (C3)

The aim of this chapter is to describe how the ABCs model was integrated into an undergraduate teacher course and how it shapes teacher candidates' readiness for action in the world within the field of interculturality and world citizenship. The name of the course is Intercultural Encounters. The primary question is How has the ABCs model promoted action readiness for teaching intercultural competence and further world citizenship? Second, how do students view the knowledge gained from this activity? Do they see it as merely fact based and instrumental, or as part of their personal development for understanding others and themselves?

Educational Setting

Intercultural Encounters is a 5-week full-time class (7, 5 ECTs), a module within a full semester (30 ECTs) undergraduate Teacher Education course (Learning 2) at School of Education, Jönköping University, Sweden. The semester is mandatory in teacher education for all students regardless of the age groups they will teach in the future, and it is also given in Swedish with a somewhat different content.

The course objectives of intercultural encounters are

> to equip the students with theoretical and practical tools for personal and professional development of competences demanded for teaching in a multicultural and internationalized society. Such specific competences are the knowledge, skills and attitudes which are required to engage actively with people from other ethnic, cultural, religious and linguistic background. (http://hj.se/download/18.50c4975f12d701edc7a80002775/Learning+2+-+Intercultural+Encounters%2C+7%2C5+ECTS.pdf)

Swedish universities have a great demand for English medium instruction classes to attract students from abroad. Because I had taught a longer course previously designed, "The Intercultural Teacher" (see Lundgren, 2009) and had cultivated a research interest in interculturality for many years, I was fortunate to be given free rein to design the class my way. The class was almost entirely taught by me except for two class sessions that addressed religious values.

As the ABCs have been tried out in two of three cohorts, it has been possible to make some comparisons as to the effect of the model. It was not introduced to the first cohort, as the TRANSABCs project had then not yet started and the model was unknown to me. I am grateful for the opportunity to have taken part in TRANSABCs because, as I will demonstrate, students benefited from its inclusion in the course.

This chapter is based on data from the second and third cohorts with 26 and 28, respectively, students of six nationalities training to become teachers for various age groups within K–12. Table 9.1 shows the distribution of students and countries by cohort.

In addition to the TRANSABCs project, another Atlantis project, CIRT (Consortium for Intercultural Reflective Teachers), was integrated into the course. All the American and British students in the two cohorts and some of the Swedish students participated in the CIRT program. The rest of the Swedish students (two in cohort 2 and five in cohort 3) had chosen to take this class instead of a Swedish medium option within their ordinary teacher education program. The other international students were Erasmus students and exchange students from our non-European partner universities.

The course, Intercultural Encounters, used our university's regular electronic learning platform, PingPong, where the students could find course documents, articles for required reading, and useful links. The students' assignments were submitted there as well as the instructor's comments. The students also used PingPong as a discussion area and a place for anonymous course evaluation.

TABLE 9.1 Participants in the Classes

Cohort 2—26 students	Cohort 3—28 students
Britain (3)	Britain (5)
The Netherlands (3)	The Netherlands (1)
Hungary (1)	Hungary (1)
United States (8)	United States (10)
Spain (3)	Singapore (1)
Sweden (8)	Sweden (10)

Course Content

According to the course syllabus, the course explores the theoretical and practical aspects of intercultural understanding from an international perspective such as

- The concepts of culture, multiculture, interculture, and cultural awareness
- The international and national basis for intercultural education
- Ethnicity and identities
- Attitudes, values, stereotypes, and prejudice
- Intercultural communication
- Brief orientation about world religions and how values/believes influence behavior etc.
- Language and power, bilingualism and language support in schools
- World citizenship education
- Some political, economic, and social issues related to ethnic minorities and refugees in a citizenship perspective
- Cultural similarities and differences
- Theoretical cultural models to analyze cultural differences
- Cultural knowledge to improve classroom learning and communication

The intended learning outcomes of the course Intercultural Encounters are quoted below.

On successful completion of the module, the students will be able to

- demonstrate their understanding of key concepts of the area
- demonstrate respect for otherness
- demonstrate acknowledgement of identities
- demonstrate an ability to recognize different linguistic conventions
- demonstrate an awareness of culture-specific and culture-general knowledge of their own culture and another culture different than their own
- understand several theories related to intercultural competence
- demonstrate the ability to utilize theories to analyze cultural differences
- demonstrate the ability to apply intercultural competence theories in practice by developing practical ideas to implement in the classroom

A detailed schedule was handed out to the students at the course start. Mondays, Wednesdays, and Fridays the students were expected to attend lectures and seminars for three hours in the morning. Both seminars and lectures included interactive activities. In the afternoons and Tuesday and

Thursday mornings there was scheduled work in groups or individually. The group formations varied. The students were alternatively divided into study groups of four students of different nationalities or in pairs according to the nature of the activity/assignments. This was an arrangement to make students meet and work with new people from different cultures. According to one student,

> It was very interactive, especially working within groups. I enjoyed how there was a representative from each country present, and not with people who I would have chosen if I were able to choose. It provided me a chance to meet and make new friends. (anonymous evaluation)

Assignments were submitted individually or in groups, and the presentations were written or oral, sometimes supported by PowerPoint presentations. The ABCs model was the start and the end of the course. Students were encouraged to keep a private diary during the course to collect useful data for their final reflection.

To facilitate the students' intercultural learning process, the course was designed to hold a very structured progression, a variation of numerous individual assignments as well as group activities/assignments in fixed groups. The students were also encouraged to participate actively in classes and group discussions. There was a constant involvement of students' own cultures, as one student observed:

> I truly felt involved in my own learning during this class. I was given the opportunity to participate on many different levels of learning, through essays, oral presentations and tasks. I enjoyed being able to have many discussions with my classmates about the topics brought up in class. It gave me a much broader perspective. (anonymous student evaluation)

In reference to the aim of this chapter, the role of the ABCs and how they were integrated into the course are highlighted in Table 9.2. The students were required to fulfill the following activities and assignments as presented in seminars or submitted on PingPong.

Students' Voices About Lesson Activities (C3)

The empirical data used for this chapter are the two written students assignments, Lesson Activities, C3 (A13) and Final Reflections (A14) as well as the final anonymous course evaluations, all submitted on PingPong by the students. There may seem to be many assignments, but the students did not object, and even an initially critical student changed his mind and saw that they served a purpose:

TABLE 9.2   Assignments from the Course Intercultural Encounters

No	Title	Responsibility	Presentation	Date for presentation	Assessment
A1	Autobiography (A)	Individual	Submitted on PingPong (Pp)	Day 2	Presented according to instructions on PingPong/Contents = pass
A2	This is me	Individual	Presented orally in class and submitted on Pp	Day 4	See above
A3	Biography (B)	Individually	Submitted on Pp	Day 5	See above
A4	Values in education	In study groups	Seminar Submitted on Pp	Day 8	See above
A5	Mini ethnography	In study groups	Submitted on Pp	Day 9	See above
A6	Ethnic minorities	In groups	Seminar Submitted on Pp	Day 12	See above
A7	Cross-cultural analysis(C1 and C2)	Individuallly	Submitted on Pp	Day 16	Graded
A8	Intercultural communication	In study groups	Seminar Submitted on Pp	Day 17	See above
A9	World religions I	In groups	Seminar Oral presentation	Day 22	See above
A10	Field study in schools	In groups	Seminar Oral presentation	Day 19	See above
A11	World religions II	Individually	Submitted individually on Pp	Day 30	Graded
A12	World Citizenship Education	In groups	Submitted on Pp	Day 23	See above
A13	Lesson activities (C3)	Individually and in study groups	Discussed in groups and submitted individually on Pp Seminar	Day 31	Graded
A14	Reflection on cultural encounters as a learning process	Individually	Submitted individually on Pp	Day 36	Graded
A15	Course Evaluation	Individually	Submitted individually on Pp	Day 36	See above

Now that I have the whole picture and can look back at what we have done it feels like everything has been for a purpose. And I do not think that any of the assignments could be taken out of the course, because they all have their specific purpose. This purpose could be that we should learn new things, or merely that we as small groups with students from different countries should sit down and discuss in order to be more aware that the view we have as individuals might not be the view that a person from a different country has. (015 SEm)

Due to limited space in this chapter, only Assignment 13 is described in detail as the focus here is the ABCs activity C3 (Ruggiano Schmidt & Finkbeiner, 2006), which focuses on generating curriculum ideas based on cross-cultural comparisons between themselves and those they interviewed. However, the learning progression is specifically outlined according to the learning theories of the course Intercultural Encounters

Assignment 13

The aim was to promote the ability to apply intercultural competence theories in practice by developing practical ideas to implement in the classroom in interaction with colleagues.

The following instructions were given:

- Step A)—Individually (Day 24)
  Develop a minimum of five culturally responsive ideas for lesson activities that you would consider relevant for your future profession. Draw a potential educational context as an introduction (age group, subject, social, ethnic, religious, linguistic diversity, etc.).
    Study the rubric [see Table 9.3] below and try to meet with as many requests as possible.
    You are free to adapt your activity from any source, but do not just copy ideas straight off unless they really fit in with your very context. The point is that the lesson activity should be meaningful to your group of students in the specific setting that you teach.
- Step B)–In groups (Day 25)
  Present your ideas to your study group. Have all of the group's activity ideas discussed and peer reviewed according to the rubric. The group is a team who wants to support its members. Help each other to improve and further develop the ideas.
- Step C) Individually (Day 29)
  Be prepared to present one of your revised ideas (preferably your favorite one or one of your favorite ones) in seminar.
- Step D) Individually (Day 31)
  Write up your five revised ideas (do not forget the introduction to your educational context and post them on PingPong).

Use course literature, any additional literature and the Internet. This assignment is graded according to the rubric below [See Table 9.3].

TABLE 9.3 Rubric for Culturally Responsive Lesson Ideas/Activities for School

	A. Information and Organization	B. Connecting School to Home and/or Community	C. Critical Literacy Learning	D. Creativity and Contextual Adaptation	E. Theory Based	F. Level of Variety and Engagement
3	The idea/activity has necessary information for lesson implementation and perfect organization.	Obvious connections exist between the content area and ethnic, linguistic, and/or cultural diversity.	A critical literacy (in a broad sense) connection is highly present in the implementation of this idea/activity.	The idea/activity shows great creativity and contextual adaptation from the original source, which is stated as a reference.	The idea/activity has an analytic approach in connecting practice with theory.	The idea/activity demonstrates great variety compared to the student's other ideas and student active involvement.
2	The idea/activity has some, but not adequate information necessary for lesson implementation and the organization is difficult to follow.	Some connections exist between the content area and ethnic, linguistic, and/or cultural diversity.	A critical literacy connection is present in the lesson idea/activity.	The idea/activity has been copied from a stated source and inadequately adapted to the given educational context.	The idea/activity shows some theoretical awareness and connection to theory.	The idea/activity has little variety compared to the teacher student's other ideas and little active student involvement.
1	Only the idea is presented	The idea/activity does not demonstrate clear connections between the content area and ethnic, linguistic, and/or cultural diversity.	A literacy connection is vaguely present in the idea/activity.	The idea/activity has just been copied and no source is referred to and it has no relevance to the educational context given.	The idea/activity lacks theoretical connection.	The idea/activity lacks motivational strategies since it incorporates repetitious activities with little student involvement.

Findings

At the introduction of the course, sociocultural theories of learning and dialogism were introduced (among others, Dysthe, 2002; Vygotsky, 1962) to promote learning strategies for active participation and cooperative learning. The students learned that social mediation, sharing with others, getting reactions, and discussing what you understand and do not understand all are activities that mediate learning.

The actual course was designed to apply these theories in practice for the students' experiential learning. In short, they learned that learning is developed in social action. The relationship between social and individual learning became obvious through activities and assignments. According to students,

> Most of the activities (as the essays or the problem solving tasks) required debate, self-reflection and opinions sharing which is always a good way to learn about the topic, analyse it from many perspectives, understand what your classmates believe and to make your learning process attractive and to grow your knowledge (anonymous student evaluation). I think that the course was centered on student active learning. Everything that we did we were a part of and discussed what we thought and believed and we furthered our own knowledge by being active learners. (anonymous student evaluation).

To many of the international students, this was a new way of approaching academic studies.

The response to the course was very positive. As the ABCs was the core of it and the skeleton around which almost all the theory and practice was connected, I am inclined to give the credit to the model. The importance of the ABCs model for the course and the philosophy behind the model is obvious to the following student.

> The ABCs was the first thing we started with in this course and it did just end right before this assignment. It has been something that has been able to develop in the same time as our learning process concerning intercultural encounters. This has been the work which has tied me to the course and the course literature most personally since it involved a closer look at myself and my life. I must say that it has been an important part of the learning process and that the quote showed in the beginning when we talked about ABCs was something I got to understand the true meaning of: "*know thyself & understand others.*" (008 SEf)

Learning about yourself through others resonated with other students, such as the next informant :

ABCs helped me understand not only that there are differences, but also similarities that we can use in a classroom. We can use stereotypes and prejudice
to show that they are most likely misleading us, and that there is much more
to a person than what you first see ("Top of the iceberg"). Understanding
your own way of looking at the world, and share it with others, helps us realize that even though we are different we are very much alike. I have learned
much about not only myself, but others as well. It was an eye opener to the
fact that we are just the same, only in different "packages." Underneath the
surface, we share the same feelings, though they might occur in different
situations due to cultural differences or habits or environmental differences.
I found a new way of understanding people around me . . . ! through looking
at my own life and life experiences . . . very developing! (109 SEf)

By being personally involved in the various stages of the ABCs model
(autobiography, biography, and cross-cultural analysis), students began to
grasp the meaning of *intercultural competence*.

The ABCs project also gave me a better understanding of intercultural competence theories. Before the ABCs project I thought that intercultural competence was just when somebody knew that other cultures existed and that
people were also tolerant of these other cultures and other people's differences. In this course, I learned that my idea of just knowing that other cultures exist and being able to pick out similarities and differences is just known
as "content competency" which is a "a one-dimensional" or static character
and refers to the *knowing that-aspects* of both the "other" and the "home culture" (Stier, 2006, p. 6). After the assignment, I realized that there is much
more to intercultural competence then just knowing that other cultures exist
and being tolerant of them. (021 USf)

The female student quoted above had internalized (Vygotsky, 1962) Byram's and Stier's theories of intercultural competence and they had become personal knowledge to the student.

Data collected indicate that all the learning outcomes were met if not by
every student but by most of them.

The requirement to transform theory to practice gave the students new
insights that a teacher's role is also to promote personal development:

I think that the course was something that will benefit me in the future. It
gave a whole new way of thinking about what to teach and how to have an
open mind and not judge people right away. (anonymous evaluation)

This course has been very developing on a personal level and I would really
like to do something similar with my own students in the future. It has been
hard and tough, no point denying that. It forces you to develop on a personal
level more than any ordinary class at university has done so far. The other

ones are more about theoretical knowledge, but this course has involved that but also a personal level. (011 SEf)

Many students realized that the intercultural perspective can be brought into all subjects and is a benefit to developing a good classroom atmosphere:

> Thinking of lesson plans let me reflect on what I know, what I want my students to know, and the lens with which I have the ability to teach. After taking this course, I think that my lens has become much less narrow and I want to bring that same experience to my students as well. I also learned that whether you have a specific subject titles "world citizenship" or "citizenship education" or just plain "social studies," teachers can find links to bring intercultural competence to all subjects whether it be literature, art, music, physical education or any other subject in school. There are links in just about every subject. Intercultural Encounters has taught me that intercultural competence is important to understand others and your own culture as well. Also, that for teachers especially, intercultural competence can help make students feel welcome in the classroom, make students feel valued, give students a wider view of the world and even make the classroom atmosphere more accepting and respectful if differences are explored and made familiar. (021 USf)

Students also enjoyed the process of using their knowledge of intercultural competence to create lessons activities:

> The last step of the ABCs was to make lesson activities and this was the thing I enjoyed the most during this course. Finally I was allowed to creative [*sic*] something "useful" from what I learned and I really had a lot of fun while trying to involve as many different aspects of intercultural competence as I possibly could. I would think, now in hindsight, that it was respect for otherness that I wanted to have as my outcome of the lessons. I want my students have curiosity and openness and to believe in other cultures as in their own, which is close to how Byram puts it (Handout, 1/26/2010). I do look forward to the day when I actually can put these activities into practise and see if they worked as I have planned. (008 SEf)

A group of three Erasmus students had to go home before the course finished and developed all their lesson activities together back home in Spain and submitted all their ideas collectively. They realized that fulfilling the assignment according to the rubric was a way of rehearsing the course and implementing intercultural theories by practicing learning theories.

> I would like to comment about the planning of lesson activities. At first, I thought it would be an easy activity because we had a lot of theoretical basis and enough knowledge to plan culturally and responsible activities, relevant for my future profession and also for the kids to be aware of the importance of

intercultural encounters. However, when my group and me started planning the activities we realize that doing this paper work in a properly way would take a lot of time. Adapting fifteen activities to the context of the class with all the diversity in it was not a simple thing to do. Furthermore, I would like to say that doing this activity was useful to be aware of what we had learned during the course and it was a good way to put it on practise. Another positive aspect on that activity was that we were working cooperatively helping each other and trying to improve our activities all the time. In my opinion, this is one of the best ways to work because it give you the other's perspective and point of view and you are able to listen to it, think about it, make a reflection and change it. (019 ESf)

The students of the two classes supplied well over 250 lesson ideas together. All of them are good and a considerable number are very good, based on the assessment categories described in the rubric. Had the students been allowed more time for their learning process they would have met the requirements to an even deeper level. The rubric (Table 9.3) has been a great help to them to become aware of what is expected and at the same time it was of great value to my ability to assess their performance.

DISCUSSION

In this chapter, I have illustrated how the ABCs model has supported the aim of involving international students and their various cultures as a resource leading to action. Students' knowledge, attitudes, skills, and critical cultural awareness (Byram) were developed. The students have in many respects fulfilled the aims of world citizenship education as they are stated in the introduction of this chapter. That is obvious in their lesson ideas and reflections The ABCs combine in a fruitful way intrapersonal and interpersonal communication. The dialectics between meeting other cultures and reflecting on your own through the hands-on activities of the ABCs has led preservice teachers to a critical awareness that is a vital component of cultural competence. Consequently, their lesson ideas mostly contained a critical component, proving that they had realized that intercultural competence is not knowledge that can be transferred but has to be personally internalized. Their lesson activities show a clear ambition to work toward developing the mindsets of their own future students to take action in the world as they themselves have experienced not only cognitive development but also emotional development.

A critical remark looking back at the use of the ABCs concerns time. I believe the ABCs project requires at least 10 weeks to allow students the chance to dig deeper into the theoretical roots of identity and connecting those to the model. I also see the possibilities to use ABCs in a similar course at the master's level.

From another critical point of view, one could ask, How reliable are the data used in this chapter? The statements are taken from the students' reflections, which were graded assignments. It is possible that students could have simply delivered the reflections and comments that they thought they were expected to according to course objectives. While this is possible, the anonymous course evaluation speaks against it, though.

When the ABCs model had been included into the second and third courses, earlier criticism from the first cohort about lacking personal involvement and practical implications were no longer valid. Some comments from the first class were "Too much theory not real life." "I think we should focus more on practical things—i.e., how to teach about intercultural relations within a class. The course was rather theoretical and I am not sure how I will present knowledge from lessons once I am a teacher." In my opinion, this change for the better is very much thanks to the introduction of the ABCs model. Naturally a course would improve by being repeated and some revisions have helped, for example, a much more structured progression. But the fact that the ABCs model was very deliberately integrated into the course structure for the second and third cohort made the students aware of a continuous progression of their own personal development, and this type of development is necessary for professional action.

My two courses including ABCs have generated a lot of data of which only a small amount has been used in this chapter. Further research on the lesson activities, on identity formation, and on critical cultural awareness will bring light to the model and help to improve it for future generations of teachers and students to take action in the world.

CONCLUSION

The integration of ABCs model has been a great benefit to the course Intercultural Encounters and it promoted pedagogical and political action readiness for teaching intercultural competence and world citizenship education, not as something fact based and instrumental but as a personal development of understanding of self and others. I would, however, like to stress that the ABCs project is a mere model. To be able to fully make use of it in a course like the one described in this chapter, the model has to be anchored in theories on interculturality and in learning theories. The students must be given frequent opportunities to work at and process what they are learning through interaction with peers and instructors as well as within their own mind through dialog and reflection to promote understanding of self and others. They should be offered an experiential learning experience.

Finally, I would like to return to the initial question of this chapter, but slightly rephrased: How could the students in my future classroom learn about intercultural competence? Elsewhere (Lundgren, 2009) I have argued that intercultural competence cannot be taught—it can only be learned. One answer might be, Give students the opportunity to "live" the ABCs model, which most likely will lead to some personal development toward action in the world.

REFERENCES

Burrows, D. (2004). Proceedings from the American Council on Education Regional Conference on New Directions in International Education: *World Citizenship*. Beloit, WI: Retrieved from http://www.pkal.org/documents/World Citizenship.cfm

Byram, M. (1997). *Teaching and assessing intercultural competence*. Clevedon, UK: Multilingual Matters.

Byram, M. (2008). *From foreign language education to intercultural citizenship: Essays and reflections*. Clevedon, UK: Multilingual Matters.

Dysthe, O. (2002). The learning potential of a web-mediated discussion in a university course. *Studies in Higher Education, 27*(3), 339–352.

Jank, W., & Meyer, H. (2002). *Ditaktische Modelle*. Berlin, Germany: Cornelsen Scriptor.

Lundgren, U. (2009). Intercultural teacher. In A. Feng, M. Byram, & M. Fleming (Eds.), *Becoming interculturally competent through education and training*. Clevedon, UK: Multilingual Matters.

Nussbaum, M. (1994). Patriotism and cosmopolitanism. *Boston Review, 19*(5), 3–34.

Osler, A., & Starkey, H. (2003). Learning for cosmopolitan citizenship: Theoretical debates and young people's experiences. *Educational Review, 55*(3), 243–254.

Ruggiano Schmidt, P. & Finkbeiner, C. (Eds.). (2006). *ABC's of cultural understanding and communication: National and international adaptations*. Greenwich, CT: Information Age.

Stier, J. (2006). Internationalisation, intercultural communication and intercultural competence. *Journal of Intercultural Communication, 11*(1), 1–12.

Trotta Tuomi, M., Jacott, L., & Lundgren, U. (2008). *Education for world citizenship: Preparing students to be agents of social change*. London, UK: CiCe Guidelines.

Vygotsky, L (1962). *Thought and language*. Cambridge, MA: MIT Press.

CHAPTER 10

INCREASING TEACHER UNDERSTANDING OF DIFFERENT CULTURES THROUGH THE ABCs

Jiening Ruan

INTRODUCTION

America has witnessed a dramatic change in the ethnic composition of its population over the last few decades. Schools and teachers across the country are facing the challenge of educating an increasingly diverse student body (Nieto, 2010). However, America's teaching force is still mainly composed of white middle-class teachers. Many of these teachers have limited knowledge and understanding of the cultures of their students, and the cultural gap between teachers and students from diverse backgrounds is large and growing (Sleeter, 2001). Accompanying this trend, the achievement gap between white students and minority students continues to widen (Au, 2011; Nieto, 2010).

The southern state where the study took place has seen a large influx of minority students in recent years, especially students from Spanish-speaking countries. The academic performance of students from diverse

Getting to Know Ourselves and Others Through the ABCs, pages 163–179
Copyright © 2015 by Information Age Publishing
163

TABLE 10.1   Percentage of High School Graduates Meeting College Readiness Criteria in 2010

Subject	All	African American	Native American/ Alaska Native	Caucasian/White	Hispanic
English	67	37	60	74	48
Math	34	10	24	39	21
Reading	52	25	46	59	35
Science	25	7	19	30	14

cultural groups in the state consistently lags behind their white counterparts. The 2010 ACT report (n.d.) on college readiness for students in the state clearly shows a large divide between white and most minority students. In particular, students from African American, Native American/Alaska Native, and Hispanic backgrounds performed significantly below the state average in all subject matters. Table 10.1 displays the percentage of high school graduates who met the criteria for college readiness from four ethnic groups in the state. While the percentage of white high school graduates who met ACT's college readiness criteria is 74%, 39%, 59%, 30% in English, Math, Reading and Science, respectibvely, the percentage of minority students who were ready for college in the four subject areas is much lower.

Need for the Study

According to the 2011 school data provided by the state's Accountability Office, 89.1% of the teaching force in the state consists of white, primarily monolingual teachers. The rapid change in student population does not seem to have triggered a significant change in the ways schools and teachers educate culturally diverse students either. In particular, under the pressure of the current school accountability movement, in many schools across the state, teaching is heavily skills-focused, aiming at helping students pass the state tests. Limited attention is paid to providing culturally diverse students with teaching that is culturally responsive in order to narrow the achievement gap (Au, 2011).

Most teacher candidates enrolled in the teacher education programs in the state came from predominantly white, middle-class communities, a pattern that exists in many other teacher education programs across the nation (Ladson-Billings, 2000; Nieto, 2002). These teacher candidates have had limited interaction with people from different cultural backgrounds, and many lacked adequate understanding of their own cultures and of other cultures (Ladson-Billings, 2000; Nieto, 2002; Ruggiano Schmidt, 1998; Sleeter, 2001). While no significant increase in the number of minority teachers is likely in the near future, it is critical that teacher education programs provide teacher candidates with learning experiences that promote understanding of different cultures and help them develop intercultural awareness and competence so that they can become culturally responsive teachers after they complete the teacher education program. There is also a need for research that explores instructional practices that are effective for supporting preservice and in-service teachers in becoming more culturally aware and interculturally competent.

Theoretical Framework

This study is grounded in the socioconstructivist theory of learning and the theory of culturally responsive teaching. The socioconstructivist theory of learning proposes that human learning is socially constructed and culturally mediated (Vygotsky, 1962). It is conditioned and shaped by socioculturally specific understandings, practices, and experiences (Bruner, 1996; Ladson-Billings, 1994, 2001; Nieto, 2002; Vygotsky, 1962). We acquire valuable knowledge and perspectives about a different culture when we interact with people from that particular cultural background. People from other cultures can serve as more knowledgeable others in our effort to gain insight into their cultures. Such insight allows us to develop clarity about our own culture (Ruggiano Schmidt, 1998).

The many worlds (i.e., home, family, school, neighborhood, and community) that a child lives in constantly interact to shape the child's learning experience and academic performance (Edwards, Danridge, McMillon, & Pleasants, 2001). Limited understanding of students' cultures and unexamined stereotypes of diverse cultural groups often creates misunderstandings and tensions between culturally different teachers and parents. Cultural mismatch between teachers and students/parents often produces a disconnect between curriculum, teaching, and student learning, which can translate to low academic performance of students from culturally diverse backgrounds (Au, 2011). Effective teachers of diverse learners are keenly aware of the cultures of their students and work hard to provide them with culturally meaningful learning experiences.

Culturally responsive teaching or culturally relevant teaching (Au, 2001, 2011; Gay, 2000, 2001; Ladson-Billings, 1994, 2001; Ruggiano Schmidt & Ma, 2006) calls for the use of the cultural characteristics, experiences, and perspectives of diverse students in curriculum development and instruction. It emphasizes the importance of valuing the knowledge, experiences, and discourse patterns (Au, 2011; Moll, Amanti, Neff, & Gonzales, 1992) that culturally diverse students bring to the classroom, and of situating academic knowledge and skills within the lived experiences of all students to make learning meaningful and relevant (Au, 2011). Culturally responsive teachers understand that incongruence or incompatibility (Au, 1983) between school and home and community often leads to low academic achievement of students of diverse backgrounds, and they purposefully connect school knowledge with home and community experiences to support student learning. However, in reality, many teachers of diverse students have limited intercultural awareness and competence. As a result, their insensitivity to cultural influences on student learning makes it difficult for them to connect home and school and to provide meaningful learning experiences.

For teachers to implement culturally responsive teaching, they have to be interculturally competent. According to Finkbeiner and Fehling (2006), intercultural competence is "the ability to change perspectives and develop a meta-cognitive awareness with respect to both language and culture" (p. 94). Some essential components of intercultural competence include attitudes that relativize self and value others, knowledge of one's own and others' cultures, and skills to interpret and relate to others' cultures and to discover and/or interact with other cultures (Byram, 1997). To be interculturally competent, one needs to acquire "cultural sensitivity, cultural awareness, and empathy, as well as the ability to change perspectives and put oneself into the other person's shoes" (Finkbeiner, 2006). The process of gaining cultural competence starts with gaining understanding of one's own culture. Only when teacher candidates realize how their own cultural experiences shape their identity can they start to be sensitive to their students' cultural experiences. Developing knowledge of themselves as well as of their students, parents, and communities help them make home-school connections in their curriculum and instruction (Banks et al., 2005).

The concept of the "human global positioning system" (Finkbeiner, 2009, p. 151) is of particular relevance to the development of intercultural competence. Using people from other cultural backgrounds as valuable sources of cultural data, we can more accurately locate and position ourselves and others in the multicultural terrain that we travel. Human GPS has the power to assist us in successfully navigating across various cultural boundaries.

The ABCs of Cultural Understanding and Communication is a model developed by Patricia Ruggiano Schmidt to help preserve and in-service teachers in teacher education programs to "become culturally sensitive so that they might begin to think about ways to communicate and connect with students and families from minority populations" (Ruggiano Schmidt, 1998, p. 28). The main components of the approach have already been presented in this book. They include the following: A—Autobiography of self, B—Biography of other, and C—Cross-cultural analysis of similarities and differences of self and other, cultural analysis of differences between self and other, and communication plans for home-school connections.

Existing research investigating the effectiveness of the ABCs suggests that the ABCs model has led to preservice and in-service teachers' increased awareness of the self and other, that is, of their own cultures and those of their interviewees. They gained appreciation for cultural differences; realized the importance of connecting home, community, and school in present and future classrooms; and started to make successful efforts to establish the connections in their teaching (Ruggiano Schmidt, 1998; Xu, 2000). Finkbeiner and her colleagues in Europe (Finkbeiner, 2006, 2009; Finkbeiner & Fehling, 2006) adapted the model to fit the European context, and their research further contributed to our understanding of the power of the ABCs. By engaging in the ABCs, the participants were able to gain multiple perspectives about themselves and others and an awareness of different world views (Finkbeiner, 2009; Finkbeiner & Fehling, 2006). Furthermore, working with each other, they were also able to co-construct a new "Third Space," which is "a new mental and emotional zone" (Finkbeiner, 2006, p. 29) that connects two cultures and allows them to question their own existing beliefs, values, and feelings about themselves and others. They also co-constructed their identities together through the process of reciprocity and cooperation.

In a previous multicultural education course I taught, I implemented an abbreviated version of the ABCs model involving the writing of autobiography, biography, and analysis of similarities and differences. Informal feedback from some students in the course indicated that the activity was effective in prompting them to reflect on their own cultures and that of their interviewee, gaining in the process a greater understanding of themselves and their interviewee. This mixed-method study is an effort to systematically investigate the impact of the ABCs model on teachers' understanding of diversity issues in the context of a teacher education program that served primarily white middle-class teachers in a southwestern state in the United States.

METHOD

Participants

The participants in this study were students enrolled in a graduate-level multicultural education course that aims at developing an expanded understanding of different cultures. This course is a core course required by the program for all master's and doctoral teacher education candidates. The two main goals of the course were to (a) help students develop a better understanding of different cultures and the challenges and benefits of cultural diversity, and (b) to provide students with the background knowledge, understandings, and techniques to work effectively with learners from diverse cultural and ethnic backgrounds. This course provided a variety of readings and learning activities targeting the two goals, and the ABCs was one of the key activities that the teacher candidates were expected to complete.

Most of the graduate students in the course were in-service teachers in public K–12 schools, college teachers at regional universities or colleges, or someone who held an education-related job. Seventeen out of the 18 teacher candidates in the course volunteered to participate in the study. Six in-service educators were chosen through purposeful sampling to provide further data on the impact of the ABCs on their learning and understanding of different cultures. The criteria stipulated that participants were currently teaching and that they agreed to be interviewed.

The six informants covered a wide spectrum of subject areas and learner levels. Megan and Susan were both teacher educators. Megan was teaching math education majors at a local university, and Susan was teaching physical education to education majors at a different university. Shelby was a high school English teacher with many years of teaching experience. Kay was a 2nd-grade teacher, while Linda was a reading specialist at a local middle school. Samantha was an instructional coach who worked with teachers around the state to help them improve technology integration in teaching different school subjects.

Implementation of the Study

I followed the original protocol developed by Ruggiano Schmidt (1998) as closely as possible. First, the candidates reflected on their own cultural experiences and wrote an autobiography. Second, they interviewed a culturally different person and wrote a biography. Third, they compared and contrasted the two cultures, analyzed the differences, and developed lesson plans to connect home, community, and school.

I made two adaptations to the original model. First, I allowed the participants to share their own autobiographies and their interviewee's biographies in order to add to the richness of this ABCs experience. I instructed the class to only share the parts of the autobiography or biography that they felt comfortable sharing. The decision of what and how much to share belonged to the participants. The added dimension to the original model allows the participants to be exposed to not only the culture of their interviewee but to multiple cultures, perspectives, and viewpoints from a larger group of culturally diverse people. The second modification involved the sharing of the culturally responsive lesson plans. I held a multicultural idea fair, and the participants shared their lesson plans with the rest of the class in an interactive manner. The participants were also asked to complete pre- and postpolarity profile surveys, and pre- and postculture surveys. All participants completed all steps of the model, and the whole duration of the project took about 2 months.

Instruments and Procedures

In this mixed-methods study, I collected and analyzed quantitative data and qualitative data. Quantitative datasets include a polarity profile survey that examines participants' perceptions of the ABCs model and a culture survey that measures participants' understanding of diversity-related issues. Both instruments were administered at the beginning and end of the ABCs project.

Qualitative data include the cross-cultural analyses of cultural similarities and differences in a chart form, cultural analyses of differences papers completed by the participants, face-to-face interview data collected from the six interviewees through purposeful sampling, and final reflections written by all participants regarding the ABCs and other aspects of the course. Culturally responsive lesson plans developed by the participants were also collected to find out if they were able to effectively connect home, community, and school when planning for instruction.

For quantitative data, I conducted paired t-tests to find out if there was any statistically significant difference between participants' pre- and post-answers to the culture-related constructs measured in the pre- and post-culture surveys and their emotions and perceptions about the project.

Qualitative data analysis focused on the impact of the ABCs on participants' understanding of culture- and diversity-related issues. Content analysis (Patton, 1990) was used to analyze the qualitative data (cross-cultural analysis charts, cultural analyses of differences papers, interview transcripts, and course reflections) in this study. Using an open coding procedure, I identified prominent concepts or codes that surfaced in the charts, papers, transcripts, and reflections. Then I reread the data until all potential concepts were identified and no new ones could be found. Afterwards, I grouped similar concepts into larger concept categories.

Afterwards, axial coding was applied to find relationships among the concepts and to form themes (Strauss & Corbin, 1998). For example, the theme of taking action was developed based on the various forms of actions, such as actively challenging family members about their biases and prejudices against other cultural groups, educating fellow teachers about the importance of culturally responsive teaching to student learning, and sharing multicultural materials and culturally responsive teaching ideas with their fellow teachers after the ABCs experience. Each theme was tested against all the data for triangulation and was refined continuously throughout the recursive process of data analysis. Even though multiple themes emerged through the iterative process of data analysis, only the six most prominent themes were kept and reported in this chapter. Finally, representative data clips, from which the themes derived, were selected to illustrate the themes.

RESULTS

I did not find a statistically significant difference in participants' perception of the ABCs, based on the results of the pre- and postpolarity surveys. One construct measured in the culture survey produced a statistically significant difference. On the question, "All people should be able to speak more than one language," the change was statistically significant, indicating that the participants were more in favor of bilingualism ($t = 3.14$, $df = 22$, $p = 0.0048$) after their participation in the ABCs project.

Qualitative data supported this finding. In the analyses of cultural differences, seven participants whose interviewees spoke two languages specifically commented that knowing an additional language is an asset, and they expressed envy or admiration of their interviewees who were bilingual. In a state where the English-only sentiment is strong and culturally and linguistically diverse children are forbidden to speak their native tongue in many schools and classrooms, this finding is quite noteworthy.

One reason why I was unable to find statistical significance in the rest of the survey is because of the small sample size ($N = 17$); the limited number of participants made it more challenging to detect significance among the remaining survey items. Regarding the polarity profile, the fact that the ABCs model did not change significantly could be a result of participants' initial positive reaction to the description of the model, a reaction that remained positive at the conclusion of the project.

Several themes emerged from the analyses of qualitative data, and they are related to what the participants learned from doing the project and the impact of the project on their understanding of different cultures.

The Participants Developed a Greater Understanding of Their Own Cultures

Several teacher participants were excited to discover for the first time that, just like their culturally diverse interviewees, they too had a unique culture of their own. In her reflection, Susan wrote, "I feel I've probably changed the most in respecting and allowing that I do have a family culture. This was something I never thought about too much but now I realize I have a rich family culture."

Such a sentiment also echoed Jane's reflection that "I changed what I think about having vs. not having a culture. Never realized that I actually have a culture." Kay also had the misconception about what culture meant to her before her participation in the ABCs. While doing the project, it dawned on her that she has a culture too. In her words, "culture is not just exotic ethnicities but the way you were raised, family values." The participants' perception of what culture is changed due to their participation in this project. They realized that culture is not something exotic but a part of their very existence. In addition, they no longer regarded culture as a unidimensional concept. Instead, they began to view culture as complex and multidimensional. They understood that culture is more than ethnicity. Social economic status, gender, physical conditions, language spoken, and one's education all contribute to one's cultural identity. Through the ABCs, the participants gained a stronger sense of awareness of who they are as cultural beings.

The Participants Became Metacognitive of Self and Other

Findings also suggest that the ABCs pushed the teacher participants to engage in critical reflection on their own culture and the culture of others and to reexamine their preconceived notions of who they are and who others are. Linda described the process of the ABCs as "a self-reflective, metacognitive act, analyzing my own beliefs and understandings and comparing that to someone else's, seeing how similar or how different you are, but in unexpected ways."

Belinda contributed her growth in this area to the ABCs and said, "My largest area of growth has been examining myself fully, especially through the ABCs. I feel like I have learned a lot about myself." Jane made a similar assessment of her growth in her reflection by saying, "As far as growth, I have grown a lot! I have been able to respect other people's ideas/thoughts. I can also critically think about my ideas and thoughts." Megan contributed that she had an increased understanding and respect for people from other cultures as a result of the ABCs.

Before the experience, the participants tended to focus on similarities and had difficulty identifying differences. By doing the ABCs, the participants came to understand the importance of not only finding cultural similarities but also differences. Susan said,

> I think I really like to find the likeness but then I really need to respect the difference and value that. And so I caught myself too many times going [sic]

that we are so much alike, but then realizing that that somewhat was devaluing the importance of her culture or the differences she has.

Like many other participants, Shelby had difficulty with identifying cultural differences at the beginning of the experience, but she was able to overcome such difficulty by the end of the project. Her comments demonstrate the shift in her thinking about the similarities and differences.

> Differences can become contentious areas between two cultures, but they can also be seen as opportunities for learning about each other. While some of the differences make me uncomfortable even to the point of feeling ostracized, there are other aspects of the Hispanic culture that I admire and even envy. Just the awareness that differences exist and are not barriers among people will aid in bridging the gaps among groups and help to conquer the unknown.

The Participants Examined Personal Hidden Biases and Stereotypes

By doing the ABCs, many participants uncovered their own hidden biases and stereotypes. Megan acknowledged that the ABCs helped her realize her prior biases and prejudice against persons from diverse backgrounds. She said, "Cause [sic] you realize that you do have prejudices. You think you don't, but everybody does, and everybody has these preconceived notions."

After working with his African American interviewee on this project, Jake acknowledged that some of his existing views about African Americans were stereotypical and problematic. In his analyses of cultural differences paper, he wrote, "However, Vera did not by any means meet this stereotype. She is a nice, well-educated, African American woman who admits she has Republican values, but certainly does not 'cling to guns and religion.'" While Jake was still not stereotype-free, he was able to more clearly identify his stereotyped views of African Americans as people who tend to be poor, less well-educated, and who are Democrats. Vera also challenged his stereotypical view of Republicans as people who are "gun enthusiasts" and religious.

Awareness of personal biases and stereotypes led to changes in perspectives. Valuing and respecting the cultures of self and other frequently surfaced in the participants' reflections and papers. Chou, a Chinese American, found that she was more open-minded and developed more respect for others who are different culturally.

> I learned to be more respect(ful) to people from other cultures, including those who are disabled or homosexual. I don't look at them as a special group of people now. I know except for one aspect of their appearance, they are the same as me.

Megan also described how the ABCs changed her perspectives, pointing out that now she was able to respect and value her own and others' experiences, beliefs, and feelings.

Changes also occurred in attitudes toward culture in general. Samantha talked about the liberating effect of the ABCs. In her words,

> I am not scared of culture anymore. Having the chance to talk to people from so many different backgrounds has allowed me to overcome my fear of asking "silly" questions; I liberated myself by talking for the first time openly [about myself].

The Participants Gained Greater Awareness of Issues of Social Justice

The participants realized that they carried an invisible cultural knapsack and took for granted privileges that people from different cultural backgrounds did not have. Hearing about the ways in which her interviewee was discriminated against because of her black skin color and her Catholic religion prompted Susan to engage in critical examination of the social issues. During the interview, she said, "I have never been discriminated against because of my skin color necessarily, or for my religion. So I pretty much fit into mainstream culture." The experiences of her interviewee helped Susan to understand the ways in which she was privileged simply for being a part of the mainstream culture. Susan also mentioned in the interview that because of this new understanding, she felt the need to be more critical of her own thoughts or behaviors. Other participants also commented about how being white and middle class had shielded them from being discriminated against in their lives.

When interviewees shared experiences of being treated unfairly because of their cultural differences, strong emotions were elicited among the participants. They showed empathy toward those victims of racism and social injustice and started to form solidarity with their interviewees. Megan interviewed an African American woman who grew up in the South right before the Civil Rights Movement. She and her siblings were not allowed to play in the front yard because of their fear of being blamed if anything bad happened in the neighborhood. Her dad was not allowed to enter the front door of an ice cream shop to purchase ice cream for his children. Megan was indignant about the injustice that her interviewee's family had received for being black. She was also upset about the racist views still held by some of her family members and relatives who lived in a neighboring southern state and showed her utter distaste for their racist remarks.

The Participants Made Home, Community, and School Connections in Lesson Planning

The ABCs model has made a profound impact on how the participants view and approach teaching. In Jake's reflection, he wrote, "I think I've become a huge supporter of introducing students' backgrounds, languages, and experiences in the classroom. I will definitely try to include this type of education in my science classes." Many other participants also made similar comments about how they would change their teaching so that it is culturally responsive.

All participants scored very high on their lesson plans using the culturally responsive teaching rubric. There is clear indication that they were thoughtful about integrating students' cultural experiences into their instruction. All lesson plans developed by the participants showed their awareness of student and community cultures and reflected the critical understanding of helping their students develop awareness of and respect for cultural differences between their cultures and the cultures of others in their classroom, school, and community.

For example, Belinda developed a lesson in which her students interview their parents to find out about their religious beliefs and practices, if any exist. They then read selected messages from religious texts and decide to which religious text a particular saying belongs. The students discover that the same saying can be found in the sacred texts of all three major religions (Christianity, Judaism, and Islam). This activity is extremely valuable in light of the particular religious context of the state in which one religion dominates, and the rest are more or less marginalized. The participants who were teaching subjects such as math and science were also able to make meaningful home, community, and school connections and build their lesson activities around the cultural experiences of their students.

The lesson plans developed by the participants include a wide variety of ideas about how they would implement culturally responsive teaching in their classrooms. The following are some of the ideas mentioned by the participants:

- Incorporating individual students' cultures and backgrounds in each lesson
- Role-playing—putting students in "another person's shoes"
- Having open discussions in the classroom, getting to know students
- Encouraging dialogs and openness, actively prevent bullying and harassment
- Finding literature that promotes differences
- Doing biography and autobiographies with students
- Making sure assignments aren't based on stereotypes

- Incorporating parents' perspectives in teaching their children
- Having more interaction with parents to involve them in the class

Kay described what she did in her class as a result of participating in the project.

> There are things that happened in my classroom, discussions and things we read that I can tie back to culture learning. I have in my classroom a Chinese American girl, a Hispanic boy, and a boy from Greece. We are able to tie together their cultures in similarities and differences, and I think I pulled that from what we learned in the class.

In the interview, Kay also talked about how the ABCs changed her teaching by saying, "I feel like I am just better at it. I'm not necessarily doing anything different. I'm just more aware of what needs to be done and more conscious of it. Making more efforts to understand [my students]."

As preservice teacher educators, Megan and Susan both prepared a set of thoughtfully developed lesson plans to expose the preservice teachers in their classes to culturally responsive teaching perspectives. Megan also taught her students how to approach math from a functional perspective (e.g., mortgages and car loans) so that they could have a better understanding of the mainstream American consumer culture and learn how to use math as a tool to help improve their lives.

The Participants Became Agents of Change

Data analyses also suggest that the participants began to think about ways to make a positive change in their professional and social circles. Kay talked about her plan to share information and culturally responsive teaching ideas with the data team at her school, and her intention to work with her teacher colleagues to come up with a common value about social equity and justice. Samantha planned to talk to the teachers she worked with about the Think B4 You Speak Campaign, and to raise awareness about the detrimental effect of bullying. She also wanted to talk to teachers about authentic teaching that builds on students' home and community experiences.

Shelby also described the ways in which the ABCs prompted her to become a change agent in her school. She initiated changes by working with her teachers on raising awareness and implementing culturally responsive teaching. When asked, toward the end of the interview, if she had anything else to say about the ABCs, she responded,

> I really enjoyed the process, and I think it really did heighten my awareness, and then I took that awareness to my department. I am a department chair,

and so in our department meetings we talked about bringing in a little bit more cultural awareness into all of our lessons in all our grades. And so not only did it influence my teaching, but it influenced the other ten teachers that are in my department... It's spreading out, so I just want you to know that.

DISCUSSION

In this study, the ABCs was found to be powerful in multiple ways. By exposing teacher candidates to people of different cultures, and having them analyze differences between their own and another's culture, the ABCs project enhanced their understandings about culture and themselves as teachers.

First, the ABCs provided the teacher candidates with opportunities for authentic intercultural experiences, which helped them develop a stronger cultural self-identity. Banks and Banks (2005) argued, "Identities matter enormously, reflecting and revealing knowledge about the world" (p. 188). The results confirmed the previous finding of "Know thyself and understand others" (Ruggiano Schmidt, 1998, p. 31).

Banks (1994) highlighted the important role self-knowledge plays in helping teachers understand students from diverse backgrounds. Because the participants became more self-aware, they were able to understand and appreciate others' cultures more. The understanding of both self and others is important because knowledge about self and others are "crucial preconditions for multicultural societies" (Finkbeiner, 2006, p. 39).

Second, the ABCs clearly supported the teacher candidates' development of intercultural awareness. Intercultural awareness starts with an awareness of oneself and one's own culture, an awareness of the role of the self in interaction, and the ability to learn from interaction (Finkbeiner & Fehling, 2006). After gaining a good sense of self-awareness, many participants expressed a desire to know more about other cultures and interact with people from other cultures after they completed the ABCs. Such a desire will continue to push the teachers forward in gaining more intercultural knowledge and competence.

Third, the ABCs helped the teacher candidates develop metacognition about cultures. By engaging themselves in the ABCs, teacher candidates were able to step back and analyze their own cultures. They gained an ability to identify similarities and differences. In addition, the ABCs is a tool that helped the teacher candidates uncover white privilege, racism, and institutional inequality.

Most encouragingly, these participating teachers became change agents. They were able to plan for culturally responsive teaching. They also took actions to educate others in their family and professional community.

The ABCs is an invaluable learning tool for teachers to develop intercultural awareness and competence. In words so aptly put by Kay regarding the impact of the ABCs,

> I think that it would be very eye-opening for every teacher to experience something like that. I think that more teachers would have a better view of their classroom and understand the differences in their classroom.... Walking in other's shoes is so enlightening—if only everyone could do it.

Limitations and a Future Direction

Two limitations surfaced during the analyses of the ABCs data. First, I was faced with what to do about the remaining sense of discomfort that some teacher candidates had about other cultures, based on the analyses of differences (religion, male chauvinistic attitudes toward women) once the class was over. In the analyses of cultural differences papers, some of the participants shared that they still felt strong discomfort about certain aspects of a different culture. Overcoming such discomfort may not be easy and quick. It is important that discussion on culture-related issues is not reserved for multicultural education courses only. All teacher education courses should encourage teacher candidates to explore issues related to cultural differences and help them come to terms with cultural differences.

While it is important to realize that similarities exist between people from different cultural groups, the study also suggests that many of our teacher participants found it a challenge to identify substantial, meaningful differences between themselves and their interviewees. However, it is critical that we recognize, respect, appreciate, and embrace cultural differences (Au, 2011; Ruggiano Schmidt, 1998). How we deal with differences will determine the healthy development of a multicultural society.

Teacher education programs in the country have been criticized for not being effective in providing adequate preparation for teacher candidates to work with linguistic and culturally diverse students (Christian, 2006). The ABCs is a great model that can be utilized to better prepare preservice and in-service teachers for working with diverse student populations. Despite the tremendous effect the ABCs model has on helping our teacher candidates to become more culturally aware, it is important to point out that the process of becoming truly culturally competent is long and never ending. Educators at all levels, including preservice and in-service teachers, should continuously engage ourselves in the process of criticality and reflexivity (Barnett, 1997; Byram, 2009). We should constantly examine our own and society's biases and stereotypes about people from other cultural backgrounds and take a more active role in fighting biases and prejudice and work harder to establish cross-cultural understanding and communication. Only then can we truly grow in our understanding of self and other and ultimately effectively support our students from all cultural backgrounds to succeed academically, intellectual, and socially.

REFERENCES

ACT (n.d.). *ACT profile report—state: Graduating class 2010, Oklahoma*. Retrieved from http://www.act.org/news/data/10/pdf/profile/Oklahoma.pdf

Au, K. H. (1983). Cultural congruence in classroom participation structures: Achieving and balance of rights. *Discourse Processes, 6*(2), 145–167.

Au, K. H. (2001). Culturally responsive instruction as a dimension of new literacies. *Reading Online, 5*(1).

Au, K. H. (2011). *Literacy achievement and diversity*. New York, NY: Teachers College Press.

Banks, J. (1994). *An introduction to multicultural education*. Boston, MA: Allyn & Bacon.

Banks, J., & Banks, C. (2005). *Multicultural education: Issues and perspectives* (5th ed.). Hoboken, NJ: John Wiley & Sons.

Banks, J., Cochran-Smith, M., Moll, L., Richert, A., Zeichner, K., LePage, P. . . . McDonald, M. (2005). Teaching diverse learners. In L. Darling-Hammond & J. Bransford (Eds.), *Preparing teachers for a changing world* (pp.232–274). San Francisco, CA: Jossey- Bass.

Barnett, R. (1997). *Higher education: A critical business*. Buckingham, UK: Open University Press.

Bruner, J. (1996). *The culture of education*. Cambridge, MA: Harvard University Press.

Byram, M. (1997). *Teaching and assessing intercultural communicative competence*. Clevedon, UK: Multilingual Matters.

Byram, M. (2009). Afterword. In A. Feng, M. Byram, & M. Fleming (Eds.), *Becoming interculturally competent through education and training* (pp. 211–213). Bristol, UK: Multilingual Matters.

Christian, D. (2006). Foreword. In K. Tellez & H. C. Waxman (Eds.), Preparing quality educators for English language learners (pp. vii–ix). Mahwah, NJ: Lawrence Erlbaum.

Edwards, P., Danridge, J., McMillon, G. T., & Pleasants, H. M. (2001). Taking ownership of literacy: Who has the power? In P. Ruggiano Schmidt & P. Mosenthal (Eds.), *Reconceptualizing literacy in the new age of multiculturalism and pluralism* (pp. 111–114) Greenwich, CT: Information Age.

Finkbeiner, C. (2006). Constructing third space: The principles of reciprocity and cooperation. In P. Ruggiano Schmidt & C. Finkbeiner (Eds.), *ABC's of cultural understanding and communication: National and international adaptations* (pp. 19–42). Greenwich, CT: Information Age.

Finkbeiner, C. (2009). Using "human global positioning system" as a navigation tool to the hidden dimension of culture. In A. Feng, M. Byram, & M. Fleming (Eds.), *Becoming interculturally competent through education and training* (pp. 151–173). Bristol, UK: Multilingual Matters.

Finkbeiner, C., & Fehling, S. (2006). Investigating the role of awareness and multiple perspectives in intercultural education. In P. Ruggiano Schmidt & C. Finkbeiner (Eds.), *ABC's of cultural understanding and communication: National and international adaptations* (pp. 19–42). Greenwich, CT: Information Age.

Gay, G. (2000). *Culturally responsive teaching: Theory, research, and practice.* New York, NY: Teachers College Press.

Gay, G. (2001). Preparing for culturally responsive teaching. *Journal of Teacher Education, 53*(2), 106–116.

Ladson-Billings, G. (1994). *The dreamkeepers: Successful teachers for African-American children.* San Francisco, CA: Jossey-Bass.

Ladson-Billings, B. (2000). Fighting for our lives: Preparing teachers to teach African American students. *Journal of Teacher Education, 52,* 206–214.

Ladson-Billings, G. (2001). *Crossing over to Canaan: The journey of new teachers in diverse classrooms.* San Francisco, CA: Jossey-Bass.

Moll, L. C., Amanti, C., Neff, D., & Gonzalez, N. (1992). Funds of knowledge for teaching: Using a qualitative approach to connect homes and classrooms. *Theory into Practice, 31*(2), 132–141.

Nieto, S. (2002). *Language, culture, and teaching: Critical perspectives for a new century.* Mahwah, NJ: Lawrence Erlbaum.

Nieto, S. (2010). *The light in their eyes: Creating multicultural learning communities* (10th ed.). New York, NY: Teachers College Press.

Patton, M. (1990). *Qualitative Evaluation and Research Methods.* Newbury Park, CA: Sage Publications.

Ruggiano Schmidt, P. (1998). The ABCs cultural understanding and communication. *Equity and Excellence in Education, 31*(2), 28–38.

Ruggiano Schmidt, P., & Ma, W. (2006). 50 literacy strategies for culturally responsive teaching, K–8. Thousand Oaks, CA: Corwin.

Sleeter, C. E. (2001). Preparing teachers for culturally diverse schools: Research and the overwhelming presence of whiteness. *Journal of Teacher Education, 52*(2), 94–106.

Strauss, A. L., & Corbin, J. (1998). *Basics of qualitative research.* Thousand Oaks, CA: Sage Publications.

Vygotsky, L. S. (1962). *Thought and language.* Cambridge, MA: MIT Press.

Xu, H. (2000). Preservice teachers integrate understandings of diversity into literacy instruction: An adaptation of the ABCs model. *Journal of Teacher Education, 32*(4), 505–531.

CHAPTER 11

THE ABCs AS A TOOL FOR CRITICAL INTERCULTURAL DEVELOPMENT

Ewa Bandura

INTRODUCTION

Critical cultural awareness and critical literacy are important cognitive components of intercultural competence. These orientations involve deconstructing the cultural context of the situation, recognizing stereotypes, interpreting cultural differences, and evaluating on the basis of explicit criteria. The critical dimension involves questioning what is taken for granted and being inquisitive in searching for explanations. It assumes an active approach to learning and readiness to put acquired knowledge and skills into practice. Criticality is necessary for both intercultural and intracultural understanding and communication. Therefore, foreign language teacher candidates need to develop their critical abilities in order to participate in inter- and intracultural communication themselves as well as prepare their pupils to do so.

This research project examines how the ABCs model (Ruggiano Schmidt & Finkbeiner, 2006) can be used to strengthen participants' criticality at

Getting to Know Ourselves and Others Through the ABCs, pages 181–196
Copyright © 2015 by Information Age Publishing

various junctures—while writing about themselves (Step A); while listening to their interlocutors and writing about them (Step B); while reading about and comparing cultures (C1); as well as trying to relate theories and views from set articles to the trainees' specific cultural and educational contexts in academic essays (Step C2); or while designing teaching activities to develop criticality in their pupils (Step C3). I examined the extent to which the ABCs project enhances teacher candidates' critical reflexivity as individuals, future teachers, and citizens. Specifically, I ask how the teacher candidates could benefit from it in terms of their personal, professional, social and political growth. Based on an investigation of the trainees' cross-cultural analysis essays and their intercultural teaching activities, I will deliver some important insights about the ways the ABCs model could be used to foster critical intercultural development of future foreign language teachers.

Sociocultural Context and Setting

Contemporary Polish society has been described and perceived by the majority of its members as monolingual and monocultural. Indeed, as compared to many other European and non-European countries, Poland is considerably homogeneous in terms of ethnicity, religion, race, and the first language of its inhabitants. One standard version of both written and spoken Polish used in official documents, literature, media, and education is considered the mother tongue for almost all Poles. On the other hand, there are still several local Polish dialects, with differing degrees of prestige, used for communication in families or regional communities. Moreover, there are a number of other languages, such as Belarusian, German, Kashubian, Lithuanian, Romani, Rusyn, Ukrainian, some of which are official auxiliary languages in a number of communes and languages of instruction in schools.

The question of cultural clashes as a result of immigration to Poland is still a marginal issue. The most noticeable groups who are seeking a permanent residence in Poland are the Vietnamese, and the citizens of former Soviet republics, whose ancestors were Polish citizens or ethnic Poles. Recently, a number of Western European students, workers, professionals, and their families have been settling temporarily in Poland.

Sociocultural diversity in Polish society takes its roots mainly in the different financial status of either individuals or families, as well as where people live, either in big cities or in small towns and villages. Both factors affect educational opportunities and aspirations of young Poles to a large extent. As a result, the question of diversity in Polish classrooms would be a controversial and complex issue to discuss in the classroom. Teachers and pupils alike may either find it difficult to notice the phenomenon as such, if they look for more obvious manifestations of diversity in school, such as race, ethnicity and religion; or consider it inappropriate and are uncomfortable speaking openly about inequalities related to pupils' economic background or where they live.

In view of that, the ABCs project in Poland, which involved teacher candidates of English as a foreign language, focused primarily on developing their intercultural competencies, such as knowledge, awareness, skills and attitudes necessary for successful communication with the representatives of different countries or nations. An ability to transmit or introduce elements of the target culture has been traditionally considered a foreign language teacher's professional competence, whereas the need to develop EFL pupils' awareness of the nature of intercultural communication itself would not be perceived as such an obvious objective by the teacher candidates. We hoped that the project participants would improve their understanding of the concept of culture and of the nature of intercultural differences, and thus become aware of less noticeable aspects of sociocultural diversity in both the target culture and as their own. It was our contention that if teacher candidates were to develop competencies as intercultural mediators in international contexts they would become more adept communicators in Polish monolingual classes by being more sensitive to diversity in the apparently monolithic national culture.

The Educational System

The present educational system in Poland is the result of the educational reform of 1999. Six years of elementary school (primary education) and 3 years of "gymnasium" (lower secondary school) are compulsory. Beyond this, most future teachers would take 3 more years of upper secondary education in lyceum, which is the general secondary school. Lyceum students are externally assessed through Matura, the standardized national secondary school achievement examination. The maturity certificate makes its holder eligible for higher education studies in Poland. Admission to higher education is based on the results of this exam, and foreign language teacher training institutions require their candidates to take both oral and written parts of the exam in the target foreign language at an advanced level.

In order to become a foreign language teacher, an 18- or 19-year-old lyceum graduate would normally enter a teacher training college or university in order to complete the first cycle studies. It takes 3 years to get the title of licentiate and to be qualified to teach in all types of schools. At the same time, the first degree gives access to the second cycle studies, which allow candidates to obtain the master's (MA) degree in 2 years. Full-time, daytime, and evening students attend classes during weekdays and part-time students during selected weekends.

Tertiary education, including foreign language teacher education, is supervised by the Ministry of Science and Higher Education. According to its regulations, graduates of the first cycle studies in modern languages should reach the advanced level (C1) of the target language, and during the second cycle, graduates further develop their skills to achieve the next level (C2). Licentiate graduates are supposed to acquire a good knowledge of the target language and culture as well as teaching skills. They are assumed to be able to communicate in different social situations, express their views and opinions, and understand the historical roots and diversity of cultures. MA students are additionally expected to develop an attitude of openness to foreign languages and cultures, and to get acquainted with different aspects of intercultural communication (Regulation by the Minister of Science and Higher Education of 12 July 2007).

Polish pupils start learning their first foreign language in the beginning of primary education, and the second one in gymnasium, with English being not only obligatory at some stage but also the most popular language. Hence, each lyceum candidate must have had at least 3 years of English instruction. The core curricula (Podstawa Programowa, 2009) are defined by the Ministry of Education for each subject in each school type, and must be respected by the school and in the syllabi chosen or prepared by the teachers, as well as in the recommended textbooks. According to the ministerial guidelines the cultural dimension should be present at every stage of foreign language education, but the degree of depth varies.

Teachers of all subjects are required to consider general educational aims such as preparing pupils to act effectively and responsibly in a contemporary world, through developing their self-esteem, cognitive curiosity, and respect for a multitude of varying traditions, including their own. Various sections of the ministerial document suggest that foreign language teaching include elements of intercultural education. The primary and lower secondary schools aim to develop knowledge of the target and Polish culture, understanding of European integration and the intercultural context, and attitudes of curiosity, tolerance, and openness toward other cultures. Foreign language curricula for lyceum include topics concerning the problems encountered when different cultures and communities are in contact. Only at more advanced levels, however, are pupils expected to participate in discussions, to present, rebut, and comment on arguments, or to recognize cultural references and less observable elements of cultural contexts.

Neither the guidelines for school curricula nor for teacher education programs seem to put enough emphasis on equipping teachers with didactic competencies that would enable them to develop their pupils' critical intercultural skills and awareness of an intercultural mediator. The intercultural dimension in foreign language teaching seems to be a marginal issue, and the critical skills component is particularly neglected. The situation may be improved by providing teacher candidates with more instruction and awareness, thus raising experience of intercultural communication such as demonstrated by the ABCs project.

Relevant Research

Criticality has been traditionally viewed as an essential quality in the Western concept of education and, more recently, as an important attribute of any active citizen in an increasingly multicultural and multilingual world. Foreign language students and teachers have a particular reason to develop their critical skills as a highly transferable component of intercultural communicative competence, which they aim for. What needs to be investigated is how foreign language teaching and teacher education can contribute to the development of criticality among university graduates.

With a market-driven and skills-based approach to higher education becoming more dominant, academics point to the danger of giving up the university's duty to develop the student's "autonomy as a self-sufficient rational enquirer" (Barnett, 1988, p. 245). According to Barnett, the challenges and uncertainties of our contemporary world require education that is characterized by reflective knowing, and a focus on dialog and argument, as it "allows for the continuing examination and construction of self, society and culture, including our ways of knowing and of understanding the world about us and of acting in it" (Barnett, 1997, pp. 42–43).

Philology departments share these concerns, including the danger of "discarding critical self-reflection as the object of education" (Crosbie, 2005, p. 299). Foreign language education should aspire to be more than training for a job market and encourage teaching and learning with "a committed, reflective engagement—a willingness to continually pause, reflect, listen and evaluate" (Crosbie, 2005, pp. 296, 298), and interdisciplinary efforts are needed to make the students of linguistics view language as key to understanding others and expressing one's own identity (Duszak, 2009, pp. 49, 51).

The critical component is present in an intercultural approach to foreign language education. Byram's model of intercultural competence involves a learner's critical cultural awareness, that is, "an ability to evaluate, critically and on the basis of explicit criteria, perspectives, practices and products in one's own and other cultures and countries" (Byram, 1997, p. 63). An intercultural speaker gives priority to analytical thought and can relativize his or her own cultural values (Byram, 1997, pp. 63–64). Those who want to see foreign language teaching realize the goals of political or citizenship education claim that a foreign language curriculum should be "active, political and transformative in nature in order to help create 'the critical intercultural speakers,' i.e., critically and socially responsible citizens for the future" (Guilherme, 2002, pp. ix, 15).

Drawing on Byram's concept of intercultural competence, which allows learners to mediate between cultures, and on critical approaches, M. Pegrum (2008) calls for changes in language pedagogy and proposes a model of "critical intercultural literacies," defined as the skills necessary to "read" cultures in a variety of sources and languages, as well as to reflect on them and oneself critically in light of one's own previous knowledge, experiences and perspectives (p. 137).

Yamada's (2010) research concerning the development of critical cultural awareness among foreign language students was to a large extent exemplary to the study presented below. She defines criticality as comprising scepticism, question-raising in response to new knowledge, and the ability to suspend judgment, as well as reflect on what has been taken for granted (pp. 152, 161). Criticality can be seen as a purely academic quality necessary for persuading and justifying one's claims or for critical citizens who actively engage in transformative actions (pp. 156–157). Yamada concludes that "focused lessons," with carefully designed teaching activities, can better stimulate the development of criticality than ordinary lessons can, although the latter can also develop criticality to some extent (p. 156). Thus, the earlier findings are consistent with those of Brumfit, Myles, Mitchell, Johnston and Ford (2005), whose study on university language learning programs proved that an explicit focus on criticality helps to reflect on "the mechanisms through which we both understand and communicate" (p. 166).

Similarly, overt instructions and training seem necessary to learn didactic skills for intercultural teaching. As revealed in my own study, although teachers say it is necessary to develop intercultural competence among foreign language learners and claim that they are willing to do so, they often do not actually practice it in their classrooms (Bandura, 2007). It needs to be considered while exploring the teacher candidates' attempts to design intercultural activities in the ABCs project.

The Study

The ABCs project was incorporated into the existing courses taught in the Philology Faculty at Jagiellonian University in Kraków. The result was twofold: first, the time frame of the project had to be adjusted to the two-semester organization of the academic year and the frequency of classes for specific groups; second, the use of the ABCs model in research had to be justified in the formal course syllabi and then presented to the students.

In both the 2009–2010 and 2010–2011 cycles of the ABCs project, the participants went through the same stages and submitted their work according to similar deadlines. The workload and assessment requirements for individual courses had to be taken into consideration while planning the pace of the ABCs work. Therefore, at the beginning of an academic year, in October, the students were introduced to the project and started their writing. In November they spent 3 weeks conducting interviews and writing. They were asked to submit their final academic essays in January and were expected to complete the project at the beginning of the following semester in February.

Study Participants

In 2009–2010, there were 20 participants from the first cycle studies (second year, full-time) and 9 from the second cycle studies (second year, part-time). In the following year, 2010–2011, there were 25 participants from the first cycle studies (second year, full-time) and 10 from the second cycle studies (first year, full-time).

The participants in both first cycle studies groups (TT09/10 and TT10/11) had a lot in common. They were either 19- or 20-year-old students undergoing their initial teacher training; they had an upper-intermediate level of English on average, no teaching experience, and were studying intensive German as a second foreign language (and sometimes a third foreign language too). Their English and German curricula included introductory classes in culture, literature, and history of the target countries and very little practice of academic skills.

The participants in the second cycle studies groups were on average 2 to 3 years older and had done their teaching practice, as well as introductory culture, literature, and history classes during their first cycle studies. Some MA09/10 part-time students were practicing teachers. However, in terms of their knowledge of other foreign languages, including English and academic skills, they were less developed than the MA10/11 full-time students.

All students taking part in the project were Polish, spoke Polish as their mother tongue, and were predominantly female. Many were from smaller towns.

Procedure

The ABCs procedure and instruments were identical in both cycles of the research. The initial, main, and final stages were followed in each case. The initial stage:

- Participants sign the letter of consent and their names are coded.
- Take the pre (culture) survey, fill out student information sheet and prepolarity profile.
- Introduce the ABCs model.

The main stage:

- Autobiography writing.
- Interviewing and biography writing.
- Identify similarities and differences using the iceberg Venn diagram.
- Cross-cultural analysis essay writing, in which the students were to refer to their autobiographies, biographies, and relevant literature in order to analyze the types and sources of similarities and differences; describe what they have learned about themselves and others; and demonstrate they ways in which they might use this experience for intercultural understanding or communication.
- Design five intercultural teaching activities based on the ABCs experience and relevant theories.

The final stage:

- Take post (culture) survey and fill out post-polarity profile.
- Interview the participants in the follow-up year.

All stages of the project were incorporated into the syllabi, contents, and requirements of the specific obligatory courses taught to the students as part of the curriculum.

The ABCs model proved quite flexible in that we repeated the 2-year experience of the project procedure, adapting it to different syllabus requirements. It was particularly challenging to incorporate the project into the syllabus content, partly because the project facilitator needed to take into account the pace and organization of an academic year as well as the likelihood that the process of assigning grades might undermine student motivation. After finishing the second cycle of the project, the question of fitting the ABCs steps into an obligatory course syllabus was discussed with the MA10/11 students. Following their reading of Unit 13: Ethics and Trustworthiness (Rallis & Rossman, 2009), I invited students to comment on ways in which the ABCs research design and implementation might be improved.

The students pointed out the problems connected with the ways in which research and regular teaching impact each other. First, they found it difficult to accept the double role of their new lecturer as both researcher in their group, and evaluator, that is, the person who assigned them grades. Their sense of insecurity was connected with the fact that had it not been for the research, more guidance and specific assessment criteria would have been provided. They blamed their "Polish mentality." There are several interpretations of what this might mean: it could be a reference to learning styles shaped by the teacher-centered approach dominating most Polish classrooms, or it could refer to their lack of independence and an over-reliance on the teacher's help in order to meet the course requirements. Most participants felt confused during the initial A and B steps and wanted to know all the details of the project procedure, research questions, data analysis, and expected results. They kept complaining about the fact that their participation in the project was obligatory and restricted by deadlines and writing specifications, including number of pages, while at the same time they admitted that they liked the experience and benefited from it as teachers (even though they didn't trust that participation was voluntary).

Findings

The study aimed at exploring the usefulness of the ABCs model in assessing and stimulating the critical awareness and reflexivity of the participants. We analyzed student performance in two stages of Step C, cross-cultural analysis essays and intercultural activities. The former were expected to initiate criticality development, that is, notice the differences and similarities between cultures and engage in critical reflection, whereas the latter were assumed to illustrate its consequence, that is, to be ready to take action in their specific teaching contexts.

Cross-Cultural Analysis Essays

The following aspects were taken into consideration in analyzing the participants' essays:

- most frequent areas of intercultural comparisons, e.g., relationships, beliefs, identity, education, intercultural contacts, etc.
- ways of engaging in critical reflection by questioning what has been taken for granted about the target and native cultures, questioning self and other perception, or by trying to explain the cultural phenomena through speculating or drawing on literature.
- declared changes of views or behaviors in the students' lives as individuals or professionals.

In their interviews, the students focused on several common topics, which naturally provided material for future comparisons in cross-cultural analysis essays. While comparing or contrasting their own and their interlocutor's experience, the students often gave examples of the nonobservable aspects of culture, such as values, beliefs, and attitudes. Most frequently chosen topics such as family life/values/relationships, including family regarded as a fundamental value in itself, were discussed by 80% of all the participants, and childhood by half of them. Interestingly, some participants generalized about the connection between the level of Europeanization and type of family bonds. The role of women in the family was referred to as "a hidden dimension" of the picture (10/11TT05).

Commonly investigated in cross-cultural essays was the role of faith/religion in their lives. As many as 70% of participants chose to comment on the impact of their own and their interlocutors' religious beliefs on shaping them as cultural beings and on mutual understanding. All participants referred to the issues related to identity, for example, one's native language or traits of charter associated with particular nationalities, or explicitly to their sense of national identity (70%) as opposed to all-European one. They referred to historical factors (e.g., wars, the role of Catholic Church), political context (e.g., communist period), socioeconomic status of the country, Catholic religion, national holidays, cuisine, traditions, and such.

Quite understandably, two other topics close to students' experiences included the role of education in their lives (60%) and traveling experiences/intercultural contacts (50%). Noticing the differences and similarities frequently led to some sort of critical reflection. Many students (65%) would make comments about their change of perspective following the interview, thus questioning their previous assumptions or knowledge underlying their self-perception or perception of others. Typically, they would use the following expressions: "It just occurred to me how different . . ."; "I realized how I had been wrong"; "It turned out I was seriously mistaken"; "My interlocutor changed partly my way of thinking," and so on.

Often, after acknowledging the limitations of one single perspective, the students declared a change of attitude:

> I've realized that my own perspective is not always the correct one and I can lose a lot trying to fit everyone to my own frame. (09/10TT17)

> In fact it has turned out that I based my judgment just on some short conversations with people from other countries and, frequently, was misled by stereotypes. I came to realize that whenever I had a chance to talk to a foreigner our conversation was focused on here and now. (09/10IFA25)

> Weronika unconsciously showed me my big mistake. I used to consider intellectual abilities as something that decides about person's value and determines whether one is worth knowing or not, but I should never divide people into those who are better and those who are worse because of the abilities of their brain. (09/10TT17)

Many students (70%) made an attempt at explaining their interlocutors' words and spotted intercultural differences, often judged negatively, by speculating on the possible reasons or referring to the set articles.

My first thought about John was that he was weird. Now, I think that in his behavior we can recognize some kind of acculturative stress—consequence of his lack of language skills. (10/11TT06)

For me he was intolerable, when it comes to his contacts with women.... Position of women in his country is different.... In time, John accepted Polish customs, but it was hard for him. He got used to different patterns. That was a source of conflict between John and his female friends. (10/11TT06)

Maybe I filled this gap in my knowledge about him too quickly with what was familiar to me, and just assumed that these periods of our lives were similar, as "Perceptions are based on implicit assumptions about prototypical representations and interpretations of certain categories within a certain socio-cultural context" (Finkbeiner, 2009). (09/10TT02)

As far as the differences between me and Diana are concerned, the most noticeable one is a level of closeness in family bonds. In my case, the relationships with my relatives are more warm-hearted.... I think it might be also the impact of Catholicism. Family is the basis of the Christian morality which is still quite visible in Polish society. (10/11MA34)

During our little conversations I did not realize the fact that struck me when I was reading extracts from Byram. "When two people talk to each other, they do not just speak to the other to exchange information, they also see the other as an individual and as someone who belongs to a specific social group" (Byram, Gribkova, & Starkey, 2002, p. 9). (10/11TT18)

Because in Japan it is still thought that good children are to be seen, but not necessarily heard, especially girls, she was perceived as an overly quiet, disciplined person. Another example appeared when I complimented her. Suddenly, she began waving her forearm in front of her face while saying "no, not at all." It was only after asking her that she realized making the gesture and explained to me that it means dismissing something and is common in Japan. Exactly as said by Finkbeiner (2009), "Discourse and negotiation about the perception of the self and the other make hidden things visible. It can help clarify misunderstandings that are caused by... choice of words, grammar, tone, medium and body language" (par. 2). (10/11TT25)

Almost all students believed that the project affected them in some way. Two thirds of the participants claimed that these changes would influence their future behavior, first in their teaching practice and second in various intercultural contacts. They declared they had learned not only about their interlocutor but also about themselves; however, the impact on the interlocutor was never mentioned. The comments described either general or more specific outcomes of the ABCs:

I think it will help me cope with certain matters of my perception of people, their environments and cultures. Being aware of disparities may prevent injustice, intolerance and inequality among people in the whole world. (09/10TT04)

In multicultural classes it is important for a teacher to be tolerant, understanding and to have an open mind on student's culture and their social backgrounds. (09/10TT15)

On my computer there are now many interesting readings about cultures, cooperation, features of a good teacher and more and I am sure that I will go back to them whenever I need some support and guidance of how to conduct my lesson and make it more interesting for my students. (09/10TT11)

My appreciation of Vietnam had certainly increased so that I perceive differently immigrants working currently in Poland and struggling with our customs, language and culture in general. (10/11MA32)

Some students demonstrated their developing critical awareness and skills in deciding to make use of their ABCs experience in their professional life:

I have decided that I will do my best to make Byram's social identity theory alive during my lesson.... Another approach I am going to introduce while teaching will be critical literacy.... In practice, it means that we should encourage students to interrogate social conditions and talk freely about issues that are significant to their lives. (09/10TT16)

I think as a foreign language teacher I can use this knowledge in creating activities, especially these that focus on speaking that would welcome different opinions on issues deeply rooted in our mentality. I think I would introduce debates on many topics that would make pupils realize their own view and be able to understand the counterarguments of those with the opposite view. (09/10MA23)

Intercultural Activities

Participants' intercultural activities were analyzed to explore how they brought a critical orientation to their own teaching contexts. Following their critical reflection in cross-cultural analysis essays, the teacher candidates had an opportunity to present their attempts to encourage critical reflection in their pupils. Their developing critical awareness and skills manifested in two practical ways:

- stating the critical aims of activities explicitly either in a general way, i.e., to develop critical skills/critical thinking, or in a specific way, i.e., to reflect/discuss/ /investigate/analyze a particular issue in order to make the learners question or find explanations of cultural differences or phenomena

* designing actual teaching activities to fulfill these aims

One third of the participants expressed a general aim to develop their pupils' critical abilities (more often the first cycle studies than MA students), and they actually developed activities with the critical focus. For instance, the pupils were to "learn to be objective and look at the situation from different points of view," and to "discover for themselves other cultures" (09/10TT09). Similarly, only one third of the participants formulated more specific aims and developed suitable activities (mostly the first cycle students, and none of the part-time master's students), which included

to help students to understand what is meant by stereotypes, how they influence the way we perceive others and how harmful stereotyping can be. (09/10TT16)

to raise awareness of the students' own culture, to show them how their country is perceived by foreigners, to make them look critically at their own culture. (10/11TT02)

to learn how others perceive you on the basis of your origins. (10/11TT09)

The younger students seemed to be more creative, open to challenge, and eager to experiment with the newly introduced teaching ideas, whereas the students who had already undergone their teaching practice tended to follow well-established techniques and materials, probably observed or tested out in practice.

According to the aims stated by the participants, the activities were to "demonstrate," "prove," "convince," "help to understand," and "make someone realize," which assumed the pupils' passive role in learning. On the other hand, many activities designed to encourage the learners' critical reflection or reconsideration of stereotypes and other common beliefs about culture obviously required their active participation in discussions, debates, negotiations of meaning, role-plays, and miniprojects presented in class. The majority of teacher candidates seemed to adhere to the idea that it is the instructor's responsibility mainly to provide cultural facts or explanations to the learners rather than stimulate them to seek for and construct knowledge themselves on the basis of independently collected materials. When they chose more active teaching techniques such as debates or projects, it was not necessarily reflected in the way activity aims were formulated, which would require more fundamental changes in the trainees' approach to autonomous learning and teaching and more exposure to specific activity types.

Interviews and Discussions

During and after the second phase of the project, I gathered some additional information that reflected students' opinions about the project in general and its role in developing the students' critical awareness in particular. Three student cases from 2009–2010 revealed not only very different perceptions of the ABCs (from positive to highly skeptical), but also the lack of an obvious relationship between their declared attitudes toward the project and the demonstrated level of critical intercultural awareness or didactic competences.

Three interviewed students from 2010–2011 gave some new insights about their approach to writing at different stages. Even if they did question what they learned at Stage B, it might have not occurred to them to express their doubts in the cross-cultural analysis essays; instead, they would write as if everything appeared unquestionable (10/11TT02). Some students remembered posing questions in their essays and admitting their inability to answer them (10/11TT14). The students were able to notice that the whole project aimed at developing critical reflection, avoiding stereotypes, and being inquisitive (10/11TT18). However, they expected to be guided and told explicitly that questioning and expressing doubts or ignorance are allowed in the essays.

The MA10/11 group of participants were asked in an open class discussion whether they found introducing activities to encourage critical reflection relevant in a Polish EFL class. They considered the issue quite "unrealistic" and "problematic" due to the "compulsory nature of education" and teacher-centred style of instruction, which is not conducive to pupils' involvement as creative and critical thinkers. Still, the students believed in the EFL teachers' role in developing their pupils' criticality, and most of them declared using "critical" activities in their own future teaching. As for their own criticality displayed in the project, they were quite sure it was visible in their essays and activities, although making it an explicit requirement of the project was considered necessary.

CONCLUSION

As far as the implementation of the ABCs model in the educational circumstances described above, its benefits were balanced with challenges. Many students found it the most interesting academic and life experience of the year; still, a considerable number could not see its usefulness or never accepted the fact of "being made" to participate in the project. All in all, alternative ways of motivating the students would have to be considered in order to ease the difficulty of justifying the use of the ABCs model in the formal course syllabi as well as the grading system.

The problem encountered by the students in monocultural societies, connected with finding suitable partners for their interviews in Stage B, can be solved in two ways. First, Internet exchanges may substitute real-life meetings and talks; second, future teachers should develop their awareness of and sensitivity to sociocultural diversity in their own country and get encouraged to use the "home ethnography" tools.

The ABCs model (Ruggiano Schmidt & Finkbeiner, 2006) proved to be successful in diagnosing the students' critical awareness and reflexivity. Most students were able to compare and contrast cultures, often questioning their findings and searching for explanations. The majority declared changes in their future behavior or attitude in terms of becoming more aware of stereotypes, more open and inquisitive; however, they rarely mentioned acquiring new habits such as referring to literature and other sources of knowledge, or to specific intercultural training. Sadly, most participants displayed their lack of didactic competencies to design intercultural activities that encourage criticality. The project results seemed to provide evidence that there is no easy transfer of an individual ability to reflect critically into pedagogic skills. Personal growth may not be enough to overcome the detrimental effect of traditional coursebooks or previous learning experience. Explicit training in the more critical use of existing teaching material or in the creative design of critical activities, as well as constant encouragement in their own critical development as students and teacher candidates is necessary to instill new attitudes and practices.

A different comparative type of study would better help to decide whether the process of writing cross-cultural analysis essays and designing culturally responsive ideas actually stimulate the development of critical awareness and reflexivity. If the model is to serve educational rather than research purposes, the students would need to be provided more explicit instruction and guidance, including theoretical background reading as well as practical examples of activities that develop the habit of engaging in critical reflection. Nevertheless, following the ABCs cycle has inspired both the facilitator and the participants to discuss the whole range of issues such as the need of critical approach and activities in developing intercultural and intracultural competencies, the role and qualifications of the foreign language teacher, or creativity and autonomy in learning, to mention just a few.

NOTE

The author would like to thank all students who contributed to this study, in particular my student assistant, Ludmiła Kotnis, who helped with data analysis.

REFERENCES

Bandura, E. (2007). *Nauczyciel jako mediator kulturowy.* Kraków, Poland: Tertium.

Barnett, R. (1988). Does higher education have aims? *Journal of Philosophy of Education, 22*(2), 239–250.

Barnett, R. (1997). Beyond competence. In F. Coffield & B. Williamson (Eds.), *Repositioning higher education* (pp. 27–44). Buckingham, UK: Society for Research into Higher Education & Open University Press.

Brumfit, C., Myles, F., Mitchell, R., Johnston, B., & Ford, P. (2005). Language study in higher education and the development of criticality. *International Journal of Applied Linguistics, 15*(2), 145–168.

Byram, M. (1997). *Teaching and assessing intercultural communicative competence.* Clevedon, UK: Multilingual Matters.

Byram, M., Gribkova, B., & Starkey, H. (2002). *Developing the intercultural dimension in language teaching: A practical introduction for teachers.* Strasbourg, France: Council of Europe.

Crosbie, V. (2005). Future directions for modern languages in the higher education landscape: An interview with Alison Phipps and Mike Gonzalez. *Language and Intercultural Communication, 5*(3/4), 294–303.

Duszak, A. (2009). Języki obce w szkole wyższej: fakty, mity, postulaty. In H. Komorowska (Ed.), *Kształcenie językowe w szkolnictwie wyższym* (pp. 41–52). Warszawa, Poland: Wydawnictwo SWPS Academica.

Finkbeiner, C. (2009). Using "human global positioning system" as a navigation tool to the hidden dimension of culture. In A. Feng, M. Byram, & M. Fleming (Eds.), *Becoming interculturally competent through education and training* (pp. 151–173). Bristol, UK: Multilingual Matters.

Guilherme, M. (2002). *Critical citizens for an intercultural world. Foreign language education as cultural politics.* Clevedon, UK: Multilingual Matters.

Pegrum, M. (2008). Film, culture and identity: Critical intercultural literacies for the language classroom. *Language and Intercultural Communication, 8*(2), 136–154.

Podstawa programowa z komentarzami. (2009). *Tom 3. Języki obce w szkole podstawowej, gimnazjum i liceum.* Warszawa, Poland: MEN.

Rallis, S. F., & Rossman, G. B. (2009). Ethics and trustworthiness. In J. Heigham & R. Croker (Eds.), *Qualitative research in applied linguistics* (pp. 263–287). New York, NY: Palgrave.

Regulation by the Minister of Science and Higher Education of 12 July 2007 on the degree programme requirements for individual fields of study and levels of study, and on the procedure for the establishment of interdisciplinary degree programmes and degree programmes in macro-fields of study and the requirements to be fulfilled by higher education institutions in order to provide such programmes. Retrieved April 20, 2011, from http://www.nauka.gov.pl

Ruggiano Schmidt, P., & Finkbeiner, C. (2006). *ABC's of cultural understanding and communication: National and international adaptations.* Greenwich, CT: Information Age.

Yamada, E. (2010). Developing criticality through higher education language studies. In Y. Tsai & S. Houghton (Eds.), *Becoming intercultural: Inside and outside the classroom* (pp. 146–166). Newcastle upon Tyne, UK: Cambridge Scholars Publishing.

CHAPTER 12

LITERACY COACHING AND THE ABCs OF CULTURAL UNDERSTANDING AND COMMUNICATION

What's the Connection?

Patricia A. Edwards and Susan V. Piazza

This is an exciting, and perhaps somewhat intimidating, time for teachers who find themselves in the middle of students and coaches. It is a time when teachers are asked to open their classrooms to someone called the "literacy coach." Literacy coaching is defined by the International Reading Association (IRA, 2010) as a "reading specialist who focuses on providing professional development for teachers by giving them the additional support needed to implement various instructional programs and practices" and the National Council of Teachers of English define it as professionals who "work with teachers individually, in collaborative teams, and/or with departments, providing pratical support on a full range of reading, writing, and communication strategies." (NCTE, 2006). They also assist teachers

Getting to Know Ourselves and Others Through the ABCs, pages 197–208
Copyright © 2015 by Information Age Publishing
All rights of reproduction in any form reserved.

in the design and teaching of lessons in other content disciplines where students continue to develop and use their literacy skills (Shanklin, 2006).

THE EXPERTISE OF LITERACY COACHES

The literacy coaching model was developed to increase support for teachers and ultimately student achievement. The model allows supportive, knowledgeable professionals to assume the role of coach in order to increase teacher effectiveness. Change in teacher practice is complex and requires much more than simple professional development or scripts (Richardson & Placier, 2001; Walpole & Blamey, 2008). The typical model of literacy coaching begins with the coach meeting with a teacher to discuss students' needs and whether the teacher feels that current practices are supporting student achievement sufficiently. The emphasis during early meetings between coaches and teachers is often on listening, steering, planning, and scheduling (Toll, 2005). Out of those initial discussions, coaches will schedule an instructional modeling session to interact with students in the classroom to demonstrate practices. Afterward, the coach and teacher will meet to dialog and reflect on the teacher's experiences and the students' responsiveness to the new instructional practices.

The traditional model of literacy coaching makes great sense in monocultural and monolingual settings; however, in multicultural and linguistically diverse settings, we suggest a broadened approach in order to achieve culturally responsive coaching. This chapter provides two case examples of developing literacy coaches who learn about others through stories and experiences presented with the ABCs of Cultural Understanding framework (Ruggiano Schmidt & Finkbeiner, 2006). In particular, we examine how the ABCs model helps literacy coaches learn to work effectively in diverse settings. Based on experiences with in-service teachers and those who are in the process of becoming literacy coaches, all of the components in a traditional literacy coaching model need to revolve around the cultural and linguistic needs of communities and schools. While there is a strong rationale for literacy coaching positions, and guidelines that define effective literacy coaching, what is often missing is a conversation about literacy coaches' abilities to talk across race and class lines. Specifically, to be effective when relating to teachers, students, administrators, and the community; literacy coaches must be able to have cross-cultural conversations to learn with and from others.

The International Reading Association's (IRA, 2010) standards for reading professionals include a new strand that focuses specifically on diversity. In those standards, it is clear that literacy coaches and reading specialists must: (a) recognize, understand, and value the forms of diversity that exist in society and their importance learning to read and write; (b) use a literacy curriculum and engage in instructional practices that positively impact students' knowledge, beliefs, and engagement with the features of diversity; and (c) develop and implement strategies to advocate for equity (http://reading.org/General/CurrentResearch/Standards/ProfessionalStandards2010.aspx).

Existing research provides the characteristics of effective literacy teachers (Pressley, Rankin, & Yokoi, 1996). These practices have proven effective for many teachers in suburban environments or with predominantly white student populations. They result in high academic performance outcomes for students in these areas. However, there are persistent achievement gaps between low-income, racial, and ethnic minority student populations and their white counterparts, even when these best practices have been implemented. The 2011 National Assessment of Education Progress (NAEP) scores demonstrate very little progress in closing the achievement gaps since 2009, and no significant change since 1992 in reading for 4th and 8th graders (NAEP, 2010). Therefore, rather than continuing to emphasize programs or practices that have been normed across a broad sample of the population, educational institutions should focus developing dispositions and cultural competencies across various sociocultural contexts. The following two sections highlight how the use of personal narratives and the ABCs framework can support this work in order to help literacy coaches learn to navigate their new roles within increasingly diverse settings.

Experiences From the Field

The authors of this chapter work with preservice and in-service teachers who either are literacy coaches or will one day be literacy coaches. Both authors are teacher educators, but they have two very different worldviews because they grew up in two different Americas during two different times. Dr. Edwards has built a successful career researching and teaching and developing programs that support culturally marginalized students and their families, as well as working with teachers and literacy coaches in challenging situations. As a black child in the south during the '50s and '60s, she attended segregated schools for 10 of her 12 years before attending an all-white high school for the last 2 years. Dr. Piazza is an early-career scholar who researches and teaches on issues of literacy and focuses on how white, middle-class, female teachers like herself can work toward becoming more culturally competent and effective in today's diverse classrooms. She has lived and worked in various parts of the United States and Canada. Together, the authors emphasize that cultural competence comes in many different forms, and it requires time, firsthand experiences, partnering with others who challenge your thinking, and a great deal of reflective practice.

Working with mostly young white females enrolled in their literacy and teacher education classes, Edwards and Piazza engage students in discussions about how they would learn to support teachers of a different race, class, or culture. Most express apprehension. Using Ruggiano Schmidt's original ABCs Model (2001) with adaptations developed by Ruggiano Schmidt and Finkbeiner in 2006, they engage their students in discussions and activities around the following: (a) autobiography, (b) biography, (c) cross-cultural analysis, (d) cultural self-analysis of differences, and (e) a communication plan for connecting home, school, and community for literacy learning. The stories shared in this chapter were collected in two midwestern teacher preparation institutions and their related field experiences. The authors analyze how the ABCs of Cultural Understanding and Communication activities can support developing literacy coaches to become more culturally responsive with both teachers and students.

Learning Through Stories

A great strength of the ABCs framework is that it encourages educators to learn from their own and others' stories. Interacting with others and learning from each others' life experiences provides a tremendous opportunity for professional growth. The following story is about Tina, a white middle-class female graduate student completing her professional preparation as a literacy coach. Her story demonstrates how personal and professional interactions with others leads to higher levels of cultural competencies in the role of coaching. At the time, she was asked to intern at a local public school grounded in an Afro-centric curriculum. Tina's first Monday in this school began in the common area where Hurambe, an African tradition celebrating community, was taking place. Shortly after, she was expected to meet with teachers and students in varioius classrooms to begin her service as a literacy coach intern. Since coaching is all about building relationships, Tina's first priority was to learn about the teachers, students, and overall sense of community in this school. She was not quite sure how to do this.

First, Hurambe, the pulling together of the school community each morning, was a brand new experience for Tina. She reported that her first day of coaching was awkward and she experienced a great deal of cultural dissonance—*culture shock* was the term she used. Had she been given the opportunity to learn about the traditions of the school and its leaders before engaging, she would have been more prepared to participate in this new experience. Nevertheless, Tina went on to work with teachers and struggled to position herself as both a learner and a leader in this community. It took Tina several weeks to find her voice as a coach who was expected to contribute to instructional ideas that supported the Afro-centric literacy curriculum, while keeping in mind the developmental and diverse needs of learners in each classroom.

The following is a key incident experienced by Tina in her placement. One of the early elementary teachers implemented the use of a lengthy Langston Hughes passage with her kindergarten class. The selection of this text was appropriate for meeting the curricular goal; however, the complexity of the text for kindergarten children was so difficult that Tina observed many children off-task and disengaged during the lesson. While her role as literacy coach was not to be an expert on the topic of antiracism and poetry, she was able to validate the selection and suggest supplemental resources and strategies that might better engage young children. It was so important that she value the curriculum objectives first and foremost and did not critique the teacher for using inappropriate materials. Instead, she affirmed the selection of a clearly high quality authentic text written by a famous African American and suggested ways to help young students engage with the text. There are endless numbers of possible solutions to resolving instructional struggles, but without cultural competencies, coaches may not have the relationship-building skills or background knowledge to provide meaningful suggestions.

Fast forward to the final week of Tina's placement. While it took Tina some time to find her place in this unfamiliar setting, she and each one of the other literacy coaches placed in this school fully embraced the Hurambe practice and genuinely wished out loud that all schools and students could begin their day of learning with such a positive experience that promotes community. Each and every interaction between coaches and teachers depends on how strong the personal and professional relationship with the teacher is. Tina's example provides a glimpse of one experiential approach that did require her to navigate her own lack of cultural competency and expertise in order to support professional development of the teacher. However, the authors would like to argue that a more systematic approach could have helped. If Tina would have had the opportunity to engage in the ABCs of Cultural Understanding and Communication with the teachers before the first day of coaching, there would have been less cultural dissonance and more effective interactions earlier on in the placement.

APPLYING THE ABCs OF CULTURAL UNDERSTANDING AND COMMUNICATION

The following example highlights how the activities within the ABCs framework were used to engage coaches during professional preparation for situations similar to Tina's. These practices have been reported as highly effective by both students and teacher educators in our classes. In a master's level course in literacy leadership, multiple roles for coaches are studied to improve literacy programs at preschool, K–12, college, and adult education levels. Coaches were asked to interview a person from a different cultural background to begin the process of learning through others' stories. These were contrasted with their own stories.

Engage in Autobiographic Writing

In-service teachers were asked to think about their own life experiences, what has made them who they are today, and how these things might inform their literacy coaching practices. The teachers were asked to write a detailed autobiography that included all of their significant life events. Next, they asked to interview a person who was racially different from them, and many of them chose to interview someone who was socioeconomically different. The reason for this was that many of the teachers in the course lived in communities where there was little or no diversity. There were seven teachers who did live in communities where they were able to interview an individual who was racially and/or ethnically different from them. We choose to highlight Colleen's case because in our opinion her, stories exemplify important components of the ABCs model. Teachers were encouraged to include their earliest memories, family origins, education, foods, celebrations, fun, victories, traumatic events, loves, honors, disappointments, and anything else they considered important. Below, you might see how Colleen connects her life experiences with her professional preparation.

> Both of my grandparents come from a Belgian lineage and my Grandpa Meganck is actually a first generation American arriving in the United States during his teen years. As it turns out, both families had migrated to Detroit in search of work where Grandma and Grandpa remained living until the 1980's. Despite my father's beliefs that I am more Irish than Belgian, I am very proud of my Belgian ancestry. My father is one of 7 children. He served in Vietnam for several years and returned to the U.S. as an emotionally scarred and depressed man. The community is very family oriented, so my brother Jeff and I always had neighbors looking out for us and close friends to play with. My mother worked as a stay at home Mom and I have always been very close with her. My father on the other hand is someone who I would consider a work-a-holic. I always felt like he made an effort to get to know my brother but that he never took an interest in getting to know me.
>
> In 6th grade, I became very close with a group of about 8 girls and one boy. We dubbed ourselves "The Clan" and hung out with each other every weekend. During 7th grade, I met a new student named Sarah and she was the most rebellious person who cared less about school and was always breaking rules at home. We became inseparable for a period of time. She eventually spread vicious rumors about me that I was a lesbian. After the shenanigans of middle school, I was ready to have a fresh start with new friends where nobody

knew me and where I would have a chance to play sports. I chose to attend a small, private catholic school named Notre Dame Preparatory....

For my internship, I was assigned to an elementary school in Pontiac. The class size was 26–30 throughout the year and was primarily African American and Hispanic students. I had students who didn't know the alphabet, families who didn't value school, and few to no resources to teach with. I hated it. I was frustrated with everything from the lack of school supports in place and lack of knowledge on how to teach students from backgrounds and value systems so different from my own.

Engage in Biographical Writing

For this portion of the assignment, Colleen chose to interview Candice, someone who grew up in Trinidad. Colleen asked about Candice's significant life events (e.g., family origins, education, celebrations, victories, traumatic events, loves, honors attained, disappointments, and anything else the interviewee deemed important). Candice shared reflections on her life history and they talked about how every person has their own identity, which is like a "cultural pie." In other words, according to Candice "who you are is made up of many different parts or 'pie slices' such as family history, traumatic experiences, great successes and more. Ethnicity is just one slice of the pie." Candice's biography, as told by Colleen, follows:

Growing up, she had friends from various religions and cultures such as Hindu and Muslims. Candice was second of four children born into the Jodhan family in Port of Spain on the island of Trinidad and Tobago. Her father Frank came from India and was the breadwinner and leader of the household. In Trinidad, everyone worked for a family business. Candice's mother Nazirah was of Spanish and Lebanese decent. When Candice was growing up, her mother made all of the clothes for the family by hand. She especially loved shoes because that's one thing her Mom was not able to make.

Trinidad was colonized by Britain, and children either attended government or catholic schools. As her luck would have it, Candice and her siblings attended Catholic school her entire life. Candice hated to study and especially despised religious education class. The highlight of school for her was the extracurricular activities that she participated in such as sports (soccer, running, tennis) and choir. In this aspect, she differed greatly from her siblings as they all enjoyed school... especially her brother. Candice said that schools were set up much like they are in America with separated grades and teachers.

On the Island growing up, grocery stores did not exist. Nazirah went to the island market every Saturday to buy fresh food for the week. Candice and her

older sister Sharon would be in charge of getting the food ready. Every summer the family took a trip to one of the small islands towardsVenezuela. Once
you left the main island by boat, it usually took about 2 hours to arrive at your
destination. For three weeks, we would live and run free.

Engage in a Cross-Cultural Analysis

When performing cultural self-analyses (Spindler & Spindler, 1987), the
teachers were asked to compare and contrast their culture with their interviewee's culture. The product of this was a list of similarities and differences. The teachers studied similarities and differences in order to analyze
cultural perspectives that might result in cultural conflicts or miscommuni-
cation. Colleen discusses the similarities between the two of them:

> Candice and I both grew up in homes where our parents had very specified
> roles. Our fathers worked very hard to make money and provide for the fam-
> ily so that we could live comfortably. In addition, we both had fathers who
> strongly valued higher education and did everything in their power to see
> that we went to college after high school. However, she was able to form a
> close relationship with her father whereas I did not because I felt like he was
> a "work-a-holic" which prevented us from ever spending time together. At the
> same time, our mothers were the matriarchs of the family. They took care of
> household duties such as cleaning, bills and raising the children. In addition,
> our mothers were the ones who made the important household decisions.

> Talking with Candice made me realize how very similar some themes are, but
> how differently we experience the world. I felt a connection to her regarding
> how different she is in this country. I thought about how prevalent racism can
> be if you really pay attention to it. As a Caucasian, I take for granted how well I
> am treated by those in society. However, I know that if I paid attention, I would
> recognize discrimination in my own neighborhood on a daily basis. It bothers
> me that I grew up, live in and work in extremely white communities. I some-
> day hope to live in a racially diverse area where it will be easier to expose my
> children to and become open minded in learning about different cultures and
> lifestyles. If I want my children to grow up accepting of others, I will have to be
> very deliberate about making sure they are exposed to various groups in society.

Cultural Self-Analysis of Differences

The teachers were asked to analyze differences, explaining the differences that caused them discomfort and those that they admired. After each
difference, the teachers were asked to explain in detail why they admire
the difference or why the difference made them feel uncomfortable. Also,

the teachers were asked to connect their analyses to power issues related to dominant and nondominant communities. As they did this, they were asked to consider race, class, and equity issues and connect with articles read in class that related to these issues. In the section below, Colleen discusses the differences between her and Candice.

> Our conversation made me realize that the era you are born in is one of the largest "cultural pie slices." Candice grew up at a time where technology did not permeate every aspect of life. You had to make your own fun using your creativity with the few toys you had. Lifestyles were also very different for her growing up because food had to be made fresh and you were only allowed to play with friends on the weekends. In addition, the politics of the time play a major role in forming who you are. Aside from the fact that I have grown up with technology, processed food and toys galore, American media and society at-large are constantly shaping my culture. Advertisements on self-image, economy and relations with countries abroad have all played a part in who I have become today.
>
> The second biggest conclusion I have come to is that each person has a "pie slice" which overpowers the rest. Personally, my entire life has revolved around the concept of education. My teachers influence who I wanted to become as an adult, friends made in middle school have become my lifelong support system and most of my major successes or challenging moments can be tied back to the school setting. For Candice however, family is the largest and most vital pie slice. She grew very close to her parents and siblings because they spent so much time together. This is very different in modern days because families are so busy running around with different extracurricular events and meetings that many families rarely eat a meal altogether. For Candice, everyone had a role and worked together to ensure the job was done. As an adult, she felt it was more important to be a stay at home mom and raise her children with values than it would be to return to work and earn money. For her, living a world apart from her immediate family has been challenging and I greatly appreciate that my family lives close enough where we can see each other on a regular basis. While family is incredibly important to me, education has played a larger role in shaping my identity.

Colleen's intimate experiences with writing her autobiography and then interviewing Candice for the biography has not prepared her to work with diverse populations; however, it is a necessary first step that all teachers must take to deconstruct some of the long-standing beliefs and unknowns about those who are culturally different from themselves. Colleen, through careful analysis of similarities and differences between her experiences and Candice's experiences, is able to think about "others" now in a much more humanistic and familiar way. It is important to acknowledge that this is a necessary first step in developing an open disposition toward learning about how to engage with teachers and students in multicultural settings. The next step is to fully engage in the communities that you will be working with.

Communication of Home, School, and Community Connections

The final step in this process was for teachers to adapt one of their lesson plans to meet the needs of someone from their interviewee's culture based on what they had learned from the project. What changes would they make to their original lesson plan based on the cultural insights that they had gained from this experience? Also, how would they address the communication between home and school so that the parents would understand what is being expected of their child for this lesson or what they hope to attain from this lesson? Colleen shared the following:

> Candice and I both come from cultural heritages that had strong educational, family, and even British influences. As a result, our cultures are very similar overall. I would like to find a way to incorporate cultural influences shared by Candice in a way that fits my existing curriculum. I regularly engage students in a year-long inquiry centered on celebrations. This is an interdisciplinary approach to language arts and social studies that allows me to teach about people, traditions, beliefs, and in this case, how people celebrate events. One approach might be to connect students from island nations to learn about their life experiences. I would be careful not to only focus on carnival, but it would be an interesting way to open the conversation and begin learning more deeply about the people. I would use the idea of carnival as the introduction to the inquiry project.
>
> On the island of Trinidad and Tobago, carnival is one of the most significant cultural events. Celebrated two days before Ash Wednesday, the event includes many special activities that would interest the children in my classes. The following are ways that I would invite students to inquire about this topic:
>
> - **Inform families**—I would create an addendum to my weekly newsletter explaining basic information about islands and traditions such as carnival. (When, why, how ...). This informational note would include key concepts that I am hoping to focus on in class as well as some materials or activities that we will do to achieve our goals. It would also specify how this inquiry project meets the curriculum standards in a holistic way.
> - **Creating Text Sets**—I would find books, photographs, websites, art, music, and other developmentally appropriate artifacts. Throughout our investigation, I would invite children to share what they learn or notice and develop questions they would like answers to.
> - **Videos**—Our district is very big on using United Streaming. I would like to find a short video or several video clips highlighting different experiences and/or events from the islands. The students could use these to begin discussions about how their own experiences may be similar or different.
> - **Classroom activities**—As much as possible, I would expose children to different kinds of information and provide students with time to explore their questions both in and out of class, both individually and in small

groups. I will also encourage discussion and sharing of information so that we create a learning community around this line of inquiry.
- **Interview**—If possible, I would invite a community member such as Candice, or Skype in an islander, who would be willing to share their life experiences and answer questions from my class.

Colleen shared with us how the ABCs of Cultural Understanding and Communication broadened her understanding of how to have a thoughtful and honest conversation with an individual who is racially different. It helped her to work through some of the discomforts she might have otherwise experienced. She admitted that she was a little nervous at first, but as she continued to interview Candice she saw the similarities and differences between the two of them as a valuable learning opportunity. When asked how the ABCs could impact her interactions with teachers once she became a literacy coach, Colleen reports seeing how it would be important to interview and openly talk with a person that was racially or ethnically different from oneself before embarking on a coaching relationship. Colleen agreed that "people can teach in the same building, but know little or nothing about each other." The ABCs would be an avenue for opening up lines of communication.

FINAL THOUGHTS

It is not the intent of this chapter to oversimplify the complex and challenging task of helping literacy coaches learn to interact with teachers in culturally responsive ways. However, we have found that the ABCs of Cultural Understanding and Communication are an effective way to begin this process. They might serve as the first steps toward helping others learn to be more culturally responsive to the diverse learners and teachers they work with. The effectiveness of these approaches has been validated by the future literacy coaches we work with who report gaining valuable insights about themselves and others. Those insights translate into professional dispositions that guide teachers and coaches toward more critical and culturally responsive practices.

Once these insights become part of a coach's professional repertoire, their supportive roles for teachers will become more meaningful and their effectiveness as a literacy coach model might be realized. Once these activities lay the foundational groundwork, it is important to have teachers and coaches engage with communities unlike themselves in order to gain firsthand experience with others. This is not always easy to accommodate but is a necessary part of applying these concepts. The ABCs of Cultural Understanding and Communication are useful tools for educators and researchers working in his area. We have learned a lot about literacy coaching over the years, such as collaborative dialog for teachers (Shanklin, 2006) across all levels of experience and locations. Yet it seems that often the discussion of race, class, language, and culture are often missing in conversations about how to prepare literacy coaches. We recommend the ABCs of Cultural Understanding and Communication as an effective tool for literacy coaches' developing cultural competencies as they learn to mentor, lead, and provide expertise in schools.

NOTE

Dr. Patricia Edwards was asked to participate in the FIPSE Grant, but due to time constraints was unable to attend the ABCs workshops. Dr. Piazza was not a participant in the grant. However, both wished to contribute to this book.

REFERENCES

International Reading Association (IRA). (2010). *Standards for reading professionals 2010.* Retrieved November 15, 2011, from http://www.reading.org/downloads/resources/standards2010.pdf

National Council of Teachers of English (NCTE). (2006). *Standards for high school and middle school literacy coaches.* Newark, DE: International Reading Association.

Pressley, M., Rankin, J., & Yokoi, L. (1996). A survey of instructional practices of primary teachers nominated as effective at promoting literacy. *Elementary School Journal, 96*(4), 363–384.

Richardson, V., & Placier, P. (2001). Teacher change. In V. Richardson (Ed.), *Handbook of research on teaching* (4th ed., pp. 905–947). Washington, DC: American Educational Research Association.

Ruggiano Schmidt, P., & Finkbeiner, C. (2006). *ABC's of cultural understanding and communication: National and international adaptations.* Greenwich, CT: Information Age.

Shanklin, N. (2006). What are the effective characteristics of literacy coaches? Denver, CO: Literacy Coaching Clearinghouse. Retrieved December 9, 2011, from http://www.literacycoachingonline.org/briefs/CharofLiteracyCoachingNLS09-27-07.pdf

Spindler, G. D., & Spindler, L. (1987). *Interpretive ethnography of education: At home and abroad.* Hillsdale, NJ: Lawrence Erlbaum.

Toll, C.A. (2005). *The literacy coach's survival guide: Essential questions and practical answers.* Newark, DE: International Reading Association.

U.S. Department of Education, Institute of Education Sciences, National Center for Education Statistics, National Assessment of Educational Progress (NAEP). (2010). Retrieved March 5, 2012.

Walpole, S., & Blamey, K. L. (2008). Elementary literacy coaches: The reality of dual roles. *The Reading Teacher, 62,* 222–231.

CHAPTER 13

WOMEN OF THREE GENERATIONS

Gender Case Studies

Lilia Ratcheva-Stratieva

INTRODUCTION

This chapter is based on my experience as the instructor of five seminars using the ABCs of Cultural Understanding and Communication model (Ruggiano Schmidt, 1999; Ruggiano Schmidt & Finkbeiner, 2006), organized in urban settings in Europe—three in Bulgaria and two in Austria—during the lifetime of the project, that is, 2009–2011. The seminars were organized in cooperation with libraries and educational institutions in an informal educational context and participation was voluntary; based on a philosophy of "learning by doing," presenters made their own contributions during the seminar. The participants were teachers (mainly teachers of English), people working in multicultural societies, professional trainers, and final-year secondary school students.

Working with the seminar participants' texts, I was struck by the changes in the situation and views of Bulgarian women over the past 50 years. Because the participants repeatedly referred to their childhood and youth, their evolving views were highlighted, as well as those of the interviewed persons.

Getting to Know Ourselves and Others Through the ABCs, pages 209–222
Copyright © 2015 by Information Age Publishing
All rights of reproduction in any form reserved.

I was deeply moved by some of the life stories; I too had many intercultural experiences, so I was especially sensitive to the topic of cultural understanding and communication. What follows is a presentation of case studies illustrating the participants' responses to multicultural encounters based on an analysis of the contributions generated within the seminars—autobiographical and biographical texts by the participants, cross-cultural analysis, pre- and postpolarity profiles, proposals for culturally responsive ideas, postinterviews on cross-cultural analysis, and observations during the discussions in class.

Sociocultural Context and Setting

Up to 25 years ago, Bulgarian society was relatively homogenous, or at least it was considered homogenous. In Bulgaria, there are no officially recognized minorities—the Constitution of the Republic of Bulgaria makes no mention of any minorities. What is generally acknowledged is the existence of "ethnic minority communities"—Turkish, Armenian, Jewish, and Roma (Constitution of the Republic of Bulgaria). In the last 25 years the situation has changed. According to the Bulgarian National Institute for Statistics, only about 3,000 to 3,500 people immigrate to Bulgaria per year, and yet there is a visible immigrant presence.[1] Society is gradually becoming less homogeneous, especially in the capital and in the border regions. At the same time, many Bulgarians study or work abroad, making it more likely that they will communicate with other cultures.

The educational system in Bulgarian schools has been traditionally focused on foreign language teaching (which includes some intercultural teaching and learning) but as a whole it is still not adapted to the continually increasing possibilities of intercultural communication. Opportunities to acquire intercultural communication skills are still not well integrated into teaching and learning.

Purposes and Method

The very essence of the ABCs project, with its philosophy of "learning by doing," provides opportunities for the participants to become active learners and for the instructor to make the seminar both a dialogic process and a student-centred interactive activity (Knowles, Holton, & Swanson, 1998). Because most of the seminar participants had some knowledge and expertise on the topic, the classes provided them with an opportunity to articulate their initial knowledge and share their experience. Most of them were cooperative, collaborative, and supportive (to use the terms of Knowles et al., 1998), and a group dynamic was created in most of the cases. In addition to my duties as lecturer I also had to coordinate the lively class discussions.

During the ABCs project, the seminar participants had to write their own autobiography, beginning with the question "Who am I?" (Step A). Step B helped them to see the perspective of another by interviewing one other person. And finally, Step C, the cross-cultural analysis, helped them achieve a third nuanced perspective. Thus, the ABCs model claims to help students get a deeper view of the self, which is the first perspective,

> captured with the autobiography. The second perspective is the story told in the interview by partner B and then written down in a biography by partner A. . . . The cross-cultural analysis is the most difficult step to be taken. It ought to entail students going beyond the surface and the binary comparison of the two stories, step back and somehow develop a new third perspective. (Finkbeiner, 2009, pp. 165–166)

The seminar participants were expected to develop the ability to articulate sets of values that defined their own cultural framework. During the seminars, they were expected to learn how to point out cultural similarities and differences. This distinction was achieved by having participants compare the autobiography with the biography, and by using the cross-cultural approach. The seminar participants were also expected to achieve a more nuanced view of their own culture and enlarge their knowledge of it. They were acquainted with the concept of the Human GPS (Finkbeiner, 2009) and were expected to use the method of positioning themselves.

This chapter seeks to present through case studies some diachronic changes in the way women of three generations have responded to multicultural encounters and environments. Their values, ideas, and views are presented briefly through an analysis of their contributions produced during the ABCs of Cultural Understanding and Communication seminars; these contributions include autobiographies, biographies, and cross-cultural observations.

In their materials, seminar participants often use such expressions as "I was surprised," "What struck me," or "What surprised me," and such. For this reason, the notion of "areas of surprise" is used in this chapter to denote surprising observed similarities and differences. A straightforward empirical approach is adopted for presenting and analyzing the case studies.

The article also considers whether a better (or changed) knowledge of their own culture has been achieved by the seminar participants.

Case Studies

An Ethnic Turkish Woman of the Older Generation

One of the teachers taking part in the seminar interviewed her cleaning woman, named F.—a woman from the Turkish "ethnic community" in

Bulgaria, belonging to the 50+ generation. For this teacher, the interview produced many "areas of surprise," including the fact that the environment of an ethnic Turkish family in Bulgaria had a very strong influence on the lives of the children in that family.

The teacher shows this through the characteristics of the family of the interviewed woman and their family life in the 1950s and 1960s.

> She has got eleven sisters and brothers and she still talks affectionately about her brothers or sisters. She used to adore her parents. . . . Despite the poverty they lived in they were happy and reliant on one another. From an early childhood she gained an insight into something very simple but valuable in life— love is the key to happiness. Of course, she still remembers well the squalor she lived in during the post-war years. But that didn't discourage her at all. Instead, she became hard-working and confident that she would always have the support and love of her large family.

The problem was that to the support received by her family, the interviewed woman had to respond in kind. The teacher who interviewed the woman from the Turkish ethnic community in Bulgaria writes,

> As soon as she graduated from secondary school she started working so that she could help in the family. She is still quite happy with the living members of that closely-knit family. . . . A few years later her family found a suitable husband for her. In those small conservative communities it is important that you have a decent family, otherwise you become an outcast. So F. married a man whom she had met twice but who was a prospective candidate—someone known in the Muslim community as diligent, honest and a suffering widower who had to look after his son after the death of his wife in a car accident.

This marriage appeared to have been a failure, but the woman could not divorce. This fact was another area of surprise, confirming the teacher in her persuasion of the influence of the family and the community on women's destinies.

> It was unthinkable to separate because they didn't want to disappoint their families. So they both put up with the situation and started pretending that things were normal. F. knew that she had to sacrifice her happiness in order not to tarnish the family's reputation.

The personal destiny being shaped and decided upon by one's own family is considered by the interviewer a "sacrifice" and an instance of forsaking one's own personal life.

The process of "learning by doing" used in the ABCs model also turned out to be a process of overcoming stereotypes and prejudices about people from other ethnicities. "Before the interview I was convinced that we were totally different," writes the teacher.

> I was wondering what similarities I could find. By contrast, as you'll see in the comparison, the features we have in common are greater in number than our differences. The latter are mainly the visible differences which are due to the different lifestyles we have.

This teacher was surprised to discover 6 visible similarities and 6 visible differences, and 27 invisible similarities, while the invisible differences, she discovered, were only 10. "As for me," writes the teacher, "I was really surprised to find out while interviewing F. that the reasons for the mutual understanding we have are deeper, not just courtesy or because we enjoy doing our jobs." Despite differences in age, religion, education, and social status, both of them "have respect for other cultures, including rites, traditions, religion." Both of them "have respect for the things they do; believe in the restorative powers of Mother Nature"; both of them

> are devoted to the families and friends; enjoy the company of children and looking after them; have had a difficult childhood but for different reasons; are enthusiastic and deeply emotional; are vulnerable; are adaptable; are loyal; are conservative, generous, from time to time naïve, honest, tolerant, grateful.

Both of them "are class-conscious; believe in a supernatural power that is in charge of the order of the world; believe in the power of good deeds; believe that Life is the greatest teacher; believe in reincarnation; believe more in the alternative medicine." Both of them "condemn terrorism." Both of them

> have a tendency to live in a fictional world when under too much stress; adore living in the country but at the same time appreciate the opportunities the big town offers; take greater pleasure when pleasing others; have a humble origin; have married once.

But life has treated them differently—one has received a good education, the other has not been able to afford that; one is satisfied with her family life, her profession, and her job, the other is frustrated and thinks "she has wasted her life."

Concerning the ability to take initiative and to persist in action (again from the invisible part of the iceberg), we observe an opposite attitude of the woman from the ethnic Turkish community. She has accepted her destiny.

> What struck me was that F. looked resigned to the whole situation, with a few touches of sadness about not being able to bear a child which, beyond doubt,

would have changed her life considerably. But she believes that it ought to be that way in order to learn a lesson from "The Book of Life."

The gender issue appears here as well, that is, masculinity versus femininity. The life story of F. is an example of a woman who, 50 years ago, had to give up the attempt to shape her own destiny.

The mutual understanding leads the teacher to better imagine the problems people from the Turkish community have. As an example, she quotes the existential problems they had during the so-called name-changing campaign.[2] "During the interview," writes the teacher,

> I asked a painful question about the name-changing campaign. Actually I found out I knew almost nothing about it despite the documentaries I had watched. Before the conversation I was acquainted with some shameful facts from our history without even trying to penetrate into the seriousness of the matter, but when I heard the personal story of a woman who had suffered the consequences from it I gained an insight into it and that gave me a reasonable answer to the question why a person should be such a conformist. F. told me the story of her rebellious sister who was sent to a working camp—one of the communist camps for nonconformists—about the tortures and hard work she was subjected to, about the mayor who had to convince the Turkish ethnic community to peacefully change their names and about his remorse when sending rebels to labour camps. F. talked about the time they were forced to leave their homes within a day and the choice they had to make what to take before plunging into the unknown. Tears, sadness, painful partings with Bulgarian neighbours with whom they had been living harmoniously for years, breaking up with previous ways of life, not knowing what lay ahead are just a few of the things F. spoke about, downcast as if she was going through the process again.
>
> Then she started talking, obviously revived and relieved, about the time of her coming back to Bulgaria. She remembered the inspiration and the excitement within her when crossing the Bulgarian border back. Home again! The place where she had spent her carefree childhood wandering in the streets of her village invariably surrounded by a group of friends, always up to some mischief and getting the buzz out of it. Trying to get her out of her reverie, I felt quite uncomfortable and, in a way, guilty of the fact that most Bulgarians don't appreciate their Motherland.

This lengthy quote, with the emotional touch used by the teacher to tell the story of the ethnic Turkish woman, shows in an indirect way her overcoming of prejudices, her decisively changed attitude to the interviewed woman, as well as her critical approach to some periods of her culture's own history and the prejudices of the social group she belongs to.

During the ABCs seminars, the participants could become aware of the stereotypes and prejudices in their own culture and have understood that better knowledge of each other leads to overcoming stereotypes and prejudices.

This is also valid for the teacher interviewing a woman from the ethnic Turkish community, who writes,

> The Turkish community is the biggest in my country and for some historical reasons it is said to be the most disliked. Luckily, this is true only among some of our politicians. My humble experience shows that hardships during the so-called transitional period here have united both Christians and Muslims and they get on pretty well, especially when they have common interests like a business, for example. The past is long forgotten and the main goal of the majority of those people is earning a decent living. People in the country have respect for the traditions of the different religions and in some small villages in the country people even celebrate their holidays together on the central square.

Women of the Active Generation

Most seminar participants were women between 30 and 50 years of age, most of them teachers of English, self-confident, and independent. Some of them were lucky to have met in their life the role model, a teacher or an older person, who had shown them the right relationships between people.

These women are able to take initiative and to persist in action. Comparing their lives with that of the interviewed person, they often find great differences in the understanding of the family life and family relations, independently of the fact that they sometimes come from one culture and have the same social background.

"My son left our home when he was 18 and I am happy with that—giving him independence and responsibility, although I like living with him"— writes one of the teachers in her autobiography. "This is unusual for our culture—children live together with parents and grandparents—which I consider not beneficial to anybody. I consider taking responsibility for your own life as essential for a person's development and achievement of maturity." This teacher shows two different responses to the family relations—one traditional for the Bulgarian culture and the other, new, which depicted the changed relations.

The women from this generation often refer to the family life, which they consider of great importance for a fulfilling life; they observe and describe in their works the changes in the family structures and the family relations. In the works of the seminar participants, the family relations in different cultures are not only an area of surprise. These participants have also become aware of the significant changes and have gained a better understanding of their own culture as a culture in a period of transition from traditional to modern family values.

If we take into consideration the differences between individualist and collectivist cultures pointed out by the cross-cultural psychologists

(Hofstede, 1997), we could conclude that although the Bulgarian family culture is in general collectivistic, and children often live together with parents and grandparents, one can observe changes in the concept of various generations in a family living together or of communicating with each other and making decisions for each other. This collectivistic family tradition is being slowly destroyed and replaced by an individualist one.

The women in this category have witnessed many changes in the traditional behavior of their compatriots. Let us take, for example, the changes in the school milieu. The cross-cultural analysis in the school milieu shows big differences in teachers' behavior and the student-teacher relations over the time. Some of the seminars participants also write about a role model, a teacher who has shown them the right relationships between a teacher and the pupils and had influenced them to select this profession.

A seminar participant shares in her autobiography how, when she went to school 27 years ago, she was impressed by the behavior of her teacher of English from the UK. The story told by this teacher shows big differences in student-teacher relations between the British culture and the Bulgarian culture.

> She was a young energetic woman in her thirties who surprised us greatly with her behaviour. She was so friendly with us that we soon forgot our fears whether we were doing well. She managed to predispose everyone in class so that they started confiding in her even the deepest secrets—no language barriers, no generation gaps, without the usual confusion when speaking to a teacher.

This is how a participant describes her teacher of English from the UK, who was supposed to be teaching pronunciation. Using words and phrases such as "surprised," "friendly" "predispose," "we forgot our fears," "confiding in her the deepest secrets," "no generation gap," "without the usual confusion when speaking to a teacher," this teacher indirectly points out that this behavior was so striking because the pupils were not used to it in their culture. Indirectly, she reveals that at that time in her culture children were afraid when going to school; they were not predisposed to confide in their teachers, feeling confusion when speaking to a teacher and perhaps even more—that the teachers were unfriendly.

Analyzing the behavior of the teacher from the UK, this participant writes, "Not only did she teach us English, but she also acquainted us with a completely different culture from ours. She showed us a very different way of communication between a teacher and a student." This is a direct statement of the way communication in the two cultures was different. Thus, through the comparison with the different culture of behavior, this teacher started obtaining critical knowledge of her own culture. The above experience occurred some 27 years ago, when the teacher in question was at the English language secondary school.

Intercultural competences are acquired in a specific and temporarily defined cultural context. It would be curious to examine a similar experience in a changed context. A school experience was related by a final-year secondary school student, who interviewed her teacher of English, now, 27 years later. This teacher is a woman with roots in two cultures—the German and the Bulgarian cultures. Her mother was German, her father Bulgarian, and she grew up bilingual in Bulgaria. The teachers' behavior and student-teacher relations shown by this student now, 27 years later, are different, and words and phrases like the ones quoted above are rarely heard nowadays. Yet another dimension in the relations between students and teachers emerges: the teacher is open to suggestions and criticism from the students. The student concludes,

> Changing is the only constant in her life because she is open to suggestions and criticism from "her children." Paying attention to the feedback made her an extraordinary teacher. I can tell from my personal observations that it is a life-changing experience to have the chance to be on the list of her friends.

Women of the Future

This generation was represented in the seminars by several young women aged 17, 18, and 19. The final-year secondary school students were more surprised about the "culture shock" they experienced in the confrontation with other cultures or even with subcultures in their own culture. They had to go through a difficult acculturation and adjustment process in order to get used to a new environment.

As Weaver (1993, p. 139) points out,

> culture shock is most probably the result of a normal process of adaptation and may be no more harmful than the psychological reactions we experience when adapting to such new environmental situations as entering college or moving to another city in our own culture.

The problems of identity crisis and acculturation are closely connected. Some of the final-year secondary school students have gone through an identity crisis. Being confronted at the same time with the identity crisis of growing up, they have started seeing the world from a different perspective. While answering the preliminary questionnaire, a question containing the expression "my country" has made those young people born in Bulgaria whose families emigrated in Austria and who live and study there hesitate, wondering whether they have to write about Bulgaria or about Austria. This shows that after some years in Austria, their identity is not clear any longer, that the very notion of their identity is unstable and blurred.

The Bulgarian students in Austria are aware of the fact that one of the reasons for their parents' immigration has been the effort to provide better education and a better future for their kids. This knowledge has not freed them from the suffering of having been taken away from their roots. Some people need an especially long time to overcome culture shock.

A female student shares the following feelings:

> I'd just finished second grade when my mother moved to live in Vienna. For me this was the moment that changed my life. I often think what it would have been like if I had stayed in Bulgaria. But this is a question that I will probably ask all my life, not being able to answer it. Life in Vienna is very different, people are different, their way of living is different, the streets, the buildings, the school system, everything is different. I was nine years old and had just been taken away from my friends, relatives and my birthplace. The good thing was that I learned the language quickly and finished third with an excellent grade, even though I was only one year in Vienna. I learned the language, I found new "friends," but to this day I cannot get used to the fact that I am not in Bulgaria. I do not deny that here I am financially very well off, but I miss my friends, my family and especially my father. Now, just like nine years ago, I am looking forward to the coming summer, when I'll go back to Bulgaria for the holidays.

Further, the student lists the differences between the two cultures. Even children's games differ in both countries and the student's preferences are on the side of the games Bulgarian children play as being free and independent. Being aware of the similarities and differences is a step in the process of acculturation in the new culture; at the same time, an awareness of an early maturity acquired through the experienced process of adjustment arises.

The process of identity crisis for those students coincides with another transitional stage, typical for those who are 15 or older, namely, the period of adolescence, which makes the adjustment process even more difficult. The fact that many adolescent novels deal with this problem is not unusual. The quotation given above points out that this adolescent has developed strategies to facilitate the process of adjustment. Thus, besides new knowledge, they have acquired new skills and changed their life perspectives.

The teacher who interviewed the woman from the Turkish ethnic community has also been able to observe radical changes in family values and family relations in the Turkish ethnic community during the last 25 years.

> F.'s niece [her younger sister's daughter] is another cause in her life. F. feels responsible for her because S. was orphaned at the age of eighteen. Her mother died of cancer and S. had to go on living. After graduating from a language school the niece continued her studies at the University of Veliko Tarnovo [the second largest in Bulgaria] majoring in French Philology. She

studied part-time so that she could support herself, and in the summers she did seasonal work in France. The year before her graduation she decided to stay in France because she had fallen in love with a French boy and a few months later she got pregnant.

Not a single trace here of the sacrifice the aunt was obliged to make, no hint of the obligation to keep the honor of the family. The teacher conscientiously gives this information in her essay in order to signal the annihilation of the traditional family structures and values even in this close-knit family of the Turkish ethnic community.

I would like to conclude with the statements of a 17-year-old female student with roots in two cultures—Bulgarian and Nigerian—named L. Although she does not mention any negative experience from her childhood in Bulgaria, in an indirect way she shows that she has had such a negative experience—through saying she was the only person in her class to show understanding and comprehension to a new student from Korea. Her understanding to people coming from other cultures who are rejected only because of the fact that their behavior or their appearance are different probably suggests that she herself had experienced an unfriendly attitude toward those who are different and that she probably also had problems with her classmates because of her mixed origin and the colour of her skin. Her own experience, as well as the experience of the interviewed person from another culture, made the student in question, despite her different talents and possibilities, more determined in her decision to work further in the field of intercultural communication.

"Differences should be treated as fortunate, not as disgraceful," writes L.

> My priority in life will be to promote the unique qualities from different cultures and by enlightening them how to preserve and take advantage of them. His story [of the interviewed person] gave me ideas how to help a foreigner to integrate in the society, and also to do something beneficial for himself/herself.

The same student starts speaking directly when she describes certain stereotypes and prejudices and expresses criticism to her own culture because of that.

The impressions of her first visit to Nigeria are of special interest. Although eager to see her grandparents for the first time, the Bulgarian student with origins in two cultures—Bulgaria and Nigeria—started her first trip to Nigeria full of preliminary stereotypes and prejudices about the country. Upon arriving there, she was surprised at the extent to which her perspectives had been manipulated "by the hardcover books and the mass media. Most people associate every African country with underdevelopment, except the countries in the northern part of the continent," writes the student.

> Travelling by road from a city to rural areas in Nigeria, I spotted some village houses with satellite dishes and moreover the national passports are issued with biometric data. I agree that there is poverty. However, people find the power within themselves to be contented and joyful.

This statement shows again one area of surprise and reminds us again that better knowledge of each other leads to overcoming stereotypes and prejudices.

> During my experience in Nigeria, the facts which I possess increased. The collision between the different cultural practices within the country and mine had given me a better understanding and comprehension of their lifestyle. Face-to-face communication can promote and enhance peaceful and cooperative relations between individuals. I travelled to Nigeria to seek enlightenment and familiarity with my relatives, but I have acquired much more—I have sustained what I have learned and applied it to my everyday life.

CONCLUSION

Comparing these women's responses to intercultural encounters or their life stories is problematic, as they all have different social backgrounds. Also problematic is to what extent they may be seen as representative of Bulgarian women as a whole. Yet it is evident that the women of today who took part in the seminars are no longer prepared to sacrifice their lives; they are no longer victims of the idea of "loyalty" to their families. Although family life continues to be the most important for them, these Bulgarian women have become self-confident and independent, satisfied with their careers and their status in society. This process must have been difficult for the women from the ethnic minority, on the one hand due to the values of loyalty to the family and the perceived necessity to sacrifice their life for the family and, on the other hand, due to the fact that belonging to an ethnic community they have perhaps suffered more from the prejudices and the stereotypes of the larger society. As far as the the youngest generation is concerned, from the materials the young people delivered we could conclude that it is confronted with much greater and more multifaceted intercultural challenges.

The case studies show that as the result of the seminars, the quoted participants have been able to compare cultural similarities and differences, to articulate sets of values that defined their own cultural framework. The described "areas of surprise" have helped them achieve a more nuanced view of their own culture and enlarge their knowledge of it.

They have themselves underlined that through the process of "learning by doing" and of analyzing different behaviors, they have managed to overcome stereotypes and prejudices. They say that they have also started seeing their own culture from a different, critical perspective. As evident from the postinterviews, they are satisfied with the knowledge and skills they acquired during the seminars. They have become aware of the necessity of intercultural competencies and are motivated to further introduce such competencies in their classes. A teacher states in the postinterview that as a result of the ABCs seminars she has introduced lessons about culture shock in her English classes. Becoming acquainted with the concept of the Human GPS (Finkbeiner, 2009), the students have become aware that the "Human GPS Journey is never over. It is a journey of a lifetime."

NOTES

1. These data are for the period when the seminars were organized. The external migration from Bulgaria at this time was between 15,000 and 27,000 per year. The latest data of the Bulgarian National Institute for Statistics, from the year 2013, show that the external migration to Bulgaria increased to 18,570. Meanwhile the external migration from Bulgaria decreased somewhat to 19,600 from its peak of 27,000. The statistical data do not indicate the nationality of the people who migrated to Bulgaria. We can assume that due to the economic crises many Bulgarians lost their jobs abroad and came back to the country. Even so, their children have spent many years abroad (some were even born abroad) and a process of acculturation is necessary even for them, and even more necessary for non-Bulgarians coming to the country.

2. In late 1984 and in 1985 in Communist Bulgaria, there was a process of a forced changing of the Turkic names of people of Turkish ethnicity with Bulgarian names; then in 1988 and 1989 followed a similarly forced process of driving such people into emigration, when about 360,000 representatives of the Turkish ethnicity emigrated from Bulgaria into Turkey; later about 150,000–160,000 of them came back to Bulgaria.

ACKNOWLEDGMENT

The author would like to acknowledge the following: Luben Karavelov Regional Library, Ruse; Foreign Language Reading Hall, Teodora Stoyanova, Luben Karavelov Regional Library, Ruse; the Pencho Slaveykov Regional Library, Varna, American Corner; Tsvetelina Voycheva, Pencho Slaveykov Regional Library, Varna; the Foreign Language School, Varna; Pavla Ivanova, teacher of English, Foreign Language School, Varna; American Corner, the Sofia City Library; Kameliya Koneva and Diana Velkova, American Corner, Sofia City Library; Eva Rohrer, Professional Trainer, Vienna, Austria; Bulgarian-Austrian Free Time School, Vienna, Austria; Irina Vladikov, Director of the Bulgarian-Austrian Free Time School, Vienna, Austria.

REFERENCES

Constitution of the Republic of Bulgaria, Article 6, paragraph 2 [Конституция на Република България, чл. 6, ал. 2]. Национален статистически институт, България National Institute for Statistic, Bulgaria.

Finkbeiner, C. (2009). Using "human global positioning system" as a navigation tool to the hidden dimension of culture. In A. Feng, M. Byram, M. Fleming (Eds.), *Becoming interculturally competent through education and training* (pp. 151–153). Bristol, UK: Multilingual Matters.

Hofstede, G. (1997). *Cultures and organizations: Software of the mind.* New York, NY: McGraw-Hill.

Knowles, M. S., Holton, E. G., & Swanson, R. A. (1998). *The adult learner: The definitive classic in adult education and human resources development.* Houston, TX: Gulf.

Ruggiano Schmidt, P. (1999). Know thyself and understand others. *Language Arts,* 76(4), 332–340.

Ruggiano Schmidt, P. & Finkbeiner, C. (2006). *ABC's of cultural understanding and communication: National and international adaptations.* Greenwich, Connecticut: IAP

Weaver, G. R. (1993). Understanding and coping with cross-cultural adjustment stress. In R. M. Paige (Ed.), *Education for the intercultural experience* (2nd ed., pp. 137–167). Yarmouth, ME: Intercultural.

CHAPTER 14

FUTURE DIRECTIONS FOR THE Abcs OF CULTURAL UNDERSTANDING AND COMMUNICATION

Althier M. Lazar and Claudia Finkbeiner

INTRODUCTION

The authors of this book participated in a grand experiment. We set out to see how two groups of scholars—one from the United States and one from the European Union—could advance research on the ABCs Model of Cultural Understanding and Communication (Ruggiano Schmidt & Finkbeiner, 2006). On either side of the Atlantic, each group of scholars agreed to test the model's usefulness in a variety of contexts. This joint effort has succeeded in developing more nuanced perceptions of how the ABCs model works to engender greater cultural understanding, language awareness, and acceptance (Fehling, 2008).

Cultural understanding is an essential goal in today's complex world. As technology has made the world a smaller place, people of different backgrounds are able to cross cultural boundaries in ways that would have been unfathomable half a century ago. Technology has both the power to forge

Getting to Know Ourselves and Others Through the ABCs, pages 223–234
Copyright © 2015 by Information Age Publishing
223

greater human understanding and acceptance but also to capture or even trigger cultural conflict in the world. Television, the Internet, and smart phones can instantly bring to our screens the often cruel outcomes of cultural conflict.

Within larger contexts of control and power, conflicts can be precipitated by hatred of certain kinds of individuals and/or groups that have differing beliefs, practices, and worldviews. Hatred can be rooted in fear and/or cultural misunderstanding, which often originates in a lack of cultural knowledge and awareness as well as an absence of empathy and a resistance to changing perspectives. However, conflicts can also be triggered through concern or even greediness about access to resources or sometimes simply through the natural drive to survive.

Cultural misunderstanding can be the reason why some people seem to be indifferent to others' oppression and suffering. The culturally marginalized are all too often considered expendable. Also pervasive are problems of cultural conflict that undermine productivity in school and at work as well as in the workplace. For all of these reasons, the topic of cultural conflict is critical, not only for teachers who have a great responsibility to raise the level of cultural appreciation among their students but for all of us who relate to culturally different others across a wide variety of work settings. All of us need to be invested in understanding ourselves in relation to each other in order to bring about a more peaceful and productive world.

We particularly recognize the responsibility of teachers to advance cultural understanding. As documented in this book, many American and European teachers are serving rising numbers of culturally diverse students, and many of these students live in underserved, high-poverty communities. These students have a background different from those in dominant mainstream groups and speak a language other than the official instructional language. Their rich multicultural and multilingual funds of knowledge are often unrecognized or unvalued in school. The ABCs can provide windows into the rich knowledge traditions that students bring to the classroom.

The authors of this book are most interested in bringing the power of the ABCs model to teachers and other professionals so they may better understand and validate the cultures of those they serve, educate, and cooperate with as well as those as yet unknown to them. We need not only to prepare for the known of today but also for the unknown of tomorrow because the only thing that we can predict is that the future is unpredictable. For these reasons, we provide research that shows the possibilities and limitations of the ABCs model as a tool for enhancing cultural understanding.

In this chapter, we will summarize what has been learned so far from these studies and how this research can inform future practice and inquiry. Specifically, we will explore what teachers and teacher educators can do to deepen and extend the model in order to maximize its potential.

New Assertions About the ABCs Model

Most of the chapters in this book describe how the ABCs model worked to further teacher candidates' knowledge of themselves and others and point out that this knowledge is key for enhancing their understanding and appreciation of others. The central goal of the TRANSABCs project was to advance our understanding of the ABCs model by disseminating and examining as well as evaluating it across nations and populations as well as specific groups and by focusing on particular perspectives.

The researchers in this book have examined the application of the ABCs model cross-nationally and with respect to specific subgroups. This includes gender and cultural profiles, such as involving openness towards cultural heterogeneity (Finkbeiner; Neer & Neer); content areas such as literacy (Xu; Lazar; Edwards & Piazza); issues of identity, critical thought, and readiness for action (Fehling; Bandura; Lundgren); matters of gender (Ratcheva-Stratieva; Cots; Finkbeiner); and certain professional roles, such as reading coaches (Edwards & Piazza). A few researchers focused on what happens when the ABCs project is modified to allow participants to look for themes across autobiographies and biographies (Lazar; Ruan). The EU authors Bandura, Cots, Fehling, Finkbeiner, Lundgren, and Ratcheva-Stratieva additionally looked at the ABCs in a language environment that was different from the main instructional language in the specific national or federal context by using English as a *lingua franca* throughout the complete ABCs discourse.

After the qualitative analyses were completed, we began looking at the impact of the ABCs project within different U.S. and EU settings (Finkbeiner) and found that those who were most culturally intolerant in the United States, Germany, Poland, and Spain before participating in the project significantly increased their openness toward cultural diversity as a result of their participation in the ABCs. The tool that served as the instrument was a cultural survey (Ruggiano Schmidt & Finkbeiner, 2009); one scale gained through factor analyses turned out to be statistically valid and stable across time (Finkbeiner). Interview data across these nations affirmed that the teacher candidates and professionals participating in the study became more knowledgeable about communicating and connecting with culturally diverse students and co-workers. Furthermore, evidence suggested that these participants were able to bring new understandings about cultural diversity to classrooms and workplaces to create more culturally responsive spaces. This finding suggests that the ABCs can serve as a tool that can significantly enhance cross-cultural appreciation and understanding across nations.

Following this research, chapter authors presented assertions about the impact of the ABCs model in specific settings with particular populations. They provided evidence that the ABCs model enhanced participants' ability to

- reflect critically on the construction of self, society, and culture, including ways of knowing and of understanding the world about them and of acting in it; for many, the ABCs model led to self-interrogation (Bandura; Finkbeiner; Finkbeiner & Davidson; Neer & Neer);
- explore and analyze identity construction (Ruan; Fehling);
- become better able to take action to teach intercultural competence and further world citizenship (Lundgren; Ruan);
- become culturally more open-minded and less xenophobic as well as more accepting of differences (Finkbeiner; Neer & Neer);
- consider issues of power, privilege, and subordination as facets of culture (Lazar; Ratcheva-Stratieva; Xu);
- examine issues of access to mainstream or school-valued literacy and language practices (Lazar; Xu);
- integrate students' prior cultural and linguistic experiences into lesson planning; this includes considering home-school connections, encouraging varied levels of engagement, and offering students opportunities to practice multiple dimensions of literacy (Xu);
- expand teacher and business candidates' understandings of what culture means (all authors);
- employ a multilingual approach in the ABCs and integrate foreign language learning (Bandura; Cots; Fehling; Finkbeiner; Finkbeiner & Davidson; Lundgren; Ratcheva-Stratieva);
- enhance working relationships between coaches and teachers (Edwards & Piazza);
- develop culturally responsive ideas (Finkbeiner; Neer & Neer).

Challenges Discovered Throughout the Journey

Researchers not only learned the value of the ABCs model, they also uncovered some of its limitations. Bandura found that her students in Poland did not become independent in their ability to construct knowledge of themselves and others as they participated in the project: "They expected to be guided and told explicitly that questioning and expressing doubts or ignorance are allowed in the essays." This might suggest at first glance that unless otherwise directed by the professor or teacher, candidates would not necessarily be able to continue an inquiry of self and other when the project is completed. This raises the possibility that some candidates frame the ABCs model as a "school or university project" with no practical relevance to their future lives. Furthermore, a pure "school or university project" can create a bias as students might be driven by the ideas of constructing their life stories according to the teacher's liking. The intent of the original framers of the model was the exact opposite (Ruggiano Schmidt, 2001;

Ruggiano Schmidt & Finkbeiner, 2006), expecting that the processes used in the model would be assimilated by candidates on some level and carried with them into their future lives. In order to achieve this goal, it is necessary to make sure that ABCs participants know how to independently construct knowledge about themselves and others, and if they struggle with this part of the process, it is important to explicitly model it. Furthermore, the ABCs can only really come about in a meaningful way if there is an anxiety-free learning environment that allows participants to express their ideas freely.

This said, we need to consider an important factor: there are huge differences in cultural scripts as to what students consider "good teaching and learning" across different educational systems (Finkbeiner, 2008). Here the teachers' roles as well as the values regarding "good teaching" come into play. In educational systems where the teacher is considered the "guru" as well as the nonquestioned authority and lessons are conducted in a teacher-oriented way, the foundations to teach the ABCs first have to be laid. This was definitely a big challenge for the two participating partners who taught in countries that were located in Eastern Europe (Bandura; Ratcheva-Stratieva).

A few researchers reported the ABCs model could only take candidates so far in their understanding and appreciation of cultural diversity. Ruan, for instance, found that candidates continued to harbor assumptions and stereotypes about those they interviewed. Participating in the ABCs project will not automatically eliminate ignorance and cultural intolerance. Quite a few of the teacher candidates in these studies are described as having reached adulthood without having had many opportunities to explore who they are culturally, to really know those who are culturally different from themselves, or to have had educational opportunities that would challenge their assumptions about culturally different others. Values and attitudes developed throughout a long acculturation process from the womb, to birth, early childhood, youth, and into young adulthood (Finkbeiner, 2006) cannot be simply changed by one course project. Learned values and beliefs influence our perceptions of the world and our expectation hypotheses and thus can lead to self-fulfilling prophecies (Finkbeiner, 2003). However, the good news, as expressed in the title of this volume, is that the ABCs are a journey and not just a one-day excursion. Carefully and slowly they take the traveler to the unknown self and the unknown other. The ABCs are a homeopathic remedy. Since all of us are embedded in cultures within dynamic systems, change is constant and inevitable and part of a lifelong journey.

Overall, the studies described in this volume have produced overwhelming evidence that the model helps most teacher candidates recognize that knowing themselves and others is a necessary part of becoming culturally competent and that this is an important goal for future educators.

As mentioned before, researchers commented that the model did not teach students to question and change the status quo in their cross-cultural analysis papers (Ruan), nor did it prompt candidates to design intercultural activities that encourage criticality (Bandura). We acknowledge this limitation of the model since it does not automatically include specific instructions on how to direct participants to engage in a number of critical explorations, such as questioning the perspectives of themselves and others, interrogating how the project is conducted and studied, or using critical perspectives (such as feminist or Marxist theories) to analyze the autobiographies or biographies within the cross-cultural analysis portion of the project. Which focus to set is left to the freedom of each ABCs teacher, often in mutual agreement with the students. For example, on the Kassel and Bayreuth campuses (Fehling; Finkbeiner), critical discourse analysis by Fairclough (1992) is used for the cross-cultural analysis in Step C. Critical discourse analysis undertakes three steps of analysis: "description of the text; interpretation of the interaction processes and their relationship to the text; and explanation of how the interaction process relates to the social action" (pp. 10–11). This analysis not only allows us to look at formal aspects and the choice of the language of the autobiography, biography, and cross-cultural comparison but also at the "frame," which gives us hints as to the contextual determination of language choice. Furthermore, the form differentiating between surface, hybrid, and deep layers of the iceberg (Weaver, 1993), introduced in Finkbeiner, helped facilitate students' critical investigations into selves and others.

Another interesting approach is suggested by Cots. He had his students apply Scollon and Scollon's (1995) four major factors having an impact on intercultural communication—ideology, social organization, forms of discourse, and socialization—as well as the two factors of positive and negative politeness (Brown & Levinson, 1987).

To conclude, there is no reason why critical approaches toward the study of culture should not be used throughout the ABCs process. Therefore, Ruan's statement is worth repeating: "It is possible that additional study of critical pedagogy (Lankshear & McLaren, 1993) and critical literacy (McDaniel, 2006) would help ABCs participants see their responsibility to enhance students' critical consciousness."

It is also necessary for researchers/professors to demonstrate what critical thinking and pedagogy look like in the context of the ABCs project. Bandura, Finkbeiner, and Ruan highlight the importance of continuously involving teachers and students in the process of criticality and reflexivity.

While we recognize some limitations of the ABCs model, the evidence clearly indicates the potential of the model to enhance cultural knowledge and sensitivity. The studies in this volume have opened up possibilities for future inquiry that can affirm and strengthen the initial findings presented in this book.

The Role of Language in a Multilingual World

In further ABCs inquiries and other intercultural projects, language ought to be considered a decisive factor throughout the process (Finkbeiner & Koplin, 2002). This is also important in an assumed "monolingual" context. According to Bhabha (1994), the very concept of homogeneous cultural entities is obsolete, and there is evidence of growing hybridity. As language and culture are most closely connected, we transfer Bhabha's statement to languages. There is not a homogeneous language situation anymore. The multilingual context might not be visible immediately, and in what seems to be a "monolingual society" at first glance, multilingualism is present: this can be perceived through language awareness-raising activities such as the language silhouette (Krumm, 2002) and the learning gallery (Finkbeiner, 2009). These activities help learners become aware of who they are linguistically and help them value the language funds they can draw on. The highly creative tasks can also help them see where there is need to do more in and for a language that might not be used as much anymore in order not to lose it.

Language usually works as a motor, and without it, the ABCs journey would not be possible. However, at the same time, the language engine can stall or burn out if fueled with the wrong fluids or if not checked regularly. And if it is not fed continuously, after several runs, it will most likely not run anymore. Each motor has different settings and needs different care. This simile has several implications: Language has to be a decisive factor before we start the ABCs journey. In this context, the following questions might be helpful at the beginning of an ABCs course:

- What is the language situation like locally, institutionally, groupwise, and individually?
- Do we face a multilingual context?
- What is the language profile of each ABCs participant? In which languages does the student have "Cognitive Academic Language Proficiency" (CALP) and in which ones only "Basic Interactive Communicative Skills" (BICS) (Cummins, 1986)?
- In which language(s) does each individual feel at home and safe?
- Is there a common language the entire learning group can share, and if so which one? What are the shortcomings of common languages with respect to expressing individual life stories?
- What language design is planned and implemented for each single step?
- What competency level can we expect, and how does this influence the expression of self?
- How far do power and language (dominant language vs. minority language) come into play?

- How can we overcome power and language? What effect does it have if we pair up linguistic experts and novices?

All these questions ought to be carefully considered as we construct identity through language, and thus, the language factor has to be taken seriously (Finkbeiner & Koplin, 2002).

Future Research on the ABCs Model

The authors of this book have established new and exciting possibilities for future research. Based on the preliminary findings presented in this book, additional inquiry is needed to explore

- the impact and effect of the ABCs process on cultural openness (Finkbeiner; Finkbeiner & Davidson; Neer & Neer);
- the processes by which participants negotiate the tension between framing project partners as "others" and minimizing their cultural differences (Cots);
- methods of discourse analysis in how participants describe themselves and others (Cots; Fehling; Neer & Neer);
- the social and power relationships between participants (Cots; Ratcheva-Stratieva);
- the ways identities are formed through the process of creating autobiographies (Fehling); the addition of a more explicit focus on critical pedagogy/critical literacy and how it might impact teachers' critical thought and actions (Lazar; Bandura; Finkbeiner; Lundgren);
- participants' exposure to multiple autobiographies and biographies to deepen participants' cultural exposure (Fehling; Ruan; Lazar; Neer & Neer);
- how the different parts of the ABCs model impact identity formation (Fehling; Lundgren);
- the role of English as a foreign and international language and *lingua franca* (Bandura; Cots; Fehling; Finkbeiner; Lundgren);
- how the ABCs model is used with participants who teach in content areas (literacy, math, science) and foreign languages (Bandura; Cots; Fehling; Finkbeiner; Lundgren; Xu; Neer & Neer);
- how the implementation of the ABCs model at different stages of a teacher preparation program might impact candidates' knowledge about diversity and their ability to teach (Xu; Neer & Neer);
- the different experiences of candidates based on their racial/ethnic/language affiliations (Xu);

- how the sociocultural context and participants' attitudes influence the ABCs process (Bandura; Ruan);
- how the ABCs model can be used to improve mentor-mentee relationships (Edwards & Piazza);
- the effect of a multiperspective Human GPS approach (Finkbeiner, 2009) using the ABCs in a triangular cooperative setting.

We also offer a few words about methods of researching the ABCs. TRANSABCs used a mixed-methods research design that allowed data triangulation. We suggest that this mixed-method approach may also be used for future studies in order to better capture the impact of the ABCs model. Qualitative studies are enhanced when researchers not only report on typical themes that surface in the data corpus but also take into account how these themes are representative within the entire group of teacher candidates as well as candidates for the workplace. Including information about the percentages of typical and atypical themes that surface is necessary for readers to discern how much of an impact the model has on a particular group of participants. Quantitative studies are enhanced when researchers capture the meaning perspectives of the participants so that readers can better understand the conditions that underlie the findings. We also support the need to continue to retest the reliability and validity of the instruments used to measure the model's effectiveness, such as the pre/post tests of the culture survey (Ruggiano Schmidt & Finkbeiner, 2009) and the pre/post tests of the polarity profile tool (Finkbeiner, 2005).

New Directions and Variations of the ABCs

Researchers who changed the structure of the ABCs model to maximize its impact (Lazar; Ruan) raise some intriguing possibilities for reconceptualizing the model while retaining its core elements. Both researchers asked teacher candidates to participate in the autobiography, biography, and cross-cultural comparison parts of the model, but they also asked that some of these documents be shared with other teacher candidates. In Ruan's study, for instance, candidates were not limited to reading and reflecting on their own autobiographies and the biographies they wrote based on their interviews with one person. Rather, they read and reflected on multiple autobiographies produced by several members of the teacher candidate group and did the same for the biographies produced by the teacher candidates. As Ruan declared, this effort "resulted in sharing multiple cultures, perspectives, and viewpoints from a larger group of culturally diverse people." In this context, the ABCs were used in a reciprocal way, as suggested by Finkbeiner and Koplin (2002) in the European adaptation. If this variation is used, it is important to clarify at the beginning of the course that the stories will be shared in class, as this might change the script and content of the texts.

In Lazar's study, teacher candidates shared their cross-cultural comparison papers with each other. Positioned as researchers, these students were asked to identify the typical and atypical themes across these papers. Teachers were then asked to write about their discoveries and discuss them with their peers. This multilevel approach shifted the responsibility for research analysis to teacher candidates and positioned researchers and teacher candidates as co-investigators. Not only did the teacher candidates in this study examine many dimensions of culture across several people, they learned to apply some basic rules of qualitative research in the context of collaborative peer groups.

In addition, ABCs participants who followed up with their own school studies or studies in the workplace also followed this approach of allowing students to cooperatively create Step C together. In international collaboration, Step C was presented orally to the classes at both ends via video conference (Goebel, 2012).

We can think of many similar extensions of the ABCs model. Candidates could be asked not only to read a range of autobiographies, biographies, and cross-cultural analyses produced by a group, but each candidate could also be involved in interviewing several people to produce multiple biographies and cross-cultural analyses. Candidates would strive to select interviewees who represent a range of cultures. The complexity of such an assignment would require extended time, and it is consistent with Xu's suggestion that this project be carried out over a much longer time period, perhaps over the course of the entire teacher education program. Communication tools such as Skype would increase candidates' access to interviewees.

As many researchers have suggested, additional or alternative categories of information can be added so that candidates can produce autobiographies and biographies that would guarantee analysis of particular dimensions of culture, such as power and/or gender relationships. Furthermore, a focus can be set on career aspirations, content areas such as the role of nature in participants' lives, or survivors and witnesses of certain historical or natural events (Finkbeiner). We must caution here that extremely structured directions for self-reflection or interviewing others may result in excluding facets of one's life story that surface as a result of investigating broad categories of experience, such as one's happiest memories or greatest life challenges. Furthermore, absolute caution and maybe even a "no" is necessary in cases where events may have been perceived as traumatizing. ABCs instructors are not trained as psychologists. Ultimately, we want to retain the integrity of the original ABCs model but strengthen its capacity to produce understanding, empathy, and action.

Another iteration of the ABCs model would be a multimodal approach to capturing the life stories of oneself and others as modeled by Wilden (2007). Instead of writing narratives, candidates might be involved in combining images, spoken words, and print in ways that reflect the cultural lives of self and others. These can be incorporated into rich visual displays using either PowerPoint as done in the follow-up project by Goebel (2012) or any number of web-based tools such as those that produce posters (Edu. glogster.com), timelines (http://timeline.thinkport.org), or presentations (www.prezi.com and http://www.capzles.com/#). To protect the anonymity of candidates and interviewees, talking avatars can be used as stand-ins for real people (www.voki.com).

FINAL THOUGHTS

The scholars in this book, representing the United States and the EU, have decided to begin to address the problem of cultural intolerance by inviting hundreds of undergraduate and graduate students to participate in the *ABCs Model of Cultural Understanding and Communication* (Ruggiano Schmidt & Finkbeiner, 2006). Findings from these studies have demonstrated the potential of the model to produce more reflective and culturally aware individuals. We have defined some of the limitations of the model and hope that our suggestions for augmenting it will be taken up without compromising its core function—to "know thyself and understand others" (Ruggiano Schmidt, 1999) through deep interpersonal contact and analysis. Our goal is that the positive momentum generated by this research multiplies to such an extent that the ABCs model becomes the tool of choice for those who wish to begin their journey toward greater cultural awareness. Given the level of hatred, intolerance, and apathy in the world today, this must be a global imperative. However, given the level of cross-cultural cooperation and support that we experienced during the global TRANSABCs project, we believe there is not just hope but also trust in that we can do something to better this world. As the wing of a butterfly can change the world (Lorenz, 1963), we do believe in the power of small steps of many.

REFERENCES

Bhabha, H. (1994). The location of culture. London, UK: Routledge.

Brown, P., & Levinson, S. (1987). Politeness. Some universals in language usage. Cambridge, UK: Cambridge University Press.

Cummins, J. (1986). Empowering minority students: A framework for intervention. Harvard Educational Review, 56(1), 18–36.

Fairclough, N. (1992). Critical language awareness. London, UK; New York, NY: Longman.

Fehling, S. (2008). Language Awareness und bilingualer Unterricht: Eine komparative Studie (2nd ed.). Frankfurt, Germany: Peter Lang.

Finkbeiner, C. (2003). What teachers think about how students read. In B. Di Biase (Ed.), Developing a second language: Acquisition, processing and pedagogy of Arabic, Chinese, English, Italian, Japanese, Swedish (pp. 73–94). Melbourne: Language Australia.

Finkbeiner, C. (2006). Constructing third space. The principles of reciprocity and cooperation. In P. Ruggiano Schmidt & C. Finkbeiner (Eds.), The ABC's of cultural understanding and communication: National and international adaptations (pp. 19–42). Greenwich, CT: Information Age.

Finkbeiner, C. (2008). Culture and good language learners. In C. Griffiths (Ed.), Lessons from good language learners (pp. 131–141). Cambridge, UK: Cambridge University Press.

Finkbeiner, C. (2009). Using "human global positioning system" as a navigation tool to the hidden dimension of culture. In A. Feng, M. Byram, & M. Fleming (Eds.), Becoming interculturally competent through training and education (pp. 151–173). Bristol, UK; Tonawanda, NY; Ontario, Canada: Multilingual Matters.

Finkbeiner, C., & Koplin, C. (2002). A cooperative approach for facilitating intercultural education. Reading Online, 6(3). Retrieved from http://www.readingonline.org/newliteracies/lit_index.asp?HREF=/newliteracies/finkbeiner

Goebel, A. (2012). The self and the other in an intercultural online encounter: An explorative study between Dutch and Indian primary school children based on the ABC's of cultural understanding and communication. (teacher state examination thesis). Kassel, Germany: University of Kassel.

Krumm, H. J. (2002). "Mein Bauch ist italienisch..." Kinder sprechen über Sprachen. Grundschule Sprachen (2002), 36–39.

Lankshear, C., & McLaren, P. (1993). Critical literacy: Politics, praxis and the postmodern. Albany: State University of New York Press.

Lorenz, E. N. (1963, March). Deterministic nonperiodic flow. Journal of the Atmospheric Sciences, 20(2), 130–141.

McDaniel, C. A. (2006). Critical literacy: A way of thinking, a way of life. New York, NY: Peter Lang.

Ruggiano Schmidt, P. (1999). Focus on research: Know thyself and understand others. Language Arts, 76(4), 332–340.

Ruggiano Schmidt, P., & Finkbeiner, C. (2006). ABC's of cultural understanding and communication: National and international adaptations. Greenwich, CT: Information Age.

Scollon, R., & Scollon, S. (1995). Intercultural communication. Oxford, UK: Blackwell.

Weaver, G. R. (1993). Understanding and coping with cross-cultural adjustment stress. In R. M. Paige (Ed.), Education for the intercultural experience (pp. 137–167). Yarmouth, ME: Intercultural.

Wilden, E. (2007). Voice chats in the intercultural classroom: The ABC's on-line project. In R. O'Dowd (Ed.). Online intercultural exchange: An introduction for foreign language teachers (pp. 271–277). Clevedon: Multilingual Matters.

ABOUT THE EDITORS

Claudia Finkbeiner is professor of applied linguistics, foreign language research and intercultural communication at the University of Kassel (Germany). She has been the chair of the Association of Language Awareness (ALA) since 2006 and has served as visiting professor around the world. Her fields of interest include foreign language research, language awareness, cultural awareness and intercultural education, EFL reading and literacy development, strategies, interest, CLIL and holistic learning, and the relevance of these issues for the education of students, teachers, and people in the workplace. Her books include *Teaching English in the European Dimension, Qualification Expectations of the Society and Students' Attitudes* and *Interests, Reports and Contexts of Two Empirical Studies* (1995), as well as *Interests and Strategies in Foreign Language Reading: How Students Read and Comprehend English Texts* (2005), and with co-editor Agneta Svalberg, *"Awareness Matters: Language Culture, Literacy"* (2015).

Althier M. Lazar is professor of education at Saint Joseph's University in Philadelphia, Pennsylvania. Her research focuses on the ways teachers and teacher candidates evolve in their understandings of culture, literacy, and language, and how these understandings translate to social equity teaching. Her books include *Bridging Literacy and Equity: The Guide to Social Equity Teaching* (2012), with co-authors Patricia Edwards and Gwendolyn Thompson McMillon, *Practicing What We Teach: How Culturally Responsive Literacy Classrooms Make a Difference* (2011), with coeditor Patricia Ruggiano Schmidt, and *Learning to Be Literacy Teachers in Urban Schools: Stories of Growth and Change* (2004).

ABOUT THE CONTRIBUTORS

Michael Byram is Professor Emeritus at Durham University and Guest Professor at the University of Luxembourg. He earned his PhD in Danish literature from Cambridge University and has taught French and German in secondary and adult education. Professor Byram has trained teachers and researched linguistic minorities and foreign language education. From 2000 to 2011, he was adviser to the Language Policy Division of the Council of Europe and, with Adelheid Hu, produced in 2013 the second edition of the *Routledge Encyclopedia of Language Teaching and Learning*. His most recent book is *From Foreign Language Education to Education for Intercultural Citizenship* (2008).

Ewa Bandura is a senior lecturer at the Institute of English Studies, Faculty of Philology, Jagiellonian University in Kraków, Poland. She has taught English literature, applied linguistics and language skills (critical reading and writing), as well as supervised licentiate and MA work. She has participated in several educational and research projects initiated by the British Council, Cultnet, and recently EU-US Atlantis Programme. Her PhD dissertation "Developing Intercultural Competence in Teaching English as a Foreign Language," defended at the Faculty of Modern Languages at Warsaw University in 2005, was published as Nauczyciel jako mediator kulturowy (*The Teacher as a Cultural Mediator*), Kraków: Tertium 2007. Her current research interest lies in fostering criticality as a transversal competence through foreign language education.

Getting to Know Ourselves and Others Through the ABCs, pages 237–240
Copyright © 2015 by Information Age Publishing
237

Josep M. Cots is professor of English language and applied linguistics at the University of Lleida (Catalonia, Spain). His research has focused mostly on applied discourse analysis, foreign language teaching and learning, multilingualism, and intercultural competence. He is the author of *Teaching by Chatting* (1998), co-author of *Competencia Comunicativa* (1995), *La parla Com a Espectacle* (1997), *La Conciencia Lingüística en la Enseñanza de Lenguas* (2007), *Plurilingüismo e Interculturalidad en la Escuela* (2010), and co-editor of *Pensar lo Dicho* (2002), *The Pragmatics of Catalan* (2011), and *Universitats Internacionals i Plurilingües?* (2013).

Troy Davidson holds a master's degree in second language education from the Université du Québec à Montréal, with research interests in second language motivation. He teaches English as a second language at the Institut de tourisme et d'hôtellerie du Québec in Montréal, and has also taught at the primary and secondary levels.

Patricia A. Edwards, a member of the Reading Hall Fame, is a Distinguished Professor of Language and Literacy in the Department of Teacher Education, and a Senior University Outreach Fellow at Michigan State University. A nationally and internationally recognized expert in parent involvement, home, school, community partnerships, multicultural literacy, early literacy, and family/intergenerational literacy, especially among poor and minority children. She served as a member of the IRA Board of Directors from 1998 to 2001, and in 2006–2007 as the first African American President of the Literacy Research Association (formerly the National Reading Conference), and as President of the International Reading Association (2010–2011). Dr. Edwards has co-authored several books, including *A Path to Follow: Learning to Listen to Parents* (1999) with Heather M. Pleasants and Sarah H. Franklin, *Bridging Literacy and Equity: The Essential Guide to Social Equity Teaching* (2012) with Althier M. Lazar and Gwendolyn T. McMillon, and *Change Is Gonna Come: Transforming Literacy for African American Students* (2010) with Gwendolyn T. McMillon and Jennifer D. Turner.

Sylvia Fehling is a senior lecturer at the University of Bayreuth (Germany) in the Faculty of Languages and Literature, focusing on Teaching English as a Foreign Language and Foreign Language Research/Intercultural Communication. Previous positions held at the University of Kassel (Germany) as a research assistant, lecturer, and teacher trainer, and at the Goethe University Frankfurt (Germany) as a visiting professor. Participation in various national and international research projects such as MOBIDIC (Modules of Content and Language Integrated Learning (CLIL) in Teacher Training), TRANS-ABCs (Transcultural ABCs of Cultural Understanding and Communication) and ADEQUA (Learning strategies in self-regulated, text-based cooperative literacy events in the context of English as a foreign language). PhD: Fehling,

Sylvia. (2008). Language Awareness und bilingualer Unterricht: Eine komparative Studie (2nd ed.). Frankfurt: Peter Lang. Her research interests include content and language integrated learning (CLIL), language awareness, intercultural learning, cooperative learning, foreign language research.

Ulla Lundgren is a retired assistant professor of education at the School of Education and Communication, Jönköping University, Sweden. Her research interest is in the intersection of languages and citizenship education. She has undertaken various research in the field of intercultural issues, for example, the intercultural dimension of foreign language education, global citizenship, internationalization, and global mindedness She has a background as a teacher in secondary schools and adult education. For many years she has taught in teacher education, teaching Swedish language, English as a foreign language, and sociolinguistics. During her career, she has developed and led interdisciplinary international courses of Intercultural Encounters and continues to publish articles, papers, and book chapters.

Susan V. Piazza is associate professor of literacy studies at Western Michigan University. She received IRA's 2007 Dissertation of the Year Award, Finalist for her reading research with diverse learners. Her research interests and professional roles include critical analyses of how learners interact with texts and assessments; critical and culturally responsive literacy practices; school and community partnerships; and professional development around curriculum building and disciplinary literacy. Issues of equity and cultural competence are themes that connect her research, teaching, publication, and service. Piazza holds leadership positions in professional organizations and works with K–12 schools locally and nationally.

Lilia Ratcheva-Stratieva is a project manager for the International Institute for Children's Literature in Vienna, Austria. Of Bulgarian origin, since 1996 she has developed four (and participated in another five) major European projects on intercultural education and communication as well as on reading promotion. She was editor of Bookbird, the international journal on children's literature (2000–2004), member of the Andersen Award International Jury (1996, 1998) and member (1987, 1990) and president of the Janusz Korczak International Jury (1998, 2000). Besides fiction for children, her publications include numerous research articles on various aspects of literature for young people.

Jane L. Neer has taught high school English in Liverpool, New York from 1979 to the present and is an adjunct instructor for educational literacy at Le Moyne College, Syracuse, New York. She has recently been involved in developing a "Flipping Instruction" model for student research projects and has presented this model at several local colleges and high schools. She is a member of the English Language Arts cabinet and the Right to

Intervention Committee in her district, as well as a member of the Balanced Assessment Audit Committee.

William Neer, is an adjunct instructor at Le Moyne College in Syracuse, New York. After teaching social studies and English in public schools for 33 years, he joined the faculty at Le Moyne as a visiting assistant professor of literacy. He also served as a consultant to the New York Education Department and a curriculum writer for the Colonial Williamsburg Educational Foundation in Virginia.

Jiening Ruan is associate professor of reading/literacy education at the University of Oklahoma. Her research interests include literacy education in international contexts, culturally responsive teaching, and using technology to support teacher reflection. Her books include *Perspectives on Chinese Literacy Teaching and Learning in China* (2012) and *Perspectives on English Literacy Teaching and Learning in China* (2012), with co-editor Cynthia Leung. She also co-authored *Literacy for Young Children* (2008) with Sally Beach, Loraine Dunn, and Priscilla Griffith.

Patricia Ruggiano Schmidt is Professor Emerita of Literacy Education at Le Moyne College, Syracuse, New York. After more than 20 years of teaching at all levels of education, she earned a doctorate at the Reading and Language Arts Center, Syracuse University. Her research examines preservice and inservice preparation for culturally responsive teaching in elementary and secondary classrooms. She created the *ABCs of Cultural Understanding and Communication* in 1992 and has worked at perfecting the model ever since. It is the centerpiece of her research and coursework. Her recent books include, *Practicing What You Teach: How Culturally Responsive Literacy Classrooms Make a Difference* (2011) with Althier Lazar and *Transforming Yourself, Transforming the World* (2013) with Mary Beth Combs. During 2006–2013, Dr. Ruggiano Schmidt was an active volunteer, a principal and development director for an urban international school in the Roman Catholic Tradition. The growth of this school has produced a noticeable affect on the revitalization of a struggling neighborhood.

Shelley Hong Xu is professor of teacher education at the College of Education in California State University, Long Beach. She has taught literacy, research, technology, and bilingual Chinese-English courses in the doctoral, master's, and teacher credential programs. Her research areas focus on literacy instruction for English language learners, preparing teachers for working with culturally and linguistically diverse students, and integrating various genres of texts into literacy instruction. Her book publications include Teaching English Language Learners: Literacy Strategies & Resources for K–6 (2010), and Literacy Instruction for English Language Learners, PreK–2 (2008), co-authored with Diane Barone.

CPSIA information can be obtained at www.ICGtesting.com
Printed in the USA
BVOW08s2305120415

395704BV00004B/29/P